Reader's Guide
to
JOHN MILTON

Reader's Guide
to
JOHN MILTON

W. Cormier

CENTRUM PRESS
NEW DELHI-110002 (INDIA)

CENTRUM PRESS
H.O.: 4360/4, Ansari Road, Daryaganj,
New Delhi-110 002 (India)
Ph.: 23278000, 23261597

B.O.: No. 1015, Ist Main Road, BSK IIIrd Stage
IIIrd Phase, IIIrd Block,
Bangalore - 560 085 (India)
Tel.: 080-41723429
Visit us at: www.centrumpress.com

Reader's Guide to John Milton

First Edition, 2009

ISBN 978-93-80106-67-0

PRINTED IN INDIA

Printed at Salasar Imaging Systems, Delhi-110035 (India)

Contents

Preface

John Milton was born in London. His mother, Sarah Jeffrey, a very religious person, was the daughter of a merchant sailor. He is one of the greatest poets of the English language, best-known for his epic poem Paradise Lost (1667). Milton's powerful, rhetoric prose and the eloquence of his poetry had an immense influence especially on the 18th-century verse. Besides poems, Milton published pamphlets defending civil and religious rights.

Milton's father, named John, too, had risen to prosperity as a scrivener or law writer - he also composed madrigasl and psalm settings. The family was wealthy enough to afford a second house in the country. One of Milton'e earliest works, 'On the Death of a Fair Infant' (1626), was written after his sister Anne Phillips had suffered from a miscarriage. Milton did not adjust to university life. He was called, half in scorn, "The Lady of Christ's", and after starting a fist fight with his tutor, he was expelled for a term.

On leaving Cambridge Milton had given up his original plan to become a priest. He adopted no profession but spent six years at leisure in his father's home, writing during that time L'allegro, IL Penseroso (1632), Comus (1634), and Lycidas (1637), about the meaning of death, which was composed after the death of his friend Edward King. Milton wrote in Latin as was usual for the time. His first published poem was the sonnet 'An Epitaph on the Admirable Dramatic Poet, W. Shakespeare', which was printed anonymously in the Second Folio of Shakespeare's works (1632). In 1651 Milton became blind, but like Jorge Luis Borges centuries later, blindness helped him to stimulate his verbal richness.

Author

Chapter 1

Introduction

John Milton was born on December 9, 1608, in London, as the second child of John and Sara (neé Jeffrey). The family lived on Bread Street in Cheapside, near St. Paul's Cathedral. John Milton Sr. worked as a scrivener, a legal secretary whose duties included preparation and notarization of documents, as well as real estate transactions and moneylending. Milton's father was also a composer of church music, and Milton himself experienced a lifelong delight in music. The family's financial prosperity afforded Milton to be taught classical languages, first by private tutors at home, followed by entrance to St. Paul's School at age twelve, in 1620.

The "overdated ceremony," as Milton himself might have called it, of protesting that the best record of a great writer's life is in his works can, at least, plead this in its favour, that it applies to hardly any two persons in quite the same way. In Milton's case, especially, its application has a peculiarity partaking of that strong separation from ordinary folk which is one of the great Miltonic notes.

We are not, in his case, without a fairly large amount of positive biographical information; and that information was worked up and supplemented by David Masson with heroic diligence, with lavish provision of commentary and without that undue expatiation into "may-have-beens" and "probablys" and "perhapses" which, despite the temptation to it which exists in some cases, is irritating to the critically minded and dangerously misleading to the uncritical.

But, in order to understand the external information, we need unusually constant and careful recurrence to the internal, and, on the other hand, we are likely to misread not a little of the work if we do not know the life.

Nor is this double process one requiring mere care. The ordinary conception of Milton, among people more than fairly educated, may be fairly uniform and reasonably clear; but it does not follow that it is either correct or complete. He may not so absolutely "evade our question" as does Shakespeare. The contradictions or inconsistencies in him may not be trivial and exoteric as in Bacon.

But, like Dante, whom, of all other writers of the highest class, he most resembles, Milton gives us his life and his work, to explain each other, it may be, but offering not a few puzzles and pitfalls in the course of the explanation. Although, therefore, the immense mass of detail which has been accumulated about Milton defies distillation and condensation in such a chapter as this, it has been thought important to give all the principal points, while excluding those proper to a full "life," or a critical edition of the "works" in extenso.

The life itself was not extraordinarily eventful, but it was unusually so when compared with the average lives of men of letters; and, though the unusualness was partly due to the times, it was largely increased by Milton's own attitude towards those times, during the last forty years of his life. In the circumstances of his birth and origin, he reflected the peculiar ecclesiastical—which meant, also, the political—history of England for the past three generations.

He was born on 9 December, 1608, in the city of London, at The Spread Eagle, Bread street, Cheapside, where his father (and namesake) carried on the business of a scrivener—that is to say, a lawyer of the inferior branch, who had specially to do with the raising, lending and repayment of money on landed or other security.

The sign of the office or shop was the crest of the family—an Oxfordshire one of the upper yeomanry; and the reason of the elder John's taking to business was that he had been disinherited by his father for abandoning Roman Catholicism and conforming to the Church of England.

The poet's younger brother Christopher reversed the

process, became a judge and a knight under James II and (probably on that account, for we know very little else about him) has been generally spoken of in a depreciatory manner by biographers and historians.

But the brothers seem always to have been on good terms. There was also an elder sister, Anne, who married, and became the mother of John and Edward Phillips, both men of letters, in their way, the latter our chief original source of information about his uncle. Of the poet's mother, we hear but little, and it is by inference rather than on direct evidence that her name is supposed to have been Sarah Jeffrey or Jeffreys.

Milton's father, however, was not only a prosperous man of business, but one of rather unusual culture. His son derived from him his interest in music; and that the father was not indifferent to poetry—perhaps not to romance—is evident from his connection with a contemporary version of Guy of Warwick, which exists in MS. and to which he contributed a sonnet.

He sent his son to St. Paul's school, giving him, also, a private tutor, Thomas Young, who was a good scholar but an acrid presbyterian and, later, the "ty" of Smectymnuus. And Milton seems to have had no objection to being "brought on" in the Blimberian sense—working by himself when a boy of twelve, till the small hours.

Although it is impossible to deny the indebtedness of some of the good qualities of his work to this "overpressure," it must have had bad results in various directions, moral and physical. And, though his blindness cannot have been actually caused by this over-exertion of his eyes, it was certainly not staved off by the process. For the time, however, all went well.

Alexander Gill, high master of St. Paul's, was an excellent teacher, and his son continued to be a great friend of Milton when Gill went to Oxford and Milton to Cambridge. There, he was admitted at Christ's on 12 February, 1625, when he had just entered his seventeenth year; and he began to keep terms at Easter. His college sojourn begins the Milton legend and controversy—tedious and idle like all controversial legends and to be kept down as much as possible. He certainly did not get on with his tutor Chappell, and was sent away from college; though not technically "sent down" or rusticated, inasmuch as he did not lose a term. And his transference to another tutor has been held (though the fact is not quite conclusive) as proof that there were faults on both sides. He himself admits "indocility" and grumbles that he was not allowed to choose his own studies.

That he was unpopular with his fellow undergraduates is not certain, though it is not improbable. The celebrated nickname "the lady of Christ's" admits of—and has been fitted with—both interpretations—that of a compliment to his beauty and that of a sneer at him as a milksop. He certainly must have been as different as possible from the "Square-Cap" of his contemporary Cleiveland's lively glorification of the graduates and undergraduates of Cambridge.

But he protested, later, that the Fellows treated him "with more than ordinary respect" and wished him to stay up at the end of his seven years, when, in 1632, he took the M.A. degree. The upshot of the whole seems to be that he was studious, reserved and not quite like other people—once, at least, and, probably, more than once, becoming definitely "refractory." He was always to be studious, reserved and not like other people; and, in his nearly seventy years, the times of truce were not very common and the times of war very frequent.

It is impossible to say what he would have done if his father had not been unusually, though by no means unwisely, indulgent, and of means sufficient to exercise indulgence. That Milton could work hard at mere routine when it suited him, the disastrous secretaryship afterwards showed; but it is impossible to imagine him in any ordinary profession. He had been "destined of a child" to the church.

But, though there is no positive evidence of anti-Anglican feeling in his work before Lycidas, and, though Lycidas itself might have been written, in a quite possible construction, by an orthodox and even high Anglican who was an ardent church reformer, Milton's discipleship to Young and the Gills, his difficulties with Chappell, who was a Laudian, and his whole subsequent conduct and utterance, explain his abandonment of orders. No (or only the slightest) obstacles were put in his way, and no force was used to urge him out of it. His father had given up business, and settled at Horton in the south of Bucks, less than twenty miles from London, on the river Colne, within sight of Windsor, and in a pretty, though not wildly romantic, neighbourhood. Here Milton lived, and read, and thought, and annotated, and wrote, for five years, directing his attention chiefly to linguistic, literary and historical study, but, at last, setting seriously to work at poetry itself.

Besides smaller pieces, Comus (1634) and Lycidas (1637) certainly date from this time; and the ingenious attempts of Mrs. Byse 1 can hardly be allowed to carry L'Allegro and Il Penseroso on to the period that followed. In 1635, he was admitted ad eundem as M.A. at Oxford.

Milton worked for Oliver Cromwell and the Parliament of England and thus wrote first-hand for the Commonwealth of England. Arguably, the failed rebellion and reinstallation of the monarchy left him to explore his losses within Paradise Lost. Some critics say that he sympathized with the Satan in this work, in that both he and Satan had experienced a failed cause. Milton incorporates Paganism, classical Greek references and Christianity within the story. He greatly admired the classics but intended this work to surpass them. The poem grapples with many difficult theological issues, including fate, predestination, and the Trinity.

Drawn from about 1,500 books, scholars estimate, Paradise Lost (Published in 1667) is an epic account of The Fall of man. Milton begins his poem by invoking the aid of the (Holy) Spirit for his task, and sets forth the purpose of his song: "that..I may assert the Eternal Providence and justify the ways of God to man". The poem then depicts Satan and his fallen angels, already expelled from heaven and burning in the fire, as they start to talk among themselves. The rest of Books I and II, are then recounted from the perspective of Satan and his minions.

Satan goes on to tell how those of Hell deliberated with him as to whether or not they should war with those in heaven yet again and attempt to overthrow it. Once agreed upon, Satan struggles through Chaos from Heaven to Hell. Traditional Christians may argue that this is an unbiblical ability according to the Gospel of Luke chapter 16 in the story of the rich man and Lazarus, "...between us and you a great chasm has been fixed, so that those that want to go from here to you cannot, nor can anyone cross over from there to us".

Perhaps the ability to transfer from one immaterial place to another differs between composites of form and matter or soul and body (humans) and pure spirit. However, this is not even an issue in this context, even though Hell is a state of mind, "the hell within him; for within him Hell he brings, and round about him, nor from Hell one step, no more than from himself, can fly by change of place". Later on in the poem, Satan goes on to introduce Death and Sin. Sin was birthed from the head of Satan, an allusion to the birth of the Greek god Athena.

Sin is half beautiful woman and half serpent, the lower portion of her body destroyed after giving birth to Death. Hell-hounds are attached to the waist of Sin, constantly running in and out of her being re-birthed and devouring Sin's body. In book 4, Adam and Eve are introduced for the first time. Milton's idea of marriage is very much influenced in this section.

Their relationship is one of inequality, but not a relation of domination or hierarchy. There is a mutual friendship between the two and they also model the ideal ruler and subject. For Milton, this marriage is political ideal just as much as it is a personal ideal. Satan also describes their personalities. Eve is a described as a '"coy", flirtatious, beautiful, sex object that Adam is overwhelmed by"' (Rust), or "too much, too ornament."

Adam is seen as more of an intellectual. Though there is no sin within paradise, Adam and Eve have an argument about the care of the land. Eve thinks the garden is growing too fast and that the two should split up while working to cover more ground, thus accomplishing more. Adam disagrees and says that time is not an issue for them, therefore they were meant to enjoy their work and not rush it. This disagreement would begin the stirring up their hearts, making them more vulnerable to the temptation that was to come. Adam consents to Eve's wishes and they split up during their work. Satan, as the serpent in the garden, made ready to fool Eve through the process of reduction.

In the last three chapters after the Fall, the Son of God intercedes for Adam and Eve and the Father accepts. However, he commands the angel Michael to ban Adam and Eve from the garden. In doing so, Michael gives Adam a vision of the Flood, and life and death of Christ, revealing to him the way of redemption. Adam and Eve's lives carry on but they are driven out from the Garden of Eden.

CAREER

In 1625, Milton was admitted to Christ's College, Cambridge. While Milton was a hardworking student, he was also argumentative to the extent that only a year later, in 1626, he got suspended after a dispute with his tutor, William Chappell. During his temporary return to London, Milton attended plays, and perhaps began his first forays into poetry. At his return to Cambridge, Milton was assigned a new tutor, Nathaniel Tovey. Life at Cambridge was still not easy on Milton; he felt he was disliked by many of his fellow students and he was dissatisfied with the curriculum. It was at Cambridge that he composed "On the Morning of Christ's Nativity" on December 25, 1629.

In 1632, Milton took his M.A. cum laude at Cambridge, after which he retired to the family homes in London and Horton, Buckinghamshire, for years of private study and literary composition. His poem, "On Shakespeare", was published in the same year in the Second Folio. From this period hail also his "L'Allegro" and "Il Penseroso." Milton's Comus, a masque, was performed at Ludlow Castle in 1634, to be first published anonymously in 1637, music by the famed court composer Henry Lawes.

In April 1637, Milton was nearing the end of his studies when his mother died and was buried at Horton. Only a few months later, in August, Milton's friend Edward King died as well, by drowning. In November, upon his memory, Milton composed the beautiful elegy, Lycidas. It was published in a memorial volume at Cambridge in 1638.

As customary for young gentlemen of means, Milton set out for a tour of Europe in the spring of 1638. He met famed scholar Hugo Grotius in Paris, where he stayed briefly before continuing on to Italy. Milton arrived in Florence in the autumn, where he probably met with Galileo, who was then under house arrest by order of the Inquisition.

In Rome, he was a guest of Cardinal Barberini, the Pope's nephew, and visited the Vatican Library. In Naples, Milton met Giovanni Batista, biographer of Torquato Tasso. Milton wrote Mansus in his honour.

Upon reaching Geneva to visit with Calvinist theologian Giovanni Diodati, Milton found out about the death of his childhood friend, Charles Diodati in London. Milton's tour of Europe was cut short with rumors of impending civil war in England, and he returned home in July 1639. Shortly after, Milton composed Epitaphium Damonis, a Latin poem to the memory of his dearest friend.

Milton settled down in London, where he began schooling his two nephews, later also taking in children of the better families. The Civil War was brewing — King Charles I invaded Scotland in 1639, and the Long Parliament was convened in 1640. Milton began writing pamphlets on political and religious matters; Of Reformation, Animadversions, and Of Prelatical Episcopacy were published in 1641, The Reason for Church Government in February, 1642.

In the spring of 1642, Milton married Mary Powell, 17 years old to his 34, but the relationship was an unhappy one, and Mary left him to visit the family home briefly thereafter, and did not return. Matters were not improved when the Powells declared for the King in the Civil War which broke out in August.

This prompted Milton to write his so-called 'Divorce Tracts' speaking for divorce on the grounds of incompatibility. In 1643, Milton published the Doctrine and Discipline of

Divorce, which had its second, longer edition in early 1644. In 1644, Milton also published The Judgement of Martin Bucer Concerning Divorce. The 'Divorce Tracts' caused an uproar both in parliament and amidst the clergy, as well as with the general populace, which earned him the nickname "Milton the Divorcer."

It is in reference to the attempted censorship of the same by the Stationers' Company, that Milton published his eloquent Areopagitica, an oration advocating freedom of the press, in late 1644. Milton had also had time to write a treatise Of Education, which prescribed a rigorous course of study for English youth. In 1645, Milton published Tetrachordon and Colasterion, and registered Poems of Mr. John Milton, Both English and Latin. Milton had made plans to remarry, when Mary Powell returned.

The two seem to have reconciled, since their daughter Anne was born in 1646. The whole Powell clan moved in with the Miltons, because Royalists had been ousted from Oxford. The situation was not savory. The year 1647 saw the death of both Milton's father and his father-in-law. The Powells eventually moved out and the Miltons moved to the neighborhood of High Holborn, where their daughter Mary was born in 1648.

It is probable that Milton witnessed the public execution of Charles I on January 30, 1649. Tenure of Kings and Magistrates was published two weeks later.

In March, the Cromwellian government appointed Milton Secretary for Foreign Tongues and ordered him to write an answer to Charles I's purported Eikon Basilike ("Royal Image"). After publishing Observations on the Articles of Peace, Milton published Eikonoklastes ("Image Breaker") in October, 1649. In 1650, the Council of State ordered Milton to write a response to Salmasius' Defensio Regia the Continental outcry against the English action ("Defence of Kingship"). Defensio pro populo Anglicano was published in February, 1651. Milton's first son, John, was born in March and the Miltons moved to Westminster.

The year 1652 was one of many personal losses for Milton.

In February, Milton lost his sight. This prompted him to write the sonnet "When I Consider How My Light is Spent." In May, 1652, Mary gave birth to a daughter, Deborah, and died a few days later. In June, one year-old John died.

In 1654, Milton published Defensio Secunda, the response he had been ordered to write for Pierre du Moulin's Regii sanguinis clamor ("Clamor of the King's Blood"). Andrew Marvell had become his assistant, and he had aides to take dictation, to facilitate the carrying out of his duties as Secretary. In 1655, Defensio Pro Se ("Defence of Himself") was published.

In 1656, Milton married Katherine Woodcock, but the happiness was short-lived. Milton's daughter Katherine was born in late 1657, but by early 1658, both mother and daughter had passed away.

It is to the memory of Katherine Woodcock that Milton wrote the sonnet "Methought I saw my late espousèd saint." Lord Protector Oliver Cromwell died in October, 1658, and the days of the Commonwealth were coming to a close. In early 1659, Milton published A Treatise of Civil Power and Ready and Easy Way To Establish a Free Commonwealth.

For his propaganda writings, Milton had to go into hiding, for fear of retribution from the followers of King Charles II. In June, 1659, both Defensio pro populo Anglicano and Eikonoklastes were publicly burned. In early autumn, Milton was arrested and thrown in prison, to be released by order of Parliament before Christmas.

King Charles II was restored to the throne on May 30, 1660. In 1663, Milton remarried again, to Elizabeth Minshull, a match his daughters opposed. He spent his time tutoring students and finishing his life's work, the epic, Paradise Lost.

Among the greatest works ever to be written in English, the feat is all the more remarkable for Milton's blindness — he would compose verse upon verse at night in his head and then dictate them from memory to his aides in the morning. Paradise Lost finally saw publication in 1667, in ten books. It was reissued in 1668 with a new title-page and additional materials.

The book was met with instant success and amazement;

even Dryden is reported to have said, "This man cuts us all out, and the ancients too."

History of Britain was published in 1670; Paradise Regain'd and Samson Agonistes were published together in 1671. Of True Religion and Poems, &c. upon Several Occasions were published in 1673. In summer 1674, the second edition of Paradise Lost was published, in twelve books.

Milton died peacefully of gout in November, 1674, and was buried in the church of St. Giles, Cripplegate. His funeral was attended by "his learned and great Friends in London, not without a friendly concourse of the Vulgar." A monument to Milton rests in Poets' Corner at Westminster Abbey.

Chapter 2

Milton and History

Americans tend to forget that they weren't the first to have a revolution. The English had theirs more than 130 years before the Thirteen Colonies rebelled. The English revolution consisted of a bloody Civil War from 1642 to 1649, the beheading of King Charles I in January 1649, and ten years of Puritan republican rule; it ended finally with the restoration of the monarchy under King Charles II in 1660.

These events aren't merely the background to John Milton's life: they were his life. We usually think of the war as a conflict between the Cavaliers and the Roundheads. John Milton was a Roundhead. The Cavaliers, or Royalists, supported the king and tended toward Catholicism. They believed in an aristocracy that had the right to special privileges, both in politics and in religion. The Roundheads, or Puritans, believed in a wider distribution of political and economic power and the right of every man to enjoy direct access to God.

Milton was so strongly committed to the Puritan cause that he accepted a government position under Oliver Cromwell, who ruled as Lord Protector from 1649 to 1658. Milton was a radical Christian individualist who objected strongly and vocally to all kinds of organized religions which, he believed, put barriers between man and God. Milton was therefore a rebel because he identified himself with a revolutionary cause. Paradise Lost, his masterpiece, is about rebellion and its consequences.

One way of looking at the poem is to see it as Milton's working out of his own position. Although many readers have thought that Milton is really Satan, he probably saw himself as Abdiel, the angel who refuses to go along with Satan. Milton was arrogant in his belief that he understood the truth and had a duty to explain it for everyone's good.

The revolution he lived through changed every aspect of English life. When he was born in 1608, Shakespeare was still alive and Queen Elizabeth was only five years dead. Her influence was still felt. She had been an absolute monarch who regarded Parliament as a necessary evil in order to get money for her projects.

When Milton died in 1674, Charles II reigned as constitutional monarch without any real power except that granted to him by Parliament. Milton's circumstances changed drastically during his life. His family was reasonably well-to-do. They lived in London, which was Milton's home for most of his life. His father was a scrivener, a sort of combined notary and banker, who was wealthy enough to afford private tutors for his son, then schooling at St. Paul's and Christ's College, Cambridge University. Perhaps just as important for Milton's development was the fact that his father was a musician and composer.

One of the most attractive features of Milton's poetry is its marvelous musical qualities. Since Milton had a small private income, he did not seek a profession when he left Cambridge, but stayed at home writing poetry and increasing his already amazing stock of knowledge. Some people have said that Milton was one of the most learned men England has ever known.

He wrote poetry in Latin, Greek, and Italian, and read almost all the literature surviving from the Greek and Roman periods. He even read the Bible in Hebrew. Just before the religious and political quarrels in England came to a head, Milton went abroad for fifteen months, meeting and talking with learned and famous men all over Europe. He met Galileo and looked through his telescope, a fact Milton mentions more than once in Paradise Lost.

When he returned, he put his learning and considerable rhetorical force at the service of the Puritan cause. He wrote a series of scorching political and religious pamphlets: he condemned bishops, not only the Catholic ones but those of the Protestant Church of England; defended the liberty of the press against censorship; even advocated divorce. Many of the controversies in which he engaged with heat and passion we find difficult to sympathize with now, but Milton championed them with vigour and made himself not only well known but also well hated.

The Civil War deeply affected his personal relations. His brother Christopher adhered to the Royalist side. Milton married into a Royalist family in 1642. He was swept off his feet by a fun-loving seventeen-year- old, Mary Powell, whose family was originally the source of Milton's private income (they had bought property from Milton's father). The Powells kept Mary away from Milton, in Oxford where King Charles I made his headquarters, and did not let her travel to London to live with her husband until 1645.

By that time Milton had been extremely vocal publicly on the subject of divorce (he even advocated polygamy at one time) and had had an affair with a Miss Davies. His was a lively household, for he looked after and educated his dead sister's three sons. (One of them became Milton's biographer and the source of most of what we know about Milton's life.) He took his duties as schoolmaster very seriously; the boys were beaten if they did not learn their Latin and Greek grammar. The civil disturbances flowed in and out of the house as Milton's pamphlets provoked angry opposition and his supporters cried for more.

Only six weeks after King Charles I's head rolled from his body (Milton's friend Marvell wrote a famous ode on the occasion), Milton became Latin secretary to Oliver Cromwell. It was his duty to compose all the government's diplomatic correspondence in Latin, a job probably concerned as much with public relations as with accurate translation.

By this time Milton was blind, probably as a result of a cyst or tumor of the pituitary gland. For the rest of his life he depended on others to read to him and to write at his dictation. Because he was not a patient man-he had the arrogance of a person conscious of his talents-reading and writing for him was not easy. His daughters objected to the tyranny he showed in demanding their time and then complaining when they read incorrectly.

Mary died in 1652, leaving a blind man with three young daughters, the eldest mentally retarded. Milton married again in 1657, but his second wife, whom he called in a famous sonnet his "espoused saint," lived only fifteen months and died after giving birth to a daughter, who also died. Milton married a third time, to a woman who looked after him for the rest of his life and managed to bring order to a household full of quarreling daughters, relatives, and visitors to the famous writer.

In 1658, Oliver Cromwell had died, leaving England in the incompetent hands of his son, Richard. The passions that had caused the Civil War had cooled, and the king's son was asked to return, but on the conditions which brought about the English constitutional monarchy.

The coming of Charles II meant the end of Milton's government job. For a time he was in danger of his life and had to be hidden by friends-one of his pamphlets had argued strongly in defence of Charles I's beheading. Milton retired from public life and devoted himself to the composition of Paradise Lost.

By the time he had finished dictating it to whoever got up early in the morning, two other events had disturbed Milton's never very tranquil life. In 1665 he was forced by the Great Plague to leave London and live in a Buckinghamshire village. A year later, in the Great Fire in 1666, Milton lost the last piece of property he owned. He lived the last few years of his life in considerable poverty, quite unlike the comfort of his first pampered years in his father's house.

Paradise Lost (1667) is the culmination of his life's work. His early poems, the exquisite "L'Allegro," "Il Penseroso," "Lycidas," the masque Comus, and the sonnets would all secure him a place among the finest English poets. But it is Paradise Lost which makes it impossible for you to ignore Milton. He wrote Paradise Regained afterward, but it has nothing like the stature of Paradise Lost. (It is not, as you might think, about Christ's sacrifice, but about his three-day temptation in the desert by Satan.) Milton's final work, Samson Agonistes, is a Greek drama as impressive as Paradise Lost in everything except size.

Milton died in 1674, just after the second edition of Paradise Lost appeared. The poem was for that time a modest best seller. It sold 1,300 copies in the first eighteen months and earned Milton a total of ten pounds. By the end of the seventeenth century, the book had gone through six editions, including one published in 1678 with large engraved illustrations.

It has never lost its status as a classic, and it has never stopped being a source of controversy. People love or hate Paradise Lost, for as many reasons as it has readers. The poem has retained its interest because it deals with subjects that will always concern us-good, evil, freedom, responsibility. And because, like any great work of literature, it's exciting to read.

Chapter 3

Youthful Works and Poetic Ambitions

Pastoral elegy: Read over Lycidas quickly don't sweat the details, but note that it is a pastoral elegy written in 1637 in memory of a college classmate, Edward King. As one of Milton's earliest works, it puts him squarely following in the footsteps of Virgil, who, as we recall from our discussion of Spenser, went from writing pastoral poetry in his youth to the epic in his maturity.

Review pastoral works read earlier this quarter; know what poets (vernacular and classical) were models for Milton in this regard. Note that the memorial volume in which Lycidas was published included twenty poems in Latin, three in Greek and only thirteen in English, clearly demonstrating the humanist training of these university students who (as Ascham and others advocated) learned to imitate classical poets in part by writing their own Latin and Greek verse.

Note classical elements that denote the nobility of poetry (e.g. references to laurels, the Muses, and Orpheus). Note also that the three explicit climaxes in Lycidas combine humanist and Christian concerns: first Phoebus Apollo, the God of poetry, answers a question concerning the reward of poetry then St. Peter, guardian of the gate to heaven, answers a question about spiritual shepherds and finally, Lycidas becomes a synthesis of both Classical and Christian "pastoral" imagery: he is in heaven with the lamb of God, an explicitly Christian God who is at once the Good Shepherd and the giver of poetic fame.

Milton also wrote 24 sonnets between 1630-1658 (i.e. between the ages of 22 and 50). His knowledge of and respect for the vernacular origins of the sonnet form are demonstrated not only by the fact that he wrote five sonnets in Italian but also in that he followed Petrarchan rather than Shakespearean (English) form; note also his use of the "tailed sonnet" form (sonneto caudato) in "On the Late Massacre in Piedmont".

Another formal innovation is his tendency to avoid end-stopped lines, a technique borrowed from another Italian poet, Giovanni Della Casa.

This technique is analogous to the 'Metaphysical poets' desire to emulate the cadences of natural speech because it focusses attention on sentences rather than lines of verse ("On the Late Massacre in Piedmont" also offers a good example of this tendency).

Read over the assigned sonnets quickly. Unlike Lycidas (or Donne's Holy Sonnets), most of Milton's sonnets are not explicitly Christian in content; they also diverge from earlier sonnet tradition by their lack of emphasis on erotic love (and by the fact that they do not together constitute a sonnet cycle).

Rather, Milton's sonnets betray his interest in the political and religious controversies that dominate his attention during and after the period of Puritan Rule (see esp. the poem dedicated to Cromwell, the military dictator of the Puritan Commonwealth and Protectorate,.

Two notable exceptions are "When I Consider How My Light is Spent", which offers a first poetic reaction to Milton's blindness (a theme he will return to in Paradise Lost), and "Methought I Saw My Late Espousèd Saint", which records Milton's grief at the death of one of his wives from complications of childbirth.

Note that the "night" to which he refers in the poem's final line can be understood not only as his despair at his loss but as a reference to his physical condition. Since 1652, when he became completely blind, Milton can "see" only in dreams — or in his poetry.

Polemical Tracts and Pamphlets. The introduction to "Voices of the War" mentions the wide range of "tracts" and "pamphlets" that were written during the twenty years of Puritan rule. This proliferation of literally hundreds of published polemical texts came to be known as the "Pamphlet Wars."

Milton was an active participant in these debates, represented for our purposes by the "Plans and Projects" section of The Reason of Church Government Urged Against Prelaty. In this text (dating from 1642), note Milton's concern with the intersection between religion and politics (comparable to that found in his sonnet "

On the New Forcers of Conscience Under the Long Parliament,". Pay particular attention to statements that reveal Milton's literary ambitions and to his comments on his own education. Milton's participation in the public debate of the "pamphlet wars" era also included e.g. arguments in favor of divorce for incompatibility and his Areopagitica (written in 1644), a defence of a free press.

The title of Areopagitica is a classical allusion that implies a connection between the ancient Greek tribunal and the English parliament (as well as between the Greek orator Isocrates and Milton himself). Milton's classical education is also felt in the structure of the tract, which follows the rules of classical rhetoric.

While Areopagitica is not an assigned reading, be aware that Milton's final argument for freedom of the press introduces the theme of Free Will which he will develop in Paradise Lost: since God made man capable of free will, men should be allowed to choose between ideas In ancient Greece and Rome, poets had always requested "the muse" to fire them with creative genius when they began long narrative poems, called epics, about godlike heroes and villains.

In Greek mythology, there were nine muses, all sisters, who were believed to inspire poets, historians, flutists, dancers, singers, astronomers, philosophers, and other thinkers and artists. If one wanted to write a great poem, play a musical instrument with bravado, or develop a grand scientific or philosophical theory, he would ask for help from a muse.

.......When a writer asked for help, he was said to be

"invoking the muse." The muse of epic poetry was named Calliope [kuh LY uh pe].

However, in Book 7, Milton identifies Urania–the muse of astronomy–as the goddess to whom he addresses his plea for inspiration.

In Milton's time, writers no longer believed in muses, of course. Nevertheless, since they symbolized inspiration, writers continued to invoke them. So it was that when Milton began Paradise Lost, he addressed the muse in the telling of his tale, writing, "I thence invoke thy aid to my adventurous Song."

Chapter 4

Milton's Epic Poetry

EPIC POETRY

Most epics follow the example of the Iliad in starting with a call on the muses (the nine daughters of Zeus are the muses of classical mythology, but more details on that are for our reading of Homer). Homer starts with the plea "Sing, goddess, the anger of Pelus' son of Achilleus..." indicating that it is not Homer's poem, but that the muse is singing through Homer. The Odyssey begins "Tell me, Muse, of the man of many ways..." This is not universal, though; Virgil doesn't start with the traditional call on the muses, but starts right out "I sing of men and arms," making clear that this is his poem.

Milton follows the Homeric model, starting with a call on the muse (and exactly who he is calling on is an interesting issue we will discuss elsewhere); the first sentence of the poem is complex, but unpacking the grammar the basic sentence structure is "Sing, Heavenly muse, of man's first disobedience...." And as we will see, he returns to call on the muse at other points in the poem.

An epic is by definition in verse, and uses one of the "heroic" meters. We must keep in mind that poetry is much older as a narrative art form than prose. Homer used a dactylic hexameter form, a form with six dactyls to the line, a dactyl consisting of one long and two short beats. Some translators have tried to copy this form, with more or less success; others have used meters more familiar to Western ears, often iambic pentameter, which is the meter that Milton uses in Paradise Lost.

But in all cases, epic poetry uses relatively long lines, as opposed to, say, a ballad, which is also a sung narrative but normally uses much shorter lines.

Another aspect of epic poetry is solemnity. In ancient times, epic poetry was often recited during religious festivals, and was accompanied by the solemnity and ritual elements of religion and priesthood. (Greek drama, for example, was written to be performed during religious festivals.)

Milton's poetry did not have the same surrounding accouterments of solemnity, not being designed to be recited during church services, so he sought to impose the same sense of seriousness and solemnity through his language. Compare his language, for example, with Longefellow's in The Song of Hiawatha, also a long narrative poem but one which does not even attempt to match the gravitas of the traditional epic.

Another aspect of most epic poetry is its continuity of language. Epic poetry does not go thumpety-thumpy as, say, Kipling is wont to do. Nor does it have the short, sometimes enigmatic lines of, say, Dickinson. Since the classical model is sung, the poetry must keep flowing, must keep our thoughts intact as we move from line to line.

Thus you will find Milton makes extensive use of very long sentences with interior pauses marked by commas and semicolons, but with as few full stops – periods – as possible. This effect is most noticeable when the poetry is read aloud; you will hear this if you listen to a recording of PL, or read it aloud to yourself. Laurel commented that it sounds like organ music, which is a very appropriate comparison.

Epic poetry also makes extensive use of simile. This was a favorite technique of Homer, and was carried forward by Virgil and adopted, probably from their examples, by Milton. These, then, are some of the principal common elements of epic poetry: heroic meter, solemnity of language, continuity of language, and extensive use of simile.

We will identify others as our reading of Paradise Lost progresses, but I hope this will help a bit to identify some of the basic elements which mark Paradise Lost as an epic poem. Milton's great epic (1667) is built upon the stories and myths

— in the Bible and in the classical tradition — through which Western men and women have sought to understand the meaning of their experience of life. Attention to some of these materials and to the ways in which Milton draws upon, and departs from, other versions and interpretations of those stories will enrich the reading of his poem.

The foundation story, of course, is the Genesis account of the Creation of the world and of Adam and Eve, culminating in the drama of their temptation and Fall. By Milton's time, the seventeenth century, that story had been reformulated in many translations in many languages and had accumulated many centuries of interpretive commentary, Jewish and Christian. Milton, in undertaking an imaginative, poetic re-creation of that story, had necessarily to accept, revise, or counter the views offered by such influential commentators as Saint Augustine and the Reformation theologian John Calvin.

He probably did not know Rachel Speght's commentary, A Muzzle for Melastomus, or Aemilia Lanyer's poem Eve's Apology in Defence of Women, but these texts provide the first examples of women turning Genesis commentary to feminist account.

The various commentators' views — about Adam and Eve, about the Edenic garden, about prelapsarian conditions of life, about the Tree of Knowledge, about the nature of man and woman as created, about marriage as first instituted, and about the causes of the Fall — can be usefully compared to Milton's own analyses in his theological tract Christian Doctrine, which remained unpublished until the nineteenth century, as well as his poetic representations of such matters in Paradise Lost.

During his tour of Italy in 1638–39, Milton probably saw some of the numerous representations of aspects of the Genesis story in Renaissance paintings and tapestries. We do not know which ones he saw, but certain remarkable images may have stimulated his imagination. A representative sample is included here: Veronese's Creation of Eve, Cranach's Adam and Eve, Dürer's The Fall, two of the Medici tapestries presenting The Fall and The Judgement of Adam and Eve, and Masaccio's The Expulsion.

Milton's poem also draws on such repositories of classical myth as Ovid's Metamorphoses and other literary analogues. Ovid's narrative of the myth of Narcissus resonates throughout the story told by Milton's Eve about her first coming to consciousness.

Two allegorical interpretations of the Narcissus myth — by Milton's contemporary George Sandys, the translator of Ovid, and by Sigmund Freud — may highlight how Milton reworks that myth. The poetic version of the Fall story in Guillaume Du Bartas's hexameral poem The Divine Weeks and Works provides another kind of literary analogue.

In Joshua Sylvester's translation that work was extremely popular, and Milton certainly knew it. Finally, the epic tradition itself was a major literary resource for Milton: it is sampled here through the opening passages — propositions and invocations — of four epics central to Milton's idea of that genre: Homer's Iliad and Odyssey, Virgil's Aeneid, and Torquato Tasso's Jerusalem Delivered.

Milton's epic proposition and invocation may be compared to these, and also Milton's defence of his better kind of tragic epic. Homer and Virgil did not use rhyme, and Milton scorned it in heroic poems as a "troublesome and modern bondage"; accordingly, the classical epics are represented here by modern unrhymed translations.

Tasso did employ rhyme, as did his Elizabethan translator Edward Fairfax. The first important criticism of Milton's epic was provided by his good friend the poet Andrew Marvell, in a commendatory poem published in 1674 along with the second edition of Paradise Lost.

It invites comparison with later prose criticism by Addison and Samuel Johnson. Responding visually to Paradise Lost are a set of engravings by John Baptist Medina that were included in the elaborate folio edition of Paradise Lost in 1688. Several of the Medina images, notably those included here, provide their own interesting interpretations of crucial scenes in the poem.

METAPHYSICAL POETRY

During the period of Milton's Paradise Lost as well as myriad of poets construction of an epoque submerged in metaphysical literature, a number of significant events both socio-political, entwined with a systematic religious metamorphism of the sixteenth and seventeenth century led to a time of unrest and discovery. The creators and author's of work of this periods placed their emphasis not specifically on a level of morality or self understanding but rather a rediscovery of the body and soul, almost a form of existensionalism or physical cosmos with a geography. 'All things are subject to the Mind..

It measures in one thought the whole circumference of heaven and by the same line it takes the geography of the earth. The seas, the air, the fire all things of either, are within the comprehension of the mind. It has an influence on them all, whence it lakes all that may be useful, all that may be helpful in government.

No limitation is prescribed to it, no restriction is upon it, but in a free scope it has a liberty upon all. And in this liberty is the excellence of the mind; in this power and composition of the mind is perfection of a man..Man is an absolute master of himself; his own safety, and tranquillity by God..are made dependent on himself.'1 In this short example of Puritanism text as it stands, alone contains a number of various references to the process of colonization, of expanding, perceiving all geographically and manipulating, making man or perhaps more specifically the colonisers omniscient and God-like.

The crusader self-reliant and independent with the knowledge that God is his guardian of safety and tranquillity. In this particular the growing number of Puritans played a significant role both in the cultivation and transformation of the Christian religion and foreign territories.

The Puritans themselves comprised of those in the Church of England unhappy with limitations of the Elizabethan Settlement; some were Presbyterians, and all were to some extent or other Calvinists (though not all Calvinists were Puritans). They were a people of scrupulous moral rigour and favoured plain styles of dress, detesting any form of luxury or decadence. The name Puritan later became a catch-all label for the disparate groups who led much of the New World colonization and won the English Civil Wars. New World colonization began as early as 1480 by English seamen performing spectacular feats of exploration under Elizabeth I.

These seamen made various claims of territorial annexation in America in an effort to outflank their Spanish rivals however, all foundations of permanent colonies proved abortive until the early 17th century. Thereafter, there was steady progress in acquiring territories in the Caribbean and mainland North America. Much settlement in the latter had a religious motive, with colonists seeking to escape the constraints of the English Established Church.

As a result, there was an uneasy relationship between many colonial administrations and the royal government at home. Further to these tensions the 'colonies were split in their allegiances during the civil wars in Britain, but Charles I derived little useful help from those who supported his cause.

The collapse of James II regime (1688-9) proved a blow to the efforts of Westminster to encroach on self-rule in North America. The relationship between the centre and the colonies remained problematic right until the War of American Independence. The metaphysical tradition established during the seventeenth century can find its foundations in the colonization explorations and the domestic unrest caused by the civil wars.

The combination of the two contextually, both in spirituality, imagery and definitions of time and space; have the unique effect of creating a devout religious protagonist's perceptions of his environment and its history, encompassed in as often was the case one work of art, as a testimony to the period and the Church of England. Frequently such works could be found in the form of poetry, commonly regarded as the most eloquent and essential part of the English language as a means of communications, via its plurality, richness of language and syntax.

Poets of the era harnessed the tools of poetry to the

spiritual essence of their communication create an impact of divine, gospel-like proportions, which were received and regarded as perhaps the most innovative and highly appreciated works of poetry! to have arisen. One such poet was John Milton whose epic work Paradise Lost (written in 1667) was ultimately the last and great Adamite work. John Milton (1608-74), was an English poet, the son of a composer of some distinction. The preparation for his life's work included attendance at St. Paul's School, Christ's College and Cambridge for several years.

His reputation as a poet preceded him as addressed to the conscience of Europe. As fame through his work augmented so with it did his political career. 'The theme of Paradise Lost (completed 1665, published 1667) had been in Milton's mind since 1641.

It was to be a sacred drama then; but when in 1658 his official duties were lightened so as to allow him to write, he chose the epic form. The first three books reflect the triumph of the godly—so soon to be reversed; the last books, written in 1663, are tinged with despair. God's kingdom is not of this world.

Man's intractable nature frustrates the planning of the wise. The hetero! dox theology of the poem which is made clear in his late De Doctrina Christiana did not trouble Protestant readers till modern critics examined it with hostile intent. Part of the poem's greatness, apart from its length, is a function of the visual immediacy with which Milton realizes the imagined scenes.

Milton has been criticized for glossing over certain contemporary developments in scientific and intellectual thought

...What if the sun
Be centre to the world, and other stars
By his attractive virtue and their own
Incited, dance about him various rounds?
Their wander course now high, now low, then still
Progressive, retrograde, or standing still,
In sixth thou seest, and what if seventh to these

The planet earth, so steadfast though she seem,
Insensibly three different motions move?
Which else to several spheres thou must ascribe,

The poem's realism is that of a myth, and its credibility dependent on the outlines of Christian belief, rather than specific historical details. The entire concern or major theme of Paradise Lost is to confute predestination and demonstrate the freedom of will. However Satan is portrayed as an almost romantic, recognizable character with whom we share every twist and turn his thinking takes throughout his physical and mental journey.

Satan can easily be perceived as the bold intrepid colonist, not lacking the courage of his convictions, be it at the expense of being exiled from the vaults of heaven. With the strength of classical precedents, Milton's cosmology refracts a seemingly incomprehensible geography of fantastic proportions, utilising allusive language to describe the indescribable. Nevertheless this did not deter some illustrators attempting to recapture the imagery of Militon's Cosmos. Satan's fall from grace to a desolate place of fathomless voids, yet unpopulated, turns Satan's disgrace into a voyage before a quest with a mission, not unlike that of the colonisers. In Book I the voyage of these unchartered and as yet inanimate destinations began when Satan and his host are:

Hurl'd headlong flaming from th' Ethereal sky
With hideous ruin and combustion down
To bottomless perdition, there to dwell
In Admantine chains and penal Fire.
For nine days they fall through Chaos till:
Hell at last
Yawning receiv'd them whole, and on them clos'd,
Hell their fit habitation fraught with fire
Unquenchable, the house of woe and pain.

They splash down into a burning lake, and, looking around, discover themselves much changed from their original angelic form, similarly their surroundings are:

A Dungeon horrible, on all sides round
As one great Furnace flam'd, yet from those flames

No light, but rather darkness visible
Serv'd only to discover sights of woe,
Regions of sorrow, doleful shades, where peace
And rest can never dwell, where hope never comes
That comes to all; but torture without end
>From which they make their way to land:
..yon dreary Plain, forlorn and wild,

The seat of desolation, void of light, Save what the glimmering of these livid flames Casts pale and dreadful. Nonetheless, like a colonizer in a one of the worst far flung corners of the globe, claiming whatever he passes as his own, Satan makes the best of his circumstances:

Farewell happy Fields
Where Joy for ever dwells; Hail horrors, hail
Infernal world, and thou profoundest Hell
receive thy new Possessor

Meanwhile the demons begin work creating a splendiforous palace, Pandemonium, perhaps the most palatial structure in Hell's history to match that of heaven. Satan's acceptance of his situation, is analogous to a determined settler determined to cultivate his surroundings as his own before expanding further afield.

Later the demons swarm to the council to decide on an acceptable plan of action. Amidst the demons and second in rank is Envy; he tells of "another World, the happy seat / Of some new Race cal'd Man," and suggests that they subvert it "and drive as we were drive,/ The puny habitants; or, if not drive/ Seduce them to our Party." This is perhaps the most substantive and overbearing allusion to colonisation of the New World, meant literally in this context.

The eager demons might well be a metaphorical representation of the religious convoys who were frequently sent ahead with the intent of settling and were hell bent on converting the original inhabitants of the land into their own kind, to adopt them into their religion, their community, so that by manipulating and corrupting them they could seize advantage of their innocence by blatantly encroaching on their land and property, with minimal opposition.

Another part adventure to discover wide
That dismal World, if any Clime perhaps
Might yield them easier habitation

Satan's heroic-like journey continues through treacherous conditions, having to pass inhospitable terrain and fauna, before reaching "thrice threefold" gates of Hell, three of brass, three of iron, and three of adamantine rock, guarded by Sin and Death. On managing to escape Milton's world of Hell he eventually reaches earth where subtly tempts Eve with the forbidden fruit of knowledge until Eve concedes and eats leading to their loss of paradise.

An analogy could be drawn here between Satan and the colonisers of the period enduring a tiresome journey and then tempting the inhabitants (Adam and Eve) with the prospect of wealth through trade; and on acceptance, thus marking their own loss and transgression into a state of perpetual inferiority thereafter in respect of the colonisers.

Adam and Eve the original settlers are beguiled by Satan's corruptness through their own innocent naivity. In respect of Paradise Lost and the theme of colonisation we can the course marked by Satan via his journey (see diagram) is regarded as his geography, despite having finally accomplished his course of action. Further on in books V-VII we have elaborate description of the landscape of Paradise, which is used the manifesto of colonialism through religious dynamics and instability.

The schematics of geography and the final mappings that became increasingly important, in so far as territories, progression of colonization and like, even God himself charters the stars in a calculated Genesis

He took the golden compasses, prepared
In God's eternal store, to circumscibe
This universe, an all created things:
One foot he centred, and the other turned
Round through the vast profundity obscure,
And said, Thus far extend, thus far thy bounds
This by thy just circumference

Milton himself somewhat of a nationalist puritan poet in

response to the issue of reformation, firm in the belief that the English were God's chosen people addressed parliament asking:

Why else was this Nation chos'n before any other, that out of her as out of Sion should be proclam'd and sounded forth the first tidings and trumpet of Reformation of all Europ. And had it not bin the obstinat perversnes of our Prelats against the divine and admirable spirit of the Wicklef, to suppresse him as a scismatic an innovator..the glory of reforming all our neighbours had bin compleatly ours. Similarly if not more so the concepts of colonialism, the systematic functions of identifying, locating and securing are no better displayed, conveyed or apparent than in writings of the metaphysical poets.

Man is all symmetrie,
Full of proportions, one limbe to another,
And all to all the world besides:
Each part may call the furthest, brother:
For head with for hath private amitie,
And bothe with moons and tides.

In this brief extract taken from George Herberts poem Man we can see the extent to which this evangelical poem - using maps and geometry to define the protestant server and his maker. A new method of language and metaphors had become available and poets did not hasten to incorporate as many different styles as possible to create an identity, using the terminology associated to science, in order to define.

A place for everything and everything in its place, reaching the conclusion that God is omnipresent, after having used language to process His location. Likewise John Donne an acclaimed poet of his period, and as Dean of Saint Paul's Cathedral was a seemingly inexhaustible source of spirituality with which to ordain his poems.

Licence my roving hands, and let them go
Behind, before, above, between, below
Oh my America, my new found lande,
My kingdome, safeliest when with on man man'd
My myne precious stones my Empiree
How blest I am this discovering thee

In this his poem named, Elegie: To His Mistress Going to Bed the allusions to colonialism are by no means marginalised. Donne paints a scene of a woman undressing, in which his description has the duality of de-sexualising, whilst sexualising. The emphasis and attention paid on material objects such as the garments are for all intents and purposes dehumanising. The description of clothes is paralleled to the colonial, metaphysical conceits discovery and of ownership, whilst mapping.

Ostensibly what Donne endeavours to do is colonise the body of the woman. Although considerable language and detail is spent in describing the layers of clothing the purpose of which to emphasise the letting go of material objects.

The infinite quest of the spiritualist could be that longing for the return to innocence, of spirituality and spiritual embodiment can only be achieved when irrelevant and extravagant thoughts of materialism and clothes are disregarded. Once the woman is void of all external graces and is the way nature intended, only then does the journey of exploration commence, to discover the essence of human nature, the spiritual manifestation of passion merely acting as a catalyst in the celebration of sexuality.

The theme of a quest, searching, mapping territory or bodies, geography of mind, body and soul, unrest and all that is external is apparent in a large proportion of what was written in the seventeen century, religious unsettlement serving only to fuel, scepticism or convictions further. The majority of metaphysical poems have similar themes and imagery, often set in room, study or office, any private enclosure reminiscent of a confession booth. Writing poetry in the form of a confessional is used as a moment of introspection.

The new awareness of questions rising with new religious identities of new churches necessitated these occasions of profound reverence and occasional enlightenment, in a journey through their own spirituality. Poetry was writing for private readership, a confessional in the form of a diary, debating with themselves and God. The status of body, that of men and women, the relationship between themselves with one another, and God were all predominati! ng factors in their writing. Poetry was written private realms for a private readership with no public address.

A parody may even be draw between Milton circumstances and his vision of Satan, during on of his profound moments of reflection:

Me miserable! which was shall I fly
Infinite wrath, and infinite despair?
Which way I fly is hell; myself am hell;

I may be useful to think of Satan in the light of 'likening spiritual to corporal forms', partly as representative of the public world of politics and rebellion, and his presentation as an exploration of the ambitions and failures, the egotism and despair, that public life offers.

In this his role is therefore complemented in the poem by the private, domestic world of Adam and Eve, in whose interpersonal relations are enacted the possibilities and problems of freedom and self-restraint. In metaphysical poetry the body was seen as a secular vessel, embodied with a spiritual love of the world, attached to a humanist concept that pre mined to embody God within the body of man.

Colonialism expanse across the America's induced imagery through language; exploring, discovery, conquering, divine protection, geometry, geography, astronomy, navigation and science were the foundations on which metaphysical poetry evidently propelled itself to growing popularity at a time of general social, political and religious unrest. The Sunne Rising also created by Donne was slightly more satirical, yet maintaining that man was ultimately the ruler of his own world, and God being embodied in wherever he be therein.

The sun is employed as a metaphysical conceit, with man being able to block it and the other element with a single wink.

Thy beams, so reverend and strong
Why shouldst thou think?
I could eclipse and cloud them with a winke,

With reference of imperial history he no longer needs to

explore to India, for it is already traced and recorded on a map before him. His self-elevation and lack of humanity are comparable to that of Milton's Satan. Around the same period other works of post-colonial art were be developed, no doubt heavily influenced by contemporary issues.

One such example is Shakespeare's final work and tragi-comedy The Tempest (1611), interposed and concerned with the theme of the elevation of one myth above another, recurrent impact of colonialism, morality and the loss of innocence. Shakespeare's unique style of writing is as a direct result of a plethora of influences, one of which was 'Montaigne's essay Of Cannibals which discussed the value and the way of life of societies which had not been affected by civilisation of a European type. In addition to this essay a pamphlet circulate called The Discovery of the Bermudas, otherwise called the Isle of Divels, may have played a crucial role.

This pamphlet described the bold adventures of a religious group of colonist travelling in a convoy of ships from London to Virginia. However during the voyage, the flagship was separated from the remainder! of the convoy in a storm. The maverick ship inadvertently blew towards Bermuda before being tossed onto some rocks. The colonists lived on the islands until they had built boats in which to continue their voyage. The story of their almost miraculous survival aroused considerable interest in England and echoes of their adventure can be found in The Tempest.

With little regard of the more elaborate themes images the tale is one of a landing on a island, a veritable paradise, already inhabited by Caliban (often spelt 'canibal' by Elizabethans by transposing the letters 'n' and 'l') a wild, deformed uncivilised beast (representative of native settlers), who is quickly manipulated, overthrown and enslaved by Prospero (King of Milan).

Caliban and his environment are parallelled to those of the Garden of Eden and Caliban himself is elemental. As the story progresses and the tyrannical relationship between the two continually increasing, Caliban's intellect is worthy of argument against Prospero for having denied him his birthright. Prospero's aim of teaching Caliban was to increase his indisputable control over him, by subverting him into an incomplete and image of his master, defective of all other attributes ie of magic.

Caliban, similar to every colonised people before him adapted his adopted culture and power of speech inflicted upon him as a weapon to communicate his own indignation and animosity towards his oppressor. And despite being frequently referred to as a crude savage, disfigured, and evil Caliban exemplifies a better set of values than most of the 'civilised' characters in the play.

This image derives from speculation regarding the popular English belief that uncivilised pagans were below their civilised counterparts in the hierarchy which had God at its apex and inanimate nature at it base. However a few individuals were beginning to question this assumption and 'there is evidence in the play that Shakespeare believed that the corruption in a civilised man was more abhorrent than any natural albeit uncivilised behaviour.'

At a time when many books and sermons, effected a characteristic Renaissance union between moral and political implications, and concerned themselves with the task of persuading the public that exploration was an honourable and indeed a sanctified activity and Drake was compared to Moses, combining voyaging and mystagogy a practical justification of "the lawfulnesse of Discovering".

It was a somewhat sophistical argument by Purchas, in favour of the propriety of usurping the rights of native populations, and an insistence, half-mystagogic, half-propagandist, on the temperate, fruitful nature of the New World, and the unspoilt purity of its inhabitants. 'The True Declaration defends colonizing, on the ground that it diffuses the true religion and has authority from Solomon's trade to Ophir (whether it lay in the East or, as Columbus thought in the West Indies).

There is room for all; and in any case the natives cannot be regarded as civilized people.' The revelations of The

Tempest of watching Caliban suffer at the hands of Prospero afford interesting material for examination. Caliban endures his abuse and insistent that he has deprived him of what is rightfully his, and this perhaps may have been Shakespeare's way of confronting his contemporary pro-colonising audience with the problems of ownership of newly discovered lands.

MILTON'S REDEMPTION OF EPIC POETRY

Classicists, out-of-date liberal arts majors, the sort of people who belong to the Conservative Book Club, and even many Christians like to say that there are certain books or certain classes of books that are more valuable than others. They talk about "enduring values," "the condition of man," "timeless beauty," and "the common cultural consensus."

They take the view that if one has only so much time in this life which may be devoted to reading, then a good portion of that time would be better spent with these "classics" than with just any old thing that comes to hand. I must confess that as a member of three out of these four groups of people (you may rest easy as to my position in the fourth), I agree with them.

Within the best class of books — what most people would understand you to mean if you said the phrase "the classics" to them out of the blue at the drinking fountain — we find a conscious dependence upon the preceding literary tradition. At one level, this dependence is evident in an author's familiarity with a literary tradition; the terms that he uses in his own works — his "grammar"— are those of the authors who have preceded him.

They have communicated to him, and he has been receptive. So we see names from classical mythology (Achilles, Hercules, Apollo, Zeus) appearing over and over again throughout the history of Western literature as a kind of shorthand. The significance of each name is part of the "common cultural consensus," and because we agree on the meaning of those terms, they communicate far more, and better, in one word than the author might have with many paragraphs of faceless abstract words.

For example, "Trojan horse" is a more lively, enduring mental image than "clever subterfuge" and may even carry far more useful connotations.

On a deeper level, authors within the literary tradition appropriate ideas and themes and even structures handed down to them by earlier authors, and they make them better, or even make something new using the old materials. The epic formula, the ode, the drama, the lyric — all have been used, imitated, developed, matured, and added to in the twenty-five hundred to three thousand years since their first known use.

Although most of the greatest authors were in fact "original" in this sense in that they made something new, originality *per se* has not been, until the last two hundred years, the dominant virtue for which an author felt he had to strive. When that notion began to thrive under the Romantics (who wrote some beautiful poetry but had terrible theories), it took the form of a deliberate attempt to shake off the past, while pretending to appreciate it, rather than building on it.

Finally, and most importantly here, we find within the "classic" literary stream a specific kind of adoption that matures the forms: *authors in the Christian age have redeemed secular ideas, themes, and structures.* Augustine reminds us that at the Exodus, the Hebrews "borrowed" from the Egyptians "jewels of silver, and jewels of gold," to illustrate how Christians ought to treat such things as pagan mythology.

Many of the stories of the Greeks and Romans — Achilles, Aeneas, Orpheus, the gods — are wonderful jewels, and rather than abandoning them, subsequent Christian authors influenced by those stories have borrowed them, sprinkled blood on the posts, and run away with them in the night.

Redemption is possible for at least two reasons. First, since the old (pagan) terms are part of the Western literary tradition, Christians must possess some familiarity with them in order to communicate with others who operate within that tradition. Paul the Apostle used his knowledge of the pagan poets (Homer, Epimenides, Menander), dramatists (Aeschylus), and philosophers (Socrates) to communicate to the Greek world. Second, as C. S. Lewis argues in *The Pilgrim's Regress*, there may be more to the story of the origin of the myths than simply depraved creativity on the part of the early Mediterranean people. We shouldn't find it unreasonable to suppose that God had his hand in the making of at least some of them, especially in light of the obvious grain of truth many of them carry. Gold and silver are not inherently evil, and neither (considered carefully) are the myths.

Classic literature provides some of the richest ground for a Christian to study if he is interested in understanding and appreciating the classics, if he is interested in demonstrating to his less intrigued brethren the value of immersing oneself in the classics, and especially if he is interested in discovering how Christian writers in the past have exercised the cultural mandate in literary history.

One of the clearest and most fascinating examples of a Christian poet exercising redemptive stewardship over the classical literary tradition is John Milton in his use of the Roman poet Vergil. The high peaks of the Western literary tradition are the great epics, but the epics change according to the worldviews of the authors, and it is the result of that change, of the maturing of the epic form, which allowed Milton to do what he did.

Milton had a view of history which was preceded not by Homer, although Homer is the first in the epic line, but by Vergil. Homer, in his *Iliad* and *Odyssey,* reveals a view of history without design and without purpose.

In the last book of the *Iliad,* Priam, king of the Trojans, and Achilles, hero of the Greeks, mourn together for their dead; then Achilles says, "Such is the way the gods spun life for unfortunate mortals, that we live in unhappiness, but the gods themselves have no sorrows." He describes immediately afterwards the two urns at the threshold of Zeus from which the chief god bestows blessings and curses on men without any apparent order or goal.

Throughout the epic, "Destiny" is mentioned often, but it is very clear that Destiny is not about the long-range future of mankind or a nation — it is about the future of each man, and it is capricious, not teleological. In the *Odyssey,* Odysseus goes to Hades to receive a prophecy, and there meets Achilles, hero of the *Iliad,* who says,

> O shining Odysseus, never try to console me for dying.
> I would rather follow the plow as thrall to another man, one with no land alloted him, and not much to live on, than be a king over the perished dead.

Neither prior good deeds nor the well-being of one's descendants comforts a person in death. The Homeric worldview has only destiny without significance. Destiny, in Homer, is about "human and personal tragedy built up against this background of meaningless flux." Vergil's *Aeneid,* on the other hand, demonstrates just as clearly that the Romans had a radically different conception of history — that it has a purpose and a direction. From the very beginning of the poem it is apparent that Vergil is "spreading out his story both in time and space."

In the opening we discover that, as in the *Iliad,* the gods are forces that drive events, but we also see that men think differently now about this driving of events. Aeneas, throughout the book, encourages his band to carry on in the face of hardships; not simply because, as in the *Iliad,* "the Destinies put in mortal men the heart of endurance", so that they must carry on with whatever it is that the fates have spun out for them just because that's the way it is, but rather because, as the *Aeneid* says, the gods "shall raise your children to the stars and build an empire out of their city."

All through this work we are reminded of prophecies which must be fulfilled, we hear the constant call of Fate to a direction, to an end (the founding, eventually, of Rome), which the Trojans must obey over every desire of the present. The concept of duty to posterity, to the future, and to the outworking of prophesied events for the nation, though understandable to us, is a new one in the history of the epic attitude, or at least one that Homer's heroes would not have recognized. Milton redeems this attitude toward history for his (Christian) purpose.

Obviously, Milton participated in the epic tradition in a general way by using the forms and conventions of the epic.

He writes his story of the Fall in twelve books, he invokes his Muse (the Holy Spirit) at the beginning, he uses epic similes that run on for so long one almost forgets what is being illustrated by the comparison, and so on.

But Milton was able to do much more than simply imitate the structural conventions of the epic; he used for his own purposes that one feature of the *Aeneid* that could only have arisen from Vergil's teleological view of history and that lent itself admirably to telling the Christian story of the future.

In the last half of book six of the *Aeneid*, Aeneas is shown the future of his descendants by the spirit of his dead father, Anchises. We have already seen that in Homer, too, there is a visit to the land of the dead, but there the purpose is very different. The spirit of the blind prophet Tiresias is to reveal the future to Odysseus, but it has only to do with his own fate—"the way to go, the stages of your journey, and..how to make your way home".

Aeneas, on the other hand, hears from his father that "you will learn of your entire race and of the [city] walls that have been given you". This is a long range vision that is to inspire in Aeneas something more than the desire to survive and get home.

In the last two books of Milton's *Paradise Lost*, the archangel Michael shows and narrates to Adam a vision of the future of mankind (Adam's descendants) through history to the end of the world, and this vision has the same teleological drive behind it, only on a greater scale.

Because of such elements as the *locations* in which they receive the visions, the *purpose* for which the men are shown the visions, the roles of Aeneas and Adam as *federal heads* for races which partake of a common ethical quality, the central element (the *incarnate hope*) of the visions themselves, and the clear connection between teleological understanding and *ethical behaviour*, the last section of *Paradise Lost* parallels marvelously the last half of book six of the *Aeneid*.

The parallels are such that Milton, thoroughly versed in Vergil as he was from his school-days, must surely have had this section of the *Aeneid* in mind when he was writing his own vision of the future; and they are a clear illustration of the way in which Milton the Christian uses Vergil's teleological development in the epic to the advance of a new kingdom — that of Christ.

LOCATION

Aeneas, in the *Aeneid*, book 6, is in the underworld — that this is an extraordinary setting is beyond question, and all the narrative leading up to his entry into Pluto's realm is designed to make the audience feel that fact.

However, Aeneas is no longer in the place of torment, but in Elysium, the happy half of Hades, and the action has calmed down (from the previous fevered description of souls in torment), so that Aeneas, Anchises, and the Sibyl, the priestess of Apollo, are in the midst of a crowd of the blessed souls moving on their way through peaceful fields toward the upper regions and eventually to reincarnation in the world of living men.

In this quieter mood, some of the strangeness of the underworld has been lost. Vergil has a solution, but it comes in the guise of a plausible move. In order better to view the souls moving by, Anchises "gained a vantage from which he could scan / all of the long array that moved toward them", and then he proceeds to interpret all the figures moving past in terms of the future of Rome.

Although Vergil does not make much of Anchises finding a good spot from which to view the passing souls, it is important that Anchises does so, not simply to see better, but to set off what he is doing. He is no longer part of that passing crowd — the phrasing, brief as it is, has separated him, and created (in a minor, understated, way) not the original mood of strangeness but at least an image of separateness fitting for the prophetic role Anchises is about to undertake.

In the analogous portion of *Paradise Lost*, after Michael tells Adam and Eve that they must leave Paradise, he commands Adam to "Ascend / This hill", Adam responds,"Ascend, I follow thee, safe guide", and then the narrator says, "So both ascend / In the visions of God".This repetition of "ascend" emphasizes that something extraordinary is happening; we understand that Adam and Michael are going not just to a different location, but, like Aeneas, to a special one. And that place is

..a hill
Of Paradise the highest, from whose top
The hemisphere of earth in clearest ken
Stretched out to amplest reach of prospect lay.

This is a vantage point from which Michael can do most appropriately what he has been sent to do. It shows Adam the world geographically, but it also gives the feel of a separated — "consecrated" — place fitting for a supernatural occurrence. A vision of the future is not an ordinary event, and it does not occur in ordinary ways or places. Not only must the recipient be placed in a special condition physically and spiritually, but the audience must be made to realize that an extraordinary event is taking place.

Epic poets are not above giving their audiences clues to the action in their poetry. Not only epic conventions, but any device which the reader can interpret, consciously or not, is useful to the poet in conveying what he wishes to in his art. That is what happens here. Whereas in Vergil, Anchises' simply stated act is our clue, in Milton, it is the repetition that tells us to pay attention, that something unusual is afoot; and the ascent is a movement away from the scene of the previous action and to a separated place.

PURPOSE

Vergil's purpose for Aeneas' s visit to the underworld is for him to learn what future races and people depend on his continued struggle against the forces Juno throws against him in her hatred of the Trojans and to encourage him in that struggle by a vision of the greatness of some of his descendants.

This sort of encouragement could never have happened in Homer, because of the difference in worldviews. Time was no inducement to the Greek heroes. But here in the *Aeneid*, the old household gods that Aeneas brought with him out of burning Troy have appeared to him in a night dream and told him that "we shall raise / your children to the stars", and the god Apollo himself had given Aeneas hope that a land would be given him in which to settle, so that by now Aeneas knows there is a future and a reason to continue his journey, although up to this point his understanding has been vague. What is necessary now is for him to see more clearly what is to come, and that is father Anchises' job.

At each setback Aeneas receives throughout the *Aeneid,* he receives a fresh word from a prophet or a god in order to keep him going. Just when the Trojans' hopes (that the land they were in was the fulfillment of Apollo's prophecy) were being crushed by a plague sweeping through the camp, the household gods had appeared with a reaffirmation of Apollo's message.

Later, in book 5, after the Trojan women have burnt their ships in their desperation for a permanent site, Anchises' spirit appears to Aeneas and tells him to come to the underworld to seek him out so that he can "learn of all your race / and of the walls that have been given you".

When the Sibyl is overcome by Apollo in her cave at Cumae, she tells Aeneas, "Do not relent before distress, but be / far bolder than your fortune would permit". This is prefatory to Aeneas' journey to Hades and is part of the message of the trip. All of these passages illustrate the fact that Aeneas' s visit to Elysium is designed for his encouragement. Even the Elysian Fields come as a relief to Aeneas after the blow of seeing the infernal side of Hades. There he sees many reminders of his own failures — Dido, who had committed suicide when Aeneas left her at Carthage, and warriors from the Trojan War.

The vagueness of the prophecies to this point is removed when Anchises shows Aeneas exactly what will happen and who his descendants are to be. Every preceding prophecy is elucidated by the Elysium display, and this shows the importance of the event to Aeneas' future endeavors. Furthermore, one of Aeneas' descendants will be the author of a return to a golden age for a war-torn Rome, and were

Aeneas to refuse to go on, his descendants would lose the hope of this man. Not only is Aeneas encouraged, therefore, by the hope of descendants, but his knowledge that one in particular will be great is a spur to his courage. When we turn to Milton, we see a similar purpose of encouragement at work. In *Paradise Lost,* Michael says Adam is to see the future

..thereby to learn
True patience, and to temper joy with fear
And pious sorrow, equally inured
By moderation either state to bear,
Prosperous or adverse: so shalt thou lead
Safest thy life, and best prepared endure
Thy mortal passage when it comes.

Michael has already told Adam that he has been sent "To show thee what shall come in future days / To thee and to thy offspring". Thus Michael's purpose is similar to Anchises', in that he is showing the future to encourage Adam to persevere and not to give up in the face of adversity, because there are future generations depending on him, but also because man's entire hope rests on one of Adam's descendants. If Adam does not carry on in spite of the trouble he has brought upon himself, he will prevent the eventual salvation of men. Adam must carry on in his struggle just as Aeneas must. His life will now be both a battle and a journey.

Furthermore, this passage is similar to the above passages from the *Aeneid* in that Michael's appearance with a vision comes after a major setback — the Fall. Adam desperately needs encouragement, for he has experienced the same despair that Aeneas has, wishing for death, although his reaction to that discouragement has, of necessity, been different from Aeneas', because the cause of it is different. Aeneas is buffeted by fate, but Adam is buffeted by his own sin.

Nevertheless, Michael tells Adam that he and Eve should go on their way "yet much more cheered / With meditation on the happy end". The teleological perspective he is giving them is to be an encouragement; they are to locate themselves in creation and (especially here) time in order to live out the remainder of their days aright.

HEADSHIP

Milton's Adam and Vergil's Aeneas are very similar in the roles they play as federal heads of their races. Aeneas is the father of the entire Roman race — the gods had said, "we shall raise / your children to the stars". He is the first Roman man. Adam is the father of a race, too — the entire human race (including Aeneas!). He is the very first man.

In more general ways as well, Milton's description of the future through Michael follows the pattern set by Vergil. For example, Aeneas and Anchises see among their descendants not only good men and leaders, but many who are not what Aeneas might wish in his offspring. Boastful Ancus, the cruel Tarquins, haughty Brutus (1081-1084) — these are in the line of Aeneas' descendants. Worse (in Vergil's eyes), are Caesar and Pompey, descendants of Aeneas and near relatives of each other, who get along so well as mere spirits in the underworld, but will bring war against each other in their day on earth (1095-1104).

Milton has even more material to work after this fashion, for all of Adam's offspring will be tainted by the Fall, and thus evil to some extent. Not only so, but since Milton is not merely concerned with social or political good or evil, as is Vergil, but rather with absolute, spiritual good and evil, everyone, with few exceptions, will fall under the indictment of evil. Thus, whereas in the train of men that Aeneas sees there are few bad men, now in Michael's display of future men to Adam there are few good men: Abel, Enoch, Noah, the Patriarchs, Moses, Joshua, David, and after Christ, the disciples.

From another perspective, Vergil gives us a roll call of many of the great men in Roman history, with only the occasional attack on some bad ruler. Milton also gives a roll call of great men of history, but he emphasizes heavily the predominant evil that will pervade history.

THE INCARNATE HOPE

In both epics, there is a vision of the fulfillment of a promise concerning a great man to come, who will bring his people into a golden age. As Anchises and Aeneas observe the souls passing, they see the man you heard so often promised —Augustus Caesar, son of a god, who will renew a golden age in Latium, in fields where Saturn once was king, and stretch his rule beyond the Garamantes and the Indians — a land beyond the paths of year and sun, beyond the constellations, where on his shoulders heaven-holding Atlas revolves the axis set with blazing stars.

Here is a description of a man bringing in a golden age, a man who has been promised for a long time. We know that Vergil was very much the conservative, and as such wished wholeheartedly for the restoration of peace and order that Augustus seemed to promise after the civil wars that had racked the Italian peninsula prior to his reign. But Vergil felt so strongly about this that in his Fourth Eclogue he becomes messianic:

The last age, told by heralds in Cymaean song, Is come! the march of the centuries swings along.

Returns the Virgin, Saturn is king again,
A new and better race descends for men.
But only do, Lucina, deign to smile
Upon the newborn babe, whose grace shall guile
Our iron breed at last to cease its pains;
The age of gold will dawn while Apollo reigns!

The Eclogue speaks in terms of the Golden Age, written about also by Ovid in his *Metamorphoses,* wherein the earth, under the reign of Saturn before Jove overthrew him, yielded its bounty to man without being plowed or seeded; the animals were tame which now are vicious, and men were peaceable. To all this, Vergil prophesied, the world was returning.

Of the subject of the Eclogue, he says, "the world's ponderous sphere bows before thee — earth and the tracts of ocean and the empyreal vault!" The educated medieval and Renaissance world was so taken by this Eclogue that Vergil was widely considered to be a proto-Christian prophet, even though he was a pagan, and Dante chose him for his guide through Hell and Purgatory because of his standing as a prophet.

Milton uses the basic idea of the promised man in his

treatment of the Scriptural theme of Messiah, who would come to put an end to strife in a way that even Augustus himself never could. The messianic theme is the most critical element of Michael's prophecy of the future. The promised man in *Paradise Lost* is of course the "Woman's Seed"(12.327), the Son of God.

Michael refers to the prophecies several times; the first follows the appearance of Moses' successor, Joshua, in the wilderness, when he speaks of

...Joshua whom the Gentiles Jesus call,
His name and office bearing, who shall quell
The adversary Serpent, and bring back
Through the world's wilderness long-wandered man
Safe to eternal paradise of rest.

This sums up not only the fulfillment of the promised adversary of Satan but also his millennial plans — the restoration of Paradise. Later, when he has foretold the birth of Messiah, Michael says that he shall "bound his reign / With earth's wide bounds, his glory with the heav'ns"; then, in his exposition of the end of all things, he speaks of "him so lately promised to thy aid, / The Woman's Seed, obscurely then foretold". The promised man is obviously Jesus Christ, the Saviour who has been promised for the deliverance of mankind from the evil effects of the fall of Adam and Eve.

He will usher in "ages of endless date / Founded in righteousness and peace and love".This language is not unlike that used for Augustus, but Milton makes the connection between Vergil's terms and his own Christian ones even clearer in his ode, "On the Morning of Christ's Nativity." There he says that if man could but hear the music of the spheres, "Time will run back, and fetch the age of gold" (stanza xiv); in stanzas xvii and xviii we are told that it cannot be so until after the Judgment Day, but it "now begins."

This is not only reminiscent of Vergil, but it would be a mistake for the reader not to have Vergil in mind and to be summoning up the sort of images that Vergil and Ovid had when they used the phrase "age of gold." It is that kind of eschatological imagery that is operative for Milton; the truth can be grasped through the images of the poets. This promise is the key to the vision of the future. If it were not that Someone would come and restore the world and man, there would be no point in showing Adam the vision. The reason for the vision is to show Adam that even in spite of the Fall, not only should he keep living and battling with the Nature that now is turned against him, but God himself will send an answer to the problem that the first couple created. God's answer will be a restoration, through one great man promised from the beginning, of the Paradise they had lost.

ETHICAL TELEOLOGY

We find a marked structural similarity between Aeneas' exit from Elysium and Adam's exit from Paradise. Vergil describes the gates through which Aeneas and the Sibyl must pass out of Hades thus:

There are two gates of sleep: the one is said to be of horn, through it an easy exit is given to true Shades; the other is made of polished ivory, perfect, glittering, but through that way the Spirits send false dreams into the world above.

And Aeneas and the Sibyl leave through that ivory gate, so that Aeneas can reenter the world of the living and press on to found his city.

The description of the great eastern gate of Paradise in *Paradise Lost* is of a rock

Of alabaster, piled up to the clouds,
Conspicuous far, winding with one ascent
Accessible from earth, one entrance high;

And it is through this gate that Adam and Eve must exit: Michael grabs their hands "and to the eastern gate / Led them direct, and down the cliff".

There is only one gate to (or from) Paradise; there are two gates from Hades. Nevertheless, there are strong similarities in the two accounts. First, and least important, the colour of the gates is similar — Vergil's is ivory, and Milton's is "alabaster" (white). Second, the gates from Hades are restricted, as is Paradise's.

Third, in both cases the leave-taking through the gates

comes immediately after the vision of the future, so there is no further revelation, no more questions, no dawdling. In both stories, the protagonist (Adam and Aeneas) must go out into the world and struggle.

The vision of the future — foreknowledge — does not obviate the necessity for the struggle; indeed, it is given in order to hearten them for it, which implies that the struggle is necessary — there is no element of fatalism, or determinism apart from means, here; they each see the future, and must now go and bring it to pass. The vision of the direction of the future, the revelation of design and purpose, is to provoke action — teleological understanding must be ethical, must be acted upon, and cannot be merely intellectual, or it becomes disobedience.

Milton redeems this teleological drive in his epic, given to him by Vergil, in a manner not open to Vergil's ultimately futile outlook. What Vergil's epic, great as it is, could never have consistently supported—true obedience, self-denial, and long-term ethical behaviour encouraged by a consideration of future generations — Milton's could, because the One Man who is the centre of the vision is the same who in the Gospel removes the obstacles to obedience.

Chapter 5

John Milton and Blank Verse

Blank verse is often confused with free verse, though they actually have nothing in common except the fact that neither rhymes. Free verse is a medium for an era that has little understanding for or appreciation of the magical and incantatory nature of poetry. It avoids all of the various patterns of repetition which have been central to the various poetic languages of the world and substitutes instead a loose and varying rhythm that in many cases differs from prose only in that the lines do not come out to the end of the page.

Early in the 20th century such poetry in the hands of poets like Eliot and Pound sounded fresh and original. These poets, however, had ears trained by more traditional forms and could write lines that were clean and crisp and graceful. The generations that followed, without such a background mostly lack the ear to write free verse effectively and the technique to write traditional verse. One result has been that today there are probably more people writing poetry than there are willing to read it.

Blank verse, on the other hand is a traditional form—unrhymed iambic pentameter. In theory it consists of ten syllables made up of five pairs of syllables, the first unstressed, the second, stressed. In practice a passage of iambic pentameter is made of lines that range from nine to eleven syllables with five stresses to each line, though not all arranged in an iambic (x /) pattern.

The perfectly regular iambic pentameter line lies like a bass line behind the verse, but is seldom followed exactly. We seem to have some inner sense of iambic rhythm, for we hear it in the tick-tock of every clock, though in reality the sound is only in our ear. There is no actual difference between the ticks and the tocks; we merely impose the rythm upon them. Speaking of clocks, here is an amost perfect imabic pentameter line from Shakespeare: "How do I count the clock that tells the time." Here we have the pattern in almost pure form— x / x / x / x / x /. It doesn't really sound very appealing does it? Shakespeare is obviously playing off the clock image with a tick-tock rhythm.

Perhaps as compensation the next "iambic pentameter" line is almost unscannable: "And see brave day sunk into hideous night." I think the stress pattern of this is something like x / \ / / x x / x /. The word "brave" is about half-way stressed, but falling between two stresses serves as an unstressed syllable. Shakespeare probably read "hideous" as a two syllable word, though it does not matter greatly.

In this line there are ten or eleven syllables and five stresses. Standing alone it could not really be called iambic pentameter, but as part of a poem with that meter as a bass or base line, it is. One of the unfortunate features of many school books that have a unit on poetic forms is that they often quote lines and mark the stresses in a way that follows the proper pattern, but that is not at all the way anyone would really read the line.

Once when I was teaching a creative writing class I decided to explain meters, and for iambic pentameter chose Robert Frost. Most of his longer poems are in this form and, as everyone knows, Frost is very regular in his patterns. I opened a literature survey to Frost's "Mending Wall," confident that here would be a clear example.

The first word of the poem was "Something." You might possibly force the word into "sum-Thing," but no one really would. The first iambic foot of the poem was reversed, though the rest of the line was regular enough. I tried the second line: "That sends the frozen-ground-swell under it." I didn't even try to do the metrics of this line. I tried the third: "And spills the upper boulders in the sun." This would almost do. The problem is that it is only our underlying expectation of a stress that puts a stress on "in" which is weak in itself, and is part of a very non-iambic unit—"in the sun," which would normally be stressed x x /. Line four was seriously irregular.

Line five was close, though it stressed a weak "is." Lines six, seven, and eight were all seriously irregular. Finally, with line nine I almost had what I wanted: "To please the yelping dogs. The gaps, I mean." We do play down the "I" to humour the meter, but altogether, this is pretty close. My point here is not that Frost is less traditional than his reputation, but rather that English iambic pentameter leaves the writer about as much freedom as anyone could ask for. No poet in English is more strongly identified with blank verse than Milton, who first made it the norm in English for epics and other long poems.

Before Milton, though blank verse was used for dialogue in most drama, it had not been used for long poems or even for translations of long poems, though today it is nearly always used if prose is not. We can see, however, in the very first line of Paradise Lost, however, that Milton is not more regular than Frost in his usage: "Of man's first disobedience and the fruit." Milton does compensate with a fairly regular second line: "Of that forbidden tree, whose mortal taste."

Aside from popularizing blank verse, Milton also deserves credit for showing a way the deficiencies of the form can be overcome. The reason blank verse was used for dialogue is that it is a fairly faint rhythm, not too obviously different than that of normal speech. Not only is the iambic unemphatic, but so is the pentameter.

The normal rhythm in English seems to be the four stress line. The other most natural rhythm is a four stress line alternating with a three stress line, which in English is called ballad meter. In Old Norse, like English, a Germanic language, there is a close equivalent with ljodahattr meter which also alternates a four stress line with a three stress line and is often used for ballad-like poems.

The five stress line does not come naturally and does not create a strong rhythm. One can write so much of it that it becomes second nature, but it is a learned talent that no one does naturally. Thus the danger of blank verse is that it will become flat and monotonous, and in fact if often does, especially in a long poem. Frost overcomes that problem by having a good ear for voice tones, so that his verse seems to speak to us in a natural way. Milton, on the other hand, makes it work by a richness of language, and by making one line rush into the next without the usual hesitation, so that there is always a sense of pressing forward.

In Milton, for the first time, the paragraph becomes a real unit of the verse, for we have to wait for the end before we can really pause:

Of man's first disobedience and the fruit
Of that forbidden tree whose mortal taste
Brought death into the world, and all our woe,
With loss of Eden, till one greater Man
Restore us, and regain the blissful seat,
Sing, Heavenly Muse, that on the secret top
Of Oreb, or of Sinai, didst inspire
That shepherd who...

Blank verse was a slow starter in America. In the seventeenth century the puritan New Englanders, when the wrote poetry at all, mostly followed the rather harsh lyricism of the English "Metaphysical" poets. In the eighteenth they were mostly feeble imitators of the manner of Dryden and Pope and wrote heroic couplets.

In the nineteenth it was mostly rather tame, though often proficient imitations of the romantics. For most Americans, poetry = rhyme. Thus blank verse was a mysterious, very highbrow thing. Making poetry rhyme was an art, but making it not rhyme was a mystery. The great blank verse classic for America was William Cullen Bryant's "Thanatopsis," which not only didn't rhyme but also had a title in Greek, and one that meant "Prospect of Death." You couldn't possibly get more POETIC!! than that.

It is eighty-one lines long, big enough to be impressive, but not long enough to outrun the limited attention span of the ordinary reader. Though the poem is a huge cliche with a thorougly overblown reputation, it is actually pretty proficient, and worth reading. More than anything, what killed its mystique was the arrival of modernism which produced a lot more poems that didn't rhyme. It has been replaced especially by Eliot's Wasteland, which not only doesn't rhyme (most of the time), but which also has footnotes and is lots harder to understand, two other big plusses on the impressiveness scale.

Actually, to say that Bryant's poem is proficient is saying quite a bit. Many poets today, even fairly good ones seldom write a line of ten syllables, and of the ones that do, many of the lines are obviously patched together from pieces like Frankenstein's monster, rather than having any real organic integrity. There is real power in being able to make a line which ends the line above it and begins the one below it, and still has a sense of completeness, like Milton's "Of that forbidden tree, whose mortal taste."

Here is the beginning of Bryant's poem:

The poet in English most identified with perfectionism in his meter and his appropriateness and exactness of rhymes is Alexander Pope. Most of what Pope wrote, and all the best of it was in iambic pentameter lines, though not in blank verse, but in the closed, or heroic couplet. Oddly, Pope's great epic poem on the founding of Britain was to be in blank verse.

It would have been interesting to see the results, but he only lived to finish the first six lines, though the poem had been thorougly outlined. I recall reading various Victorian critics who were mostly hostile to Pope's poetry. I think two different ones, though I can't now remember who described how Tennyson was first enamored by Pope but became put off by his monotonous regularity and struck out on his own. That is a charge that shows that criticism could be as ignorant and absurd in the past as it is now. First, Pope has a far better ear and produces far more subtle effects than Tennyson.

Second, Pope, like all significant English poets uses the ten syllable line with considerable freedom. In the passage below, only the last line is solidly regular:

Shut, shut the door, good John! (fatigued, I said),
Tie up the knocker, say I'm sick, I'm dead.
The Dog Star rages! nay 'tis past a doubt

All Bedlam or Parnassus is let out:
Fire in each eye, and papers in each hand,
They rave, recite, and madden round the land.
Epistle to Arbuthnot
I will finish with something a little like a crude.

From the earliest plays on, nearly all Elizabethan plays use blank verse. After 1660 comedy went to prose, but blank verse remained in use for tragedy into the eighteenth century. An exception was the short-lived popularity of Heroic Plays which were written in rhymed couplets. Milton's Paradise Lost, Pardise Regained, and Samson Agonistes were all in blank verse. James Thompson's Seasons pioneered nature poetry for the eighteenth chentury. A number of other long and influential poems of the eighteenth century were written in blank verse as well. Some of these had a major impact on the Romantic revolution in Germany as well as in England.

Edward Young's enormous poem Night Thoughts had a great effect on the Sturm und Drang movement in German literature, and was still considered a major work long after it was nearly forgotten in the English speaking world. Wordsworth's long, autobiographical poem, The Prelude is in blank verse. Browning's dramatic monologues are all in blank verse.

Frost's longer poems are in blank verse. Steven Vincent Benet's once widely popular epic, John Brown's Body is in blank verse, as have been most efforts in the last two centuries to write an epic. Edward Arlington Robinson's book-length romance, Tristram, as well as Tennyson's romance/epic Idylls of the King are also blank verse. Edward Markam's "The Man with a Hoe" was a blank verse Marxist classic for the first part of the twentieth century, but has slipped into obscurity as well as Edgar Lee Masters' once wildly popular people's epic, Spoon River Anthology. There is much, much else less well known, as well as a number of important works I have no doubt forgotten to mention.

BLANK VERSE IN ENGLISH POETRY

Blank verse (unrhymed iambic pentameter), used in

Shakespeare's dramas and Milton's Paradise Lost, is one of the most common metrical patterns in English poetry.

Other Relevant Terms:

METER—a rhythmic pattern in poetry wherein stresses (accented syllables) recur at fixed intervals. The word "meter" comes from the Greek word for "measure."

FOOT—the basic unit of meter; a group of syllables forming a metrical unit; a unit of (usually) two or three syllables that contains one strong stress. Metrical feet are marked by using symbols to represent stressed (/) and unstressed (x; or a flattened out "u" shape) syllables.

Iamb (*Iambic Foot*)—a metrical foot consisting of an unstressed syllable followed by a stressed syllable (x /).

Pentameter—a metrical pattern in which the poetic line consists of five iambic feet; thus, a ten-syllable line with the following pattern:

Rhyme (*Exact Rhyme*)—when two or more words or phrases contain an identical vowel sound, usually accented, and the subsequent consonant sounds (if any) are identical: free/see; hit/fit; prize/lies.

Dramatic Monologue—a poem in which a single (fictional) speaker addresses an implied audience at a critical moment in an ongoing series of events.

Free Verse—("vers libre"; open form poetry); poetry with no identifiable metrical pattern or rhyme scheme.

Stanza—a group of lines of verse, usually marked by a rhyme scheme (a regular pattern of end rhymes) and a predominant metrical pattern.

Verse Paragraph—a group of lines of verse (often in blank verse) which forms a unit within a poem; especially common in long narrative poems.

"Blank verse," or unrhymed iambic pentameter, is one of the best known and most widely used metrical patterns in English poetry, probably because it is so close to the natural rhythms of English speech and so easy to adapt to different levels of language—as Shakespeare does, for example, by having characters from clowns to kings speak in blank verse, but still in distinctive and appropriate voices.

Blank verse was introduced into English verse by Henry Howard, Earl of Surrey, who along with his older friend Sir Thomas Wyatt also introduced the sonnet and other Italian poetic forms into English poetry in the sixteenth century.

Surrey used blank verse (which his publisher called "this strange meter") in his translation of the fourth and second books of Virgil's "Aeneid" (1554, 1557),perhaps modeling it on the "versi sciolti" ("freed verse") of Molza's Italian translation. Blank verse must not, however, be confused with English "free verse" ("vers libre"; "open form" poetry), which lacks both a rhyme scheme and an identifiable metrical pattern, whereas blank verse has a very specific metrical pattern.

The structure of blank verse differs from that of rhymed verse, which tends to break into stanzas. Poems written in blank verse are often divided into "verse paragraphs" of varying lengths, as distinct from stanzas, which usually have regular lengths and are defined by their rhyme scheme and metrical pattern.

The natural speech rhythm of the English language is iambic, and the typical length of an utterance is usually about ten syllables, since that is approximately how long most people can speak comfortably without pausing to take a breath. Thus it might well be said that English speech rhythms tend to fall naturally into a predominantly iambic pentametrical pattern. This closeness to the natural rhythms of speech accounts for the particular popularity of blank verse in drama, dramatic monologues, epic poems, narrative poems, and long introspective or meditative poems.

One might ask why a poet would bother to write in blank verse, when it sounds so much like everyday speech. The fact is that blank verse, despite that similarity, is not quite a "normal" speech rhythm.

True, English speech follows a rough iambic pentametrical pattern, but it frequently varies that pattern as well, and also interrupts it with pauses and widely varied inflections. Put simply, the rhythm of blank verse is far more formal, more intensely regular, than the looser rhythmic pattern of normal speech.

The formality of such regular meter creates an incantatory effect, and like all strong rhythms it tends to capture and modify the listener's heartbeat and to induce a slightly altered state of consciousness.

Formal language patterns also establish a sort of "frame" around experience, thus marking the experience of the poem as separate and somehow distinguished from mundane reality. Just as the darkened auditorium at a concert creates a state of psychological receptiveness in the audience, so too does the insistent regularity of blank verse prepare the listener for a heightened response to the effects of language and image in the poem.

Soon after Surrey introduced blank verse, it became the standard meter for Elizabethan and Jacobean poetic drama. Probably it was first used in drama in "Gorboduc" (1561), by Thomas Sackville and Thomas Norton. Christopher Marlowe's "Tamburlaine" and "The Tragical History of Dr, Faustus" (c.

1588-93) are written in blank verse, but his lines are predominantly end-stopped (i.e., the sense of the lines coincides with the ends of the lines), and thus they lack the suppleness and variation that we find in William Shakespeare's use of blank verse.

Shakespeare is the most notable practitioner of blank verse as a dramatic form, and his plays are, in fact, written predominantly, though not entirely, in blank verse. Even in the twentieth century T. S. Eliot and Maxwell Anderson used blank verse as a vehicle for staged drama, though by that time their efforts were self-consciously anachronistic.

Blank verse has also been a favored form for reflective and narrative poems. The stately, majestic cadences of John Milton's religious epic "Paradise Lost" demonstrate the extraordinary incantatory power of that pattern maintained over long stretches of poetry.

Take, for example, the single long sentence that constitutes the first sixteen lines of the "Invocation" to Book I of "Paradise Lost":

Of man's first disobedience, and the fruit
Of that forbidden tree whose mortal taste

Brought death into the world, and all our woe,
With loss of Eden, till one greater Man
Restore us and regain the blissful seat,
Sing, Heavenly Muse, that, on the secret top
Of Oreb, or of Sinai, didst inspire
That shepherd who first taught the chosen seed
In the beginning how the Heavens and Earth
Rose out of Chaos: or, if Sion hill
Delight thee more, and Siloa's brook that flowed
Fast by the oracle of God, I thence
Invoke thy aid to my adventurous song,
That with no middle flight intends to soar
Above th' Aonian mount, while it pursues
Things unattempted yet in prose or rhyme.

Milton himself likened blank verse to the unrhymed verse of "Homer in Greek, and of Virgil in Latin" and called it "English heroic verse without rhyme." He considered rhyme "no necessary adjunct or true ornament of poem or good verse, in longer works especially, but the invention of a barbarous age, to set off wretched matter and lame meter...."

Milton defended his choice of blank verse for his epic as no defect, "though it may seem so perhaps to vulgar readers," but rather an "[esteemed] example set, the first in English, of an ancient liberty recovered to heroic poem from the troublesome modern bondage of rhyming". During the late seventeenth century and the first half of the eighteenth century, blank verse, though still used, was less popular, primarily because the most prominent poets of that period favored the heroic couplet.

In the nineteenth century, blank verse was frequently used by both the Romantic and the Victorian poets. William Wordsworth's autobiographical epic "The Prelude" was written in blank verse, as was Samuel Taylor Coleridge's meditative "Frost at Midnight."

The declamatory rhythms and rhetorical flourishes of Milton's blank verse were replaced in Romantic poetry by a more personal and colloquial manner. Robert Browning used blank verse in many of his dramatic monologues (e.g., "Fra

Lippo Lippi," "Andrea del Sarto," "The Bishop Orders His Tomb at St. Praxed's Church"), as did Alfred, LordTennyson ("Ulysses," "Tithonus").

Although neither poet can be credited with technical innovations in the form, their use of it is highly skilled and flexible, employing both colloquial rhythms and a more declamatory style, as the occasion warrants.

Around the time of World War I, during the "modernist" period, long poems in blank verse fell out of fashion, but blank verse continued to be used by some twentieth-century poets. It was especially favored by Robert Frost ("Birches," "Mending Wall," "Out, Out—").

Frost often said that his aim in much of his poetry was to capture the "sound of sense," that rhythmic pattern we notice in spoken language even when we are unable to make out the words being spoken. His poems written in blank verse demonstrate how conversational blank verse can sound while still retaining the formal effects of good poetry.

Here are the first eleven lines of his well-known poem "Mending Wall":

Something there is that doesn't love a wall.
That sends the frozen-ground-swell under it,
And spills the upper boulders in the sun;
And makes gaps even two can pass abreast.
The work of hunters is another thing:
I have come after them and made repair
Where they have left not one stone on a stone,
But they would have the rabbit out of hiding,
To please the yelping dogs. The gaps I mean,
No one has seen them made or heard them made,
But at spring mending-time we find them there.

Browning, too, writing many decades earlier, during the Victorian period, used blank verse to capture the sound of normal speech, but without its banality. In the opening lines of "Andrea del Sarto," the painter addresses his young wife in language that one might almost expect to overhear in a restaurant:

But do not let us quarrel anymore,

No, my Lucrezia; bear with me for once:
Sit down and all shall happen as you wish.
You turn your face, but does it bring your heart?

Yet carried over the 267 lines of this dramatic monologue, the poem's superficially colloquial rhythms produce an effect that normal speech could never produce. We are transported to another world, as it were, and mere reality fades, just as it does in a darkened theater.

Skillfully handled, blank verse is not likely ever to be mistaken for prose, despite the erroneous belief of what Milton would call "vulgar readers" that unrhymed lines do not deserve the name of poetry.

Chapter 6

Critical Analysis of Paradise Lost

THE STORY

Satan and his followers rebel against God. But God and his mighty angels defeat the rebels in a terrible war. God casts them into a dark abyss with a lake of fire.

There, the defeated legions deplore their fate and consider their future. In a great council, the many thousands of the fallen assemble in the capital city and seat of government, Pandemonium, where Satan sits on his royal throne, to hear their leaders speak their minds on the course of action they should take. Moloc, a rebel leader who fought fiercely against the forces of the Almighty, calls for renewed war.

Belial advises a do-nothing policy, maintaining that the horror of their hell will abate in time and that their surroundings will brighten. To challenge God would only result in another defeat and more punishment. After Mammon advises peace, Beelzebub–a majestic, imposing figure–notes that God is creating a new creature, man, who will occupy a new world, earth. If they turn this new creature from his ordained course, using force or trickery, they can enjoy revenge against God, Beelzebub says. His plan is not his own; it is the plan of Satan, his master.

The assembly of devils does not respond; they do not know what to say about this proposal.

Then the leader of all the accursed, Satan, speaks up. He first bemoans their environs:

Our prison strong, this huge convex of Fire,
Outrageous to devour, immures us round

Ninefold, and gates of burning Adamant
Barred over us prohibit all egress.

But if any of them manages to break free, Satan says, he will encounter a dark void beyond which are unknown regions and unknown dangers. Nevertheless, Satan, as leader, says he will venture forth and "Through all the coasts of dark destruction seek / Deliverance for us all: this enterprise / None shall partake with me." His "enterprise," of course is to work his deceptive charms against the new creatures. He will subvert God's plan and give hell a reason to cheer. None in the assemblage spoke against this plan. Instead, all rose with a thunderous noise to give assent:

Towards him they bend
With awful reverence prone; and as a God
Extol him equal to the highest in Heaven.

And so the assembly broke up and ventured off into the regions from whence they came:

Rocks, caves, lakes, fens, bogs, dens, and shades of death,
A universe of death, which God by curse
Created evil, for evil only good,
Where all life dies, death lives, and nature breeds,
Perverse, all monstrous, all prodigious things,
Abominable, inutterable, and worse.

Meanwhile, Satan "with thoughts inflamed of highest design / Puts on swift wings, and toward the Gates of Hell /

Explores his solitary flight "Later, Satan's daughter, Sin, who was born from the archfiend's head, and his son, Death, who was born of Satan's union with Sin, decide to follow and assist their father.

In heaven, God the Father and God the Son observe Satan flying in a rage toward earth. Satan will corrupt his new creatures, the Father says, even though they possess the willpower to reject sin. Their penalty will be death. However, because they will not rebel against God but instead succumb to Satan's temptation, they will be redeemable–if someone takes on the burden of their sin by suffering and dying on their behalf.

When the Son offers himself for this task, the Father

accepts the offer and approves of his incarnation in the world of man. To reach earth, Satan must fly past Uriel, a member of the highest-ranking order of angels, the Seraphim. Uriel watches over earth from his post at the sun. Disguising himself as one of the cherubim–the second-highest-ranking order of angels–Satan asks Uriel to point out the planet where man dwells so that he may go there, admire this new creature, and praise his great Maker. Uriel instructs him, and Satan resumes his journey and arrives at earth.

The sight of Paradise disheartens him, for it reminds him of all that he lost in his rebellion against God. After struggling with self-recrimination and doubt, Satan regains himself and enters Paradise, taking the shape of a cormorant–a web-footed sea bird–and perching in the Tree of Life (a tree producing fruit which, when eaten, yields everlasting life) to observe the newly created Adam and Eve.

They are beautiful, happy creatures who surprise Satan with their ability to speak and think logically. Later, when they are asleep, Satan whispers evil thoughts into Eve's ear–of "vain hopes" and "inordinate desires." When the archangel Gabriel learns of Satan's presence in Eden, he sends two angels to expel him. When they confront him, Satan defiantly scorns them and prepares for a fight. An angelic squadron descends toward Eden under the command of Gabriel, and a sign appears in the heavens in which God weighs the adversaries in his golden scales. When Gabriel tells Satan to look at the scales, the archfiend sees that they tip in the favor of the celestial forces, and he flees.

On a mission from God, the angel Raphael warns Adam and Eve about Satan. So that they understand the nature of their foe, Raphael tells them the story of Satan's rebellion and the great war in which angels on both sides fought fiercely. It ended in Satan's expulsion from heaven, Raphael says, after the Son of God intervened on behalf of the celestial forces. A new world with new creatures was then created to fill the void left by the rebels cast into the deep.

Adam, a curious creature, asks Raphael about the earth and its place in creation. Raphael explains the universe but warns Adam to temper his desire for knowledge with humility. When Adam expresses his great satisfaction with Eve as a mate, Raphael again cautions him to be careful. Living with and loving a creature such as Eve, with all of her charm and beauty, is wonderful; however, Adam must not let her divert his attention from his responsibilities to God.

Satan returns to the Garden of Eden in the form of a snake and tempts Eve to eat fruit of the Tree of Knowledge in defiance of a divine command never to do so. If she and Adam taste the fruit, he says, they will become gods. Eve eats. After Satan leaves, Adam–though reluctant–also eats. And so Adam and Eve fall from grace, and the Son of God pronounces judgment on the transgressing humans.

When Satan returns in triumph to hell, the multitude of fiends cheer him but suddenly turn into serpents. Earth becomes a place of changing seasons; the eternal spring is no more. Adam is downcast, wishing for death, and blames Eve for leading them astray. But they reconcile and decide to go on, confessing their wrongdoing and pleading for forgiveness. God decrees that heaven will remain open for them. But He sends the archangel Michael down to evict them from Paradise.

Before Michael leaves, he tells them about events to come in the history of the world and, from a hilltop, shows Adam his progeny–Cain and Abel (and the murder of Cain by Abel) and the descendants who later will form a covenant with God after a great flood.

Michael then foretells the advent of a Redeemer, who will die for the sins of humankind–then rise from the grave and leave earth but return later in a second coming.

Adam and Eve then walk into their new life.
The World was all before them, where to choose
Their place of rest, and Providence their guide:
They hand in hand with wandering steps and slow,
Through Eden took their solitary way.
They enter the imperfect world, with all its perils.

CHARACTERS

God the Father, God the Son Two of the three divine

persons making up the all-powerful Godhead, the single deity that created and rules all that exists outside of itself. The third divine person, the Holy Spirit, does not play a role in Paradise Lost. God the Father is portrayed as just but merciful, condemning the defiant and unrepentant rebel angels but permitting redemption of the repentant Adam and Eve.

God the Son volunteers to redeem them by becoming human and enduring suffering and death. Satan (Lucifer, Archfiend) Powerful and prideful angel who, with legions of supporters, leads an unsuccessful rebellion against God and suffers eternal damnation.

To gain revenge, he devises a plan to corrupt God's newly created beings, Adam and Eve, through deceit. Modern readers often admire him for his steely defiance. He would rather rule in hell, he says, than serve in heaven. It was not Milton's intent, however, to create an admirable character; rather his intent was to create a character of colossal hatred–loathsome, execrable, incurably remorseless.

Adam and Eve The first human beings, created by God to fill the void that resulted when God cast Satan and his supporters out of the celestial realm. Adam and Eve live on the planet earth in utter happiness in a special garden where spring is the only season and love and godly living prevail.

Though they have all that they want and need, cunning Satan tells them they can have knowledge and status beyond their reach if only they eat of the fruit of the Tree of Knowledge. Eve can become a goddess, he says.

Vanity overtakes her. She eats. Adam reluctantly does the same. Gabriel, Raphael, Michael, Uriel Powerful and fearless angels on the side of God.

Beelzebub, Mammon, Belial, Moloch Powerful leaders in Satan's army. In a great council in hell, each of them speaks his mind on what policy devil-kind should follow after losing paradise.

Should they make new war? Should they make peace? Ithuriel, Zephron Angels who expel Satan from the Garden of Eden with the help of a sign from God. Satan returns to the garden later to complete his devious enterprise. Mulciber

Fallen angel who designs hell's capital city and seat of government, Pandemonium. In ancient Roman mythology, Mulciber is another name for Vulcan (Greek: Hephaestus), god of fire and the forge. As a blacksmith, he kept shop in burning mountains (volcanoes). Sin Daughter of Satan. She was born from his head in the manner of Athena, Greek goddess of wisdom and war, who sprang from the forehead of Zeus, king of the gods.

SETTINGS

The settings are heaven, hell, the firmament (Chaos), and earth.

SOLAR SYSTEM

In describing the planets and other celestial bodies, Milton models God's creation on the Ptolemaic design (also called the geocentric design) rather than the Copernican design (also called the heliocentric design). The former placed earth at the centre of the solar system, with the sun and other celestial bodies orbiting it.

Copernicus and other scientists later proved that the earth orbits the sun. Milton was aware of the Copernican theory, but he used the Ptolemaic design–either because he believed it was the more credible theory or because he believed it would better serve his literary purpose.

In Paradise Lost, Adam inquires about the movements of celestial bodies–in particular, whether earth orbits the sun or vice versa–in his conversation with the archangel Raphael, but Raphael gives no definite answer. Raphael may have been speaking for Milton.

DATE COMPLETED

Milton completed the first version of Paradise Lost in 1667. It consisted of 10 books. In 1668 and 1669, he published versions with two additions: (1) an introductory comment about the verse form and (2) a section with a summary of each book. In 1674, he published the final version, in which he divided Books 7 and 10 into two books each.

The the completed work thus had 12 books instead of 10. He also reorganized the book summaries, placing each of them at the beginning of the book it summarized.

TYPE OF WORK

Paradise Lost is an epic poem which–like the epic poems of Homer, Dante, Vergil, and Goethe–tells a story about momentous events while incorporating grand themes that are timeless and universal.

SOURCES

Milton used the Bible, Homer's Iliad and Odyssey, Vergil's Aeneid, and the stories in Greco-Roman mythology as sources of information and as writing models. The Bible's Book of Genesis is the main source for his retelling of the story of creation and the first humans, Adam and Eve.

STYLE

Milton wrote Paradise Lost in dignified, lofty, melodic English free of any colloquialisms and slang that would have limited the work's timeliness and universality. The format, Milton says in an introductory note, is "English heroic verse without rhyme"–in other words, blank verse, the same verse form used by Shakespeare in his plays.

Milton's strong religious faith infuses the poem with sincerity and moral purpose, but he does not allow his enthusiasm for his subject to overtake control of his writing: Though Milton frequently uses obscure allusions to mythology and history, as well as occasional difficult words and phrases, his language is never deliberately affected or ostentatious.

What is more, it does not preach and does not take the reader on circumlocutory expeditions. Like a symphony composer–mighty Beethoven, for example–Milton is always in control, tempering his creative genius with his technical discipline. With a good dictionary and an annotated text, a first-time reader of Milton can easily follow and understand the story while developing an appreciation for the exquisite writing.

EPIC CONVENTIONS

In Paradise Lost, Milton imitated Homer and Vergil in their use of epic conventions–literary practices, rules, or devices that became commonplace in epic poetry. Among the classical conventions Milton used are the following:

The invocation of the muse, in which a writer requests divine help in composing his work.

Telling a story with which readers or listeners are already familiar; they know the characters, the plot, and the outcome. Most of the great writers of the ancient world–as well as many great writers in later times, including Shakespeare–frequently told stories already known to the public.

Thus, in such stories, there were no unexpected plot twists, no surprise endings. If this sounds strange to you, the modern reader and theatergoer, consider that many of the most popular motion pictures today are about stories already known to the public.

Examples are The Passion of the Christ, Titanic, The Ten Commandments, Troy, Spartacus, Pearl Harbor, and Gettysburg. Beginning the story in the middle, a literary convention known by its Latin term in media res (in the middle of things). Such a convention allows a writer to begin his story at an exciting part, then flash back to fill the reader in on details leading up to that exciting part.

Announcing or introducing a list of characters who play a major role in the story. They may speak at some length about how to resolve a problem (as the followers of Satan do early in Paradise Lost).

Conflict in the celestial realm. Divine beings fight and scheme against one another in the epics of Homer and Vergil, and they do so in Paradise Lost on a grand scale, with Satan and his forces opposing God and his forces. Use of dramatic irony. Dramatic irony is a figure of speech in which a character in a story fails to see or understand what is obvious to the audience.

Dramatic irony appears frequently in the plays of the ancient Greeks. For example, in Oedipux Rex, by Sophocles, dramatic irony occurs when Oedipus fails to realize what the audience knows–that he married his own mother. In Paradise Lost, dramatic irony occurs when Adam and Eve happily go about daily life in the Garden of Eden unaware that they will succumb to the devil's temptation and suffer the loss of Paradise. Dramatic irony also occurs when Satan and his followers fail to understand that it is impossible ultimately to thwart or circumvent divine will and justice.

IMAGERY

Milton's imagery is at times graceful and elegant, as in this memorable personification in the second and third lines of Book VI:

......Morn.
Waked by the circling hours, with rosy hand
Unbarred the gates of light.

At other times, the imagery is imposing and awe-inspiring, as in this description in Book VII:

.......There Leviathan
Hugest of living creatures, on the deep
Stretched like a promontory sleeps or swims,
And seems a moving land, and at his gills
Draws in, and at his trunk spouts out a sea.

Milton describes the commission of the first sin in simple, straightforward language, followed by a succinct personification summing up the terrible effects:

Her rash hand in evil hour
Forth reaching to the fruit, she plucked, she eat:
s Earth felt the wound, and Nature from her seat,
Sighing through all her works, gave signs of woe
That all was lost.

Milton uses personification again in this beautiful passage about a quiet night, the starry sky, and the ascendancy of the moon:

........The wakeful Nightingale;
She all night long her amorous descant sung;
Silence was pleased: now glow'd the Firmament
With living Sapphires: Hesperus that led......[Hesperus: evening star which the Greeks associated with the brother

The starry Host, rode brightest, till the Moon........of Atlas; later Hesperus was associated with Lucifer's brilliant light]

Rising in clouded Majesty, at length
Apparent Queen unveiled her peerless light,
And o'er the dark her Silver Mantle threw.–Book IV.

ENJAMBMENT

Milton uses enjambment (also spelled enjambement) throughout the poem. It is a literary device in which a poet does not complete his sentence or phrase at the end of one line but allows it to carry over to the next line, as in this passage near the beginning of the poem.

In the Beginning how the Heavens and Earth
Rose out of chaos: Or if Sion Hill
Delight thee more, and Siloa's Brook that flowed
Fast by the Oracle of God...

Milton's use of enjambment helps the poem flow from one line to the next.

MAIN THEME

In Book 1 of Paradise Lost, Milton reveals the central theme of the work: to justify the ways of God to man. Justify here means to explain and defend, and ultimately to vindicate, God's course of action in dealing with Adam and Eve after they succumb to the temptation of Satan and eat forbidden fruit.

SECONDARY THEMES

Inordinate pride It leads to Satan's downfall and his continuing defiance of God.

Envy Arising from Satan's pride, it makes him jealous of God the Son, who is the favorite of God the Father.

Revenge It motivates Satan to corrupt Adam and Eve and thereby subvert God's plans.

Vanity It leads Eve to believe–under the temptation of Satan–that she can become godlike. Deceit Satan appears in many disguises and tells many lies during his mission to trick Adam and Eve. Infidelity Adam betrays God by siding with

Eve and eating the forbidden fruit. Unbridled pursuit of knowledge It leads Adam and Eve to seek knowledge beyond their ken, knowledge that will make them godlike.

Volition Angels and humans alike possess free will, enabling them to make decisions. Satan freely chooses to rebel against God, and Adam and Eve freely choose to eat forbidden fruit. The consequences of their actions are their own fault, not God's. Milton uses this theme to help support the central theme, "to justify the ways of God to man."

Disobedience All sins are acts of disobedience against God, impairing or cutting off the sinner's relationship with God. Adam and Eve and all of the devils disobey God through their sins.

Loyalty: Loyalty to God and his ways are necessary for eternal salvation. Loyalty requires obedience. All of the good angels exhibit loyalty. Repentance Even though Adam and Eve have disobeyed God, their repentance makes them eligible for eventual salvation.

Hope At the end of Paradise Lost, Adam and Eve enter the imperfect world with hope; they can yet attain eternal salvation. Redemption Through the suffering and death of the Son of God, sinful man can reconcile himself with God if he is sincerely sorry for his sins.

CLIMAX

The climax, or turning point, of Paradise Lost occurs when Adam and Eve succumb to Satan's temptations and eat the forbidden fruit. This act of disobedience results in their downfall and eviction from Paradise.

THEMES OF PARADISE LOST: JUSTIFYING THE WAYS OF GOD TO MAN

The poem explains an entire theology. It is about the coming of sin into the world through the temptation of Adam and Eve by Satan after his defeat in Heaven. If Milton has justified the ways of God to man, all our questions about our relationship to God should be answered by implication from the poem.

The success of the explanation of course depends on whether you accept the Christian world view-even whether you accept Milton's special brand of Christian individualism. The task of explaining an entire physical and moral system is not one we attempt today. We divide our systems, believing that the world is too complex for a single theory to explain.

God's Omnipotence, Omniscience, and Free Will

The poem insists that all events are brought about by choice. Satan chooses to rebel, Adam and Eve choose to eat the apple, knowing the consequences. Every man and angel has free will. At the same time, God knows everything that is to happen. But his foreknowledge has no effect on choice-the universe is like a clock God winds up and sets going: each of its parts performs without interference from God.

You will keep puzzling over this explanation throughout the poem. It sometimes seems that God is callous about his creation because if he is omnipotent, why doesn't he stop evil from happening? On the other hand, perhaps God does not have the power to stop the clock or alter it once it's got going. In that case, there must be something even more powerful than God which programs him. It's an endlessly fascinating question. The poem will give you lots of examples for a continuing argument.

INDIVIDUAL RESPONSIBILITY

Everyone makes his or her own decisions. That means no one can blame anyone else for what happens. But there is a great deal of blaming in the story. Only when people accept responsibility for their own choices do they find peace within themselves and forgiveness and mercy from God.

THE TRUE NATURE OF FREEDOM

True freedom is total submission to God's will and acceptance of what he wants in the world. It is freedom from self and self-will. Satan symbolizes the wrong kind of freedom, rebellion against just authority. You are free when you understand where you fit in relationship to God and in the hierarchy of nature.

REASON

The highest exercise of man's reason is to understand and love God-and to trust him. This means accepting what may seem illogical to human reason. It also means not trusting human reason. Human reason may deceive because it is limited and cannot necessarily penetrate God's purposes, which are beyond logic.

It was perfectly reasonable for Eve to conclude that she would not die because the serpent had not died when he ate fruit from the Tree of Knowledge. But she was limiting fallible human reason. She ought to have gone beyond the logical argument and trusted true reason-God's word.

THE HIERARCHICAL ARRANGEMENT OF THE UNIVERSE

Everything is arranged in an order, beginning with God at the highest point of all, going down through the angels to man, and from man down to beasts and plants. Each part of the hierarchy has its own order: in Heaven, the angels are lower than God and must take their orders from him. On earth, Adam is closer to God than Eve, and she must take her orders from him. The poem is about the violation of the order, first by Satan, then by Eve, and then by Adam, who puts Eve ahead of God.

HISTORY HAS A PURPOSE AND AN END

Although devastating in its results, the Fall is only part of a historical process. Adam's fall leads through many generations to the incarnation of God the Son as Jesus Christ. His fall is therefore a "happy fault" ("felix culpa") because it leads to the fulfillment of God's purpose.

When Christ dies for man, he begins the process of redemption which eventually leads to the Last Judgment and the Second Coming. This will be the end of history, for then there will be a new Heaven and a new earth.

SOURCES

The sources of Paradise Lost are Milton's voluminous

reading. The story of Adam and Eve and the temptation comes from the first few chapters of the Book of Genesis.

The story of the War in Heaven does not occur in one single place. References to it occur in the Book of Revelation, the last book in the New Testament. Other places where hints of a great war and of Hell are to be found include the Book of Isaiah in the Old Testament and what are called the apocryphal books of the Old Testament. Milton also adds some details from the Book of Ezekiel, also in the Old Testament.

STYLE: THE POETIC METER

The meter of Paradise Lost is iambic pentameter, the meter in which Shakespeare wrote his plays. It is often called "blank verse" because it doesn't rhyme. Each line consists of five heavy stresses and five minor stresses. In theory a line should read like this: da-dum, da-dum, da-dum, da-dum, da-dum

It happens to be the almost natural rhythm of the English language, which is why it is easy to read blank verse when you forget your fear of poetry.

Very few lines are strictly regular in the meter. Even the famous first line reverses the stress in at least two places, where da-dum is replaced by dum- da and dum-dum. It also has one more syllable than the ten prescribed by theory.

English poetic meter is not the simple matter of counting feet that is often taught. It is a very complex interaction of stress, length, and quality of sound. It is better to forget the complications and read the poetry as naturally as possible. You will then be able to appreciate how Milton varies his rhythm and the musical quality of the words to fit what he wants to say. Read it out loud whenever you can, especially in the places where the speeches alternate like those in a play.

Chapter 7

England as Israel in Milton's Writings

By surveying Milton's use and non-use of certain biblical images, this essay records his loss of political innocence, and also something of his pluralism. In doing so, it shows in action his view of the relation between church and state. It charts his implied.

View of Isaiah Berlin's two concepts of liberty—negative and positive, the absence of external constraints as opposed to spiritual fulfilment or self-realization—to conclude that Milton favours the first for the sake of the second. He drew the corollary, that freedom mattered last as well as first. He was, in short, a more consistent thinker than is often acknowledged. I move toward these conclusions rather gradually, for two reasons.

First, it is worth illustrating from the writings and speeches of Milton's contemporaries how much more moderate Milton's political imagery from the Bible was than that of many with whom he shared political and religious commitments.

The imagery needs substantial quotation for the reader to recognise its dynamism, and to accept that it was used extensively, not only by religious cranks and the weak-minded. Secondly, I survey Milton's own writing widely, not only to show where he does share the fervour of the sectarians but also to illustrate the degree to which he does not share it even though the occasion and subject might have seemed to have suited such fervour.

THE IMAGE OF ENGLAND AS ISRAEL IN OTHER WRITERS

The greatest of all crises for ancient Israel was the Exodus. "Exodus" means literally the "coming-out" from Egypt, but extends to the wanderings of the Israelites in the wilderness, before they crossed Jordan and entered the promised land of Canaan. They were led by Moses, who at Sinai brought them the Law which governed their lives thereafter.

This normative crisis was used in England, by Parliament and Protestants generally, to image their own long struggle against King and Anglican bishops, to arrive at true Reformation. It was more than a rallying cry: on the contrary, it was their habitual, best image of where they thought God was leading their nation.

Beyond the Exodus metaphor, naturally, lay the subsequent story of Israel, including the figures of Joshua and Samson, the strife between prophets and kings, the struggle with idolatrous neighbours and world powers, the exile, the return, the desecration of the rebuilt Temple, and more. These also appear as images in the writings of the Civil War and after, alongside images of Exodus, though subordinated to it. All images so far interpret the present in terms of Israel's past.

But by going to the prophetic books of the Bible, above all Daniel and Revelation, extreme Protestants could interpret England's present from Israel's future, the future to end all futures, as a millennial consummation of prophecy, in which they were fighting against the Whore of Babylon, Rome, and could expect a fifth and final Monarchy, that of the Messiah, to end the four known evil world-monarchies, of which the fourth was Rome.

At this time, the lost tribes of Israel would be gathered. Jews, it was argued, should be readmitted to England in order to fulfil the preconditions of the Fifth Monarchy.

THE IMAGERY AND THE POLITICAL GROUPINGS

Such strange reasoning had large practical implications. All Protestant groups shared Cromwell's reasoning, though agreeing on little else at that time. The imagery of England as

Israel, a chosen people, serves to distinguish one sect or pressure-group from another and also serves as a guide to the rapid changes in political climate. In fact, we may understand attempts to monopolize this image as wars of words among the factions, in which both the government of Cromwell and its opponents were belligerents.

Once Cromwell had become head of state, the image of England as Israel on Exodus under Moses acquired new force. Colonel John Spittlehouse's title spells it all out: "A Warning-Piece Discharged: Or, Certain Intelligence Communicated to His Excellencie the Lord General Cromwell..As also, A brief and full Parallel betwixt the History of Israel and our late and present Series of Affairs.

In which Simile, Our present General is compar'd with Moses, as he was their Deliverer, Judge, and General..." Spittlehouse's book works the parallel. Cromwell himself used the image memorably to his new Parliament in 1653: the Exodus is "the only parallel of God's dealing with us that I know. " He compliments England, but also himself as the Moses of this "only parallel," which guided not only his view of the past, but also his plan for the future, moving England "towards a place of rest." Yearning, or threatening, he repeated "I say, towards it."

Others who did not support him used the same parallel for leverage. Gerrard Winstanley, the Leveller, complained in 1649 that conquerors "to this day" are "killing the poor enslaved English Israelites."[3] In 1652, he said to Cromwell, "God hath honoured you with the highest honour of any man since Moses time, to be the head of a people, who have cast out an oppressing Pharaoh."

This flatters and attempts to influence Cromwell, while not quite equating him with Moses. But the image could also be used to humble. When Cromwell intervened in the vitriolic dispute of two sectarians, one of them recalled the words of two Israelites in Egypt whom Moses had tried to reconcile, "Who made thee a prince and a judge over us? This superb deflation not only showed Cromwell his intractability, but also it meant that they were all still in Egypt.

Nonetheless, Cromwell commanded the army, held the power, and was the only candidate to play Moses. Others had to justify themselves with different imagery. Some went no further than the earlier or subsequent history of Israel, with Cromwell as a Jacob or a Gideon.

But his most vociferous critics (after the Levellers and Diggers had been crushed) were the Fifth Monarchy Men, under James Naylor. They believed that after four world empires would come the fifth, the rule of Christ through his saints at the end of time. To bring about this millennia, the self-appointed saints attempted to overturn all carnal institutions—parliaments as well as kings. The rule of the saints, "the new Israel," would follow.

So Puritans of every stripe used these images of the nation, or some part of it, as Israel. Since they had become the vocabulary of public debate, anyone who thought or spoke on politics had to use them. *Marvell's Poems, Political and Other*: It was not only prose zealots who employed the imagery. Andrew Marvell, so aloof and elusive in some poems, manifests an attachment in other poems to precisely this "only parallel." In "Bermudas" Marvell has his religious exiles sing praise to God "That led us through the watery maze"—wittily changing the wanderings in the wilderness to perils on the Atlantic in a small boat.

"Upon Appleton House" compares mowers cutting a swathe to "Israelites / Walking on foot through a green sea"—making the Red one green. This allusion is not serious, but in 1654 Marvell devotes some fifty lines of his poem on "The First Anniversary of the Government under O.C." to the apocalyptic imagery of Daniel and Revelation.[9] Here we meet the Whore and the Beast, and the need to welcome the Jews and so bring in the Last Days.

He scorns the "lying prophecies" of the Fifth Monarchists, along with their plots, not as bigotry, but as misapplication. Cromwell is the one to fulfil "the holy oracles". Or again, "If these the times, then this must be the man." Clearly, Marvell is striving, like Spittlehouse, to win the millenarian parallel for Cromwell.

When Marvell wrote a further panegyric for Cromwell upon his death, he reverted to the past of Israel. The Exodus figure looms large, but it is combined with allusion to Israel's subsequent exploits, as well.

Joshua and David join Moses as the heroes whom Cromwell resembles: Joshua continues Moses' role and leads the chosen people into the promised land; David becomes Israel's greatest King (chosen, not born). Cromwell is compared with the three.

They welcome him promptly upon his arrival in heaven. Preposterous as the compliments may seem, they are all apt. For instance, Cromwell like David loved music. As propaganda, they send precisely the right signal.

It would be curious, then, if Milton—who shared an office (both literally and metaphorically) with Marvell, and who shared a broad political and religious allegiance with Cromwell and his coalition — were not to use similar imagery for his political praise-poetry.

The main thrust of my paper examines so how this is so, and what explanations can be provided. *Milton's Relation to This Imagery and to Its Other Users*: Milton and Marvell worked together as translators in Cromwell's Foreign Office: in fact, Milton procured the job for Marvell. That neither makes their politics, nor their political vocabulary, identical but it does suggest a comparison.

The painters' cliché of Cromwell and Milton as close colleagues, man of action and blind visionary respectively, is wrong Nevertheless, we must ask whether Milton ever adopted the language of his overlord that provided the ideological underpinnings for Milton's employment and, indeed, Cromwell's whole power base. If he did not, that would itself be a notable finding.

"Decorum" might provide a simpler explanation. This view would mean that the presence and absence of Old Testament imagery depended on the topic, occasion and genre chosen.

If this were so, we might reason on the basis of my examples, that politicians making speeches would naturally use exuberant, simplistic imagery. Conversely, poets would be unlikely to employ such imagery in their private ruminations.

The imagery, in other words, would become a major rhetorical tool in winning over an audience. It might bore a sophisticated audience, such as the poet himself.

The evidence of Marvell's work does not show him limiting Old Testament imagery to popular appeals; on the contrary, he uses the imagery for all sorts of occasions. It does not appear where we might expect it, nor is it absent where we could expect it to be avoided.

Further, all these writers choose whether to speak or not, and what genre to use. Nevertheless, as occasion and genre do play some part in Milton's practice, I shall observe chronology and genre in exploring Milton's development.

Chapter 8

Milton's Writing

MILTON'S VERSE BEFORE 1642

Before 1642 Milton's verse shows signs of becoming interested in the "only parallel." His two earliest English poems are translations of Psalms 114 and 136, both of them concerned with the Exodus, in which he amplifies the Biblical joy with his own. He returned to Psalm 114 again eleven years later, at the age of 26, rendering it into rousing Homeric hexameters. This is the psalm entitled "In exitu Israel de Egypto," "When Israel came out of Egypt." He records that he woke up with the Greek version ringing in his head, and that he knew not why or how. Though one can only speculate that the "why" included a glimpse of its applicability to pre-revolutionary England, we must note the recurrence of his interest in the theme of Exodus.

Not only did Milton translate psalms of Exodus, but also in two poems written before 1642 he resorted to biblical imagery of divine intervention, one from the time of the Kings, and one from the gospels. In 1637 Milton called on the Lord to intervene in protecting his friend, the religious exile Thomas Young: "let God act now to scare away the armies of the Catholic enemy as once he drove away the Assyrian hosts! Then in 1637, in Lycidas, he imagines the intervention of St Peter, to punish the greedy clergy:

The hungry sheep look up and are not fed..
so
..that two handed engine at the door
Stands ready to smite once, and smite no more!

This (whatever its exact meaning may be) draws on gospel or apocalyptic imagery to express some new divine deliverance of God's people, a miraculous tribulation of the same kind and degree as the plagues on Egypt or the parting of the Red Sea.

Moreover, Milton looked back with satisfaction on this denunciation as prophetic, because in 1645 with hindsight he could declare, "..the Author..by occasion foretells the ruin of our corrupted clergy then in their height." Deliverance had come in the ousting of the bishops. The stage was set for Milton to identify the newly delivered English with the children of Israel.

MILTON'S PROSE OF 1640-49

In his prose writings of the early 1640s Milton moved closer to the Exodus image we are considering. Of Reformation (1641) uses it to attack. The bishops, then still in situ, are "Egyptian taskmasters." Leaping to the other end of the Bible, from the past to the far end of the future, he imagines the people of England at the Last Day "to be found the wisest, soberest and most Christian people when thou, the eternal and shortly expected King, shalt open the clouds to judge the several kingdoms of the world." He terms his image a "supereminence of beatific vision," a theophany or apocalypse of the end-time. In this work Milton ransacks the Bible for such hopeful, exhortatory images.

Animadversions, of the same year, sounds a similar note in terms drawn more exactly from Exodus: "When thou hast settled peace in the Church..then shall all thy Saints..triumph to thee, standing on the shore of that red Sea into which our enemies had almost driven us..should'st thou bring us thus far onward from Egypt to destroy us in this wilderness though we deserve."

Soon he moves over to a more future-directed, apocalyptic imagery of God's chosen people: "thy Kingdome is now at hand, and thou standing at the dore. Come forth out of thy Royall Chambers, O Prince of all the Kings of the earth..take up that unlimited Scepter."

In Areopagitica (1644), pleading now for liberty of expression as a means to Reformation, he envisions England as "fields ripe unto harvest," employing gospel imagery this time. Neither Exodus nor the Apocalypse are used as metaphors in this poem.

He compares England to Samson, "a noble and puissant nation rousing herself like a strong man after sleep, and shaking her invincible locks". Milton goes further when he recalls the Reformers Wycliffe, the Lollards, and Henry VIII: "God is decreeing to begin some new and great period in his Church, even to the reforming of reformation itself: what does he then but reveal himself to his servants, and as his manner is, first to his Englishmen?" (Hughes 743). The hyperbolic imagery closely identifies with the chosen people, even if Milton is also obvious trying to persuade Parliament to abandon censorship.

MILTON'S VERSE OF THE 1640S

Milton's poems of the 1640s are not numerous. They comprise one Latin ode, more psalm versions, and about ten sonnets. Despite the tremendous victories for Parliament and the cause of Reformation, he wrote no victory-odes or panegyrics, though in prose he enthused about the "reforming of Reformation itself." What is more, he wrote no more prose pamphlets until after the King's execution with The Tenure of Kings and Magistrates.

The Latin ode, Ad Rousium, is suggestive here. The ode is to Bodley's Librarian, John Rouse, and marks the end of the siege of Oxford. This was a huge victory for Parliament and its army under Cromwell, since Oxford had been the King's new capital. Yet what Milton celebrates is the end of hostilities, the resumption of civilized activities, like the reading of books. The poem is, in fact, about sending a replacement copy of his own poems to Bodley's Librarian. It imitates Roman poems exchanged between friends and family members who found themselves on opposite sides of civil wars, just as Milton and his brother Christopher did. In other words, the ode celebrates the resumption of non-partisan intercourse.

The Psalm translations are different, yet no more indicative of partisan views. Dated with unusual precision to "April 1648," they may be connected with public events. Suggestions have favoured either the Westminster Assembly, which wanted a new liturgy, meaning new metrical psalms, or else the anguish felt by Independents, re-arming for a second civil war because the Presbyterians were switching to the King's side.

The first suggestion would suit psalms of Exodus, the second less so. Regardless, Psalms 80-88 "done into metre" very literally, with notes about the Hebrew, show neither trend. God's anger and the Exodus receive emphasis, yet not more than blindness, the cult of the Temple in Jerusalem, and a mixture of other themes.

The sonnets of 1640-50 are often political, though they were not made public in print. In one, written "when the siege was intended to the city" by the King's army, Milton bids the royalist officer who knocks at his house to spare it, as Alexander the Great spared the house of Pindar.

It is a witty appeal, relying on Greek allusions with no Israelite parallel whatever. Two more sonnets attack critics who break the "known rules of ancient liberty". In these, the poet claims to have made the mistake of "casting pearls before swine"—a gospel, not a Hebraic, allusion. In the mightiest of these sonnets he assails the Presbyterians, as coercers of conscience:

New Presbyter is old priest writ large.

The etymological wit depends, again, on a knowledge of Greek, not on Biblical allusion. On the way to this climax, Milton wishes that Parliament will curb the Presbyterians by "clipping their Phylacteries." Phylacteries, the little boxes holding quotations from the Torah worn on the forehead by pious Jews, provide an Old Testament reference, but not a favourable, normative one.

Phylacteries, grown ostentatiously large, are denounced by Jesus as pharisaical. Milton's allusion is, after all, from a New Testament standpoint. Most of these sonnets uphold liberty of worship for all as the prime aim of state policy.

Gospel freedoms outweigh Hebrew fixities and forms. Milton had been badly hurt by the attacks on his divorce tracts, and by the Presbyterians' willingness to force consciences when they took power from the Anglican bishops.

Does he merely not use the Israelite image, or does he actively forego it? Some absences are certainly due to occasion: one would not expect a triumphal Israelite image to be used in the ode, Rouse being either neutral or on the King's side. Other absences, however, do seem noteworthy, particularly in those psalms and sonnets addressing public topics. A pattern begins to emerge.

MILTON'S POEMS OF THE 1650S

A similar pattern emerges from the poems of the 1650s, with one great exception. The psalm versions of 1653 are as mixed, as before, in subject (in fact, they also focus on metrical experiment). The sonnets are addresses to Parliamentary leaders—Fairfax, Cromwell, Vane. All three praise the addressees, then urge them to stay vigilantly on course. The "course" in question is to preserve the cause of religion, meaning liberty of worship. The major image in each case is classical or New Testament, if not both. Israel is nowhere to be seen.

Israel's absence is, in fact, striking. If there is any one of these sonnets to public figures on public topics which might adduce the imagery of Israel and Moses on Exodus, it would be the sonnet to Cromwell himself (1652). Such imagery, however, is not found there.

The imagery is Roman, Italian, contemporary, New Testament—in short, almost anything but Hebraic. If Milton's priority is to prevent a new Establishment of paid clergy, he could well have asked whether the spiritual leaders of Israel in Exodus served for cash. Instead, he addresses Cromwell in secular or gospel terms.

The volta reads:

Help us to save free Conscience from the paw
Of hireling wolves whose Gospel is their maw.

The gospel imagery is the same as in Lycidas, fifteen years

earlier. But instead of the wolves being the Catholics, now they are the "hirelings," those Independent clergy who asked Parliament to set up a state-salaried, state-controlled ministry. Milton's image equates this with coercion, greed, and an end to toleration. He did not want a state church, nor conformity to a national religion.

In other words, he was not just critical of that particular group (the Independents, now following the bishops and the Presbyterians in seeking to run a national church with gain to themselves). It was becoming hard for Milton to see how freedom of conscience could combine with any state religion. He was finding it equally hard to see any role for the cult of ancient Israel in his imagery.

One great exception to this reliance on New Testament liberty, above an idealized Old Testament unity, is Sonnet 18, "On the Late Massacre of the Piemontese." Compared with the earlier sonnets of advice to leaders, this is more heated and less reasoned, with a prophetic tone.

The Catholic Duke of Savoy had brutally repressed the religious worship of the Waldensians, a sect of proto-Protestants in the Alps. His soldiers had thrown non-combatants, including mothers with babies, over the cliffs. The atrocity was unusually hideous and Milton was the one who put Cromwell's protests to Savoy and other European powers into Latin. Details of these despatches vivify the sonnet.

Avenge, O Lord, thy slaughter'd Saints, whose bones
Lie scatter'd on the Alpine mountains cold,
Ev'n them who kept thy truth so pure of old
When all our Fathers worship't stocks and stones.

In this case, the stronger feelings raise many Biblical images. They come from both Testaments, especially prophetic books or passages—Jeremiah, Daniel, Revelation, and Luke. But they come also from a gospel parable, and Tertullian (not to mention Greek myth, Virgil, and Petrarch).

The array and force of convergent testimony are dazzling. The sonnet abounds in voices of Israel grieving and denouncing. The implication is that the atrocities described are unholy: God must avenge them. This, at last, is the Hebraic vehemence we have been awaiting. Nevertheless, the ending invites a closer look. What is a "Babylonian" woe?

And how are the Waldensian survivors to "fly" it? "Babylonian" explodes at the end like a cluster-bomb. It means "Roman," since the Papacy is blamed and the Roman church was often identified with the wicked Babylon of both Testaments. But it also means the Babylon of the Exile, beside whose rivers Israel lay down and wept. Maybe the encouragement of that allusion expands into an apocalyptic, Fifth-Monarchy hope for the Last Days. If so, it is one of Milton's very few millennarian moments.

The choice of the verb "fly" is odd. A much more pugnacious choice could have been made, such as "end," "quench," or such. The Waldensians could "fly" the woe only by leaving their vulnerable homes, and going into exile. The poem is sometimes criticised for being impractical, but Milton envisages voluntary exile, for truth and liberty's sake. It is exactly what the family of his close friend, Charles Diodati, had done in leaving Lucca.

It is also what pilgrims had been doing all century, to Holland, Germany, Massachusetts, and Bermuda. Milton had kept the image of "coming out of" Babylon for this great occasion. (We need not object that Babylon and Egypt are not identical: metaphorically they are.)

If the image is great, however, it is also disinterested. There is no suggestion in the poem that England is the promised land. Quite the reverse is true and the other sonnets show why. Milton's foreign office employment allowed him a renewed awareness of how the rest of Protestant Europe was faring. His prose studies of Dutch practices, and Arminianism elsewhere are a critique of his own country.

MILTON'S PROSE OF 1649-1660

Much of this prose was in Latin, addressed to Europe. It was hard enough to defend regicide before this audience, and out of the question to argue that the English were the chosen people. Milton concentrates on logic and law, with Biblical exegesis supporting him. Where he does wax fervid, as in the

1658 revised ending to his countrymen, he emulates Cicero (Pater Patriae). In the main, he keeps the rhetoric satirical. In Tenure of Kings and Magistrates (1649), Milton argues that kings must uphold laws and obey them, too. There is a contract between governor and governed which, if broken by either side, incurs legal punishment. His terms are those of social contract, not sacred Covenant.

In 1651, Milton was commissioned by Parliament to write their answer to an alarmingly successful piece of royalist propaganda, the Eikon Basilike—the "Icon of the [dead] King." That "icon" purported to be the weeping of Charles I over his erring people, full of sorrowing forgiveness—like Jeremiah or Christ weeping over Jerusalem.

It is arranged in layers, with sections of self-justification, followed by a Biblical pastiche of lamentation. Although it was a very one-sided sentimental work, people read it, loved it, and wept over it. Milton's method of reply was demolition, as his title Eikonoklastes shows ("Icon-Smasher").

He drove wedges between the biblical sanctities and the actual king. In short, he did not propose a rival Biblical parallel, but stuck to logic or else to his own side's version of the facts, with Charles as a "man of blood," and a quite disastrously bad ruler, as many of Charles's own side agreed. It seems Milton had recognised that the image of England as Israel was a two-edged weapon: Israel had a long tradition of kings, despite the Bible's own preference for "Judges" and prophets.

Milton's position was different, though, at the end of the 1650s, during the crisis following the death of Cromwell in 1658. Milton, despite being blind, ill and in retirement, produced four prose works in one year.

Two advocated a gospel policy against a prelatical one, on liturgy and on tithing. The fourth insisted on a basis of civil government grounded in law and reason, with no Biblical grounding at all. The third is much the most stirring, however, and it does use the Bible, including the "only parallel." Milton was either addressing different readerships, or trying any means to stave off the Restoration of monarchy.

His Ready and Easy Way to Establish a Free

Commonwealth has a tone of prophetic warning. The prophecy comes from throughout the Pentateuch, the gospels, Jeremiah, and climactically focusses on Exodus. Milton reproves the warring sects for building "no goodly tower of a commonwealth, to overshadow kings, but a tower of Babel."

(He contrasts the United Provinces, who have built more from less.) He says England is regressing to kingship despite Jesus' rebuke of certain disciples for wanting to "lord it over others, as the Gentiles do."

This is a particularly dexterous hit, making the godly sectarians ungodly. Going back to the history of Israel, he compares the English to those who so resented the crimes of the sons of Eli the prophet that they wanted kings to rule instead of prophets, as if two bad apples proved all apples bad. He aptly mentions Aesop's fable of King Log and King Stork, as well, but the principal aim is to confute Protestant extremists with the Bible itself.

Jeremiah is cited denouncing King Coniah: "O earth, earth, earth...." The allusion is truncated, and cryptic to us, but Milton may have thought that a single word to the wise would suffice, or broke off in a spirit of "absit omen." Jeremiah's full speech is filled with premonitions of exile and reprisal: "I will give thee into the hand of them that seek thy life [saith the Lord]...And I will cast thee out..into another country..and there ye shall die.

O earth, earth, earth, hear the Lord." Milton is warning the regicides and sectarians of what will follow on the King's return: particularly exile. Last, and most vehemently, Milton denounces those who for monetary reasons, like the murmurers of the Exodus, want to "return back to Egypt."Let all sensible men, "though they seem now choosing a captain back for Egypt,..bethink themselves a little, and consider whither they are rushing." To want to go "back to Egypt"—to prefer slavery—is the ultimate shame for the people of Exodus.

Milton waited until late in the 1650s debate about polity before entering into it. In particular, he waited before trumpeting the Exodus analogue, but then he used the trumpet to blow a fine impassioned blast of rebuke, a fortissimo appassionato. The army intervened yet again, called elections, and the new MPs invited the King back. Milton went into hiding for a time. He was silent on political topics for more than a decade.

CONCLUSIONS FOR 1642-1660

From the above narrative I draw a number of inferences. They are presented as if looking back from 1660, moving from more to less recent. Then I look forward again to the sequel in Milton's life, and so, finally, to a more theoretical rationale of absence. The Exodus parallel worked strongly for Milton in a crisis.

In 1659 he could expect his fellow religionists to loathe a return to an "Egypt" of monarchy, bishops, and tithing. Its rhetoric was negative or deterrent, to shame them. As they had no agreed Moses, however, nor Aaron nor Joshua, no Law and no Ark, the parallel conveyed no information or guidance, only a vague revulsion.

Old Testament parallels had given trouble, since the King's side could use them, too, and with great effect. As with the first item, the parallel works most naturally when voicing the hopes of underdogs. It preserves morale. Seeing that even Moses faced opposition and backsliding, however, and that England after Cromwell had no Moses, morale alone proved insufficient. Protestantism was international, and Milton knew this well. To limit the new Israel to England was impossible to the sincere tolerationist. Commercial wars against the Protestant Dutch had probably helped to dampen the enthusiasm of the open-minded.

The full form of the analogy, England as Israel, appears more clearly in his early prose than in his verse of any period. It returns, as a rebuke, in his late prose. Prose genres may be simpler than verse ones and are certainly more unidirectional and advocative. Moreover, this would also help explain why many prose works omit the parallel as inappropriate to the particular topic, audience or occasion.

The fact that Eikonoklastes does not answer in kind the parallelism of Charles with Jeremiah or Jesus tacitly concedes that the imagery is ambivalent, or suits the downtrodden better than the victorious.

In any case, I have found no simple correspondence between medium or genre and the presence or absence of the Exodus image. In poems, Milton employs New Testament imagery more than Old. Even pagan or vernacular images outweigh those of ancient Israel. This is especially evident in the sonnet to Cromwell.

Advocating liberty of worship predisposes the poet against the Israelite analogy, which in practice if not in principle also resisted universalization."Curse ye Meroz" became a favorite text with preachers to Parliament and its armies, with the implication that those who do not advocate such liberty are accursed themselves.

Saul ceased to be Samuel's choice because he was not thorough enough in exterminating a defeated people. Milton's political hopes of the early 1640s were rebuked in 1644 with the rancorous reception, attended by personal attacks, to his tracts on divorce. Similarly, when Presbyterianism sought religious uniformity and conformity, Milton realised that liberty of worship was likelier under a separation of church from state. Such separation was too moderate a doctrine to affirm the only parallel.

Further reasons come to mind for the absence of the Exodus image. Milton's historical studies, especially in the later 1640s when writing the History of Britain, confirmed this scepticism. Something always went wrong, whether you looked at the history of Britain or England or Greece or Rome. Liberty was what mattered, and sins of self-interest always betrayed it.

In fact, the Old Testament told the same tale. Those among whom the image of a chosen people was strongest strayed the most often. Old Testament historiography makes its theme-song or chorus the "turning aside" of Israel and its leadership, its "walking to right or left" of the straight path, the way of the Lord. The "only parallel" may be encouraging for morale and rhetoric, but not for practical politics. Did Milton come near to using this image so often, yet fully develop it only twice, because he found it a constrictive cliché? If so, where he does use the cliché it measures the young man's hope in 1642, and in 1659 the older man's desperation.

BEYOND 1660

This summarizes the period of my survey, 1642-1660, but the remaining fourteen years of Milton's life saw his greatest writing. What do the three major poems have to say or imply about England as Israel?

It has become usual to read the prophetic books of Paradise Lost as an oblique comment on the failures of England's Protestants to achieve true Reformation, and to read Samson's indictments of betrayal by the leaders of his tribe and nation as another.Certainly the emotions correspond, but why should we relate only these emotions of Samson with Milton's life circumstances?

What about Samson's blindness, his wife, his hair-length, or his father's views on marriage-choices? To privilege the political part of a whole seems to me a narrowing to our own preoccupations. As for the prophetic books, we also narrow their scope to apply them to Restoration England; the whole purpose of Milton's change of theme, from the projected epic of Arthur or its Saxon successors to "Adam Unparadiz'd," is to universalise the theme. The parallel of Israel to England would restrict it.

Knowing that this argument will not convince readers who perceive that the prophesies of misery can be applied to Milton's own post-Restoration situation, I will elaborate. In 1667, Milton wanted readers. He got them. He got more in 1669 by adding explanations of his action and his medium. In 1674, converting ten books into twelve, he made his poem more Virgilian and epic.

This direction of attention makes it less, not more, likely that he wanted his prophecies read as a cryptogram for his own situation. Paradise Regained ought to have precluded such psychobiographical discussion. The Messiah rejects the temptation of world power or liberating Israel from Rome (III.150-202). Milton appears to have chosen his topic to express the fact that temperance is personal integrity, and that this matters more than political activism.

One need not argue that this poem is political and quietist in order to refute those who read the other two great poems as political and nostalgic for failed revolution. Rather, we should credit Milton with keeping his mind firmly on the moral and spiritual principles of each poem. All interiorize hope.

THEORIZING AN ABSENCE

"Absence" resists definition. The mere fact that it gets a name does not mean the name denotes anything (as "dog" or "tenure" do). It is more sensitive to context than most abstract nouns are, since it makes us ask what it is the absence of, and what the presence of that which is absent, would mean.

It does not work in simple binary fashion, since an absence may be partial or intermittent. Absence may mean that something is self-evident or unthinkable, unknown or disregarded or ignored. Context is vital to defining an absence. The definition of "absence" is more than mere logic-chopping.

An absence of the image of England as Israel could mean Milton was simply not patriotic, being either hostile or indifferent to that sort of feeling. He was patriotic, however, expressing the feeling with other images. We seek, then, to explain the paradox, or puzzle, that a potentially strong, in fact absolute, image of national glory did not take hold of this poet even though he was eloquently patriotic, abandoning hope of European fame through Latin in order "to be an interpreter and relater of the best and sagest things among mine own citizens throughout this island in the mother dialect."

This failure to deploy an image, this inaction, has something inherently problematic about it. If an inaction is outward and public, we can find both public and personal reasons for non-occurrence. How a conspiracy or assassination attempt never succeeded can be explained by security measures.

Something which has not awoken a gifted imagination,

or has not continued to engage it, is more difficult to perceive, let alone explain.

Nonetheless, the intermittent is easier to probe than the wholly absent. Outward circumstances, known views and hopes, changing of genres along with altering occasions and audiences, all encourage speculation.

My question, why Milton makes no more use of the "only parallel," reveals very clearly certain things about Milton's intellectual, spiritual and practical life during the long mid-century crisis of rule:

I have been charting Milton's loss of political innocence. He adopted logic, not prophetic passion to combat the royal propaganda. Concurrently, Milton became more pluralist, choosing his mode of vision for each task, each political and polemical speech-act. Above all, he was driven by the wish to heed Greek and Roman principles and exemplars, as much as Old Testament ones. The sonnets in particular manifest this preference.

We have been witnessing the unfolding of a principle of separating church from state. The principle is seen not in public advocacy alone but in the poet's own sphere, his choices of topic, stance and imagery to express them. Here I might compare Milton with Cromwell.

Cromwell's actions look erratic until one sees that he sought amongst many political forms for a way to uphold liberty of worship. A consistent principle stands behind his inconsistent actions. Milton's use of the only parallel, like his use of classical imagery, varies with his occasions and genre, but he does not swerve from belief in freedom of worship ("so that the hewn and scattered virgin Truth may be slowly remembered by her sad friends").

Milton favours what Isaiah Berlin calls "negative" liberty, the absence of external constraints, for the sake of Berlin's "positive" liberty, which consists in spiritual fulfillment or self-realization.

Not only the events of the Interregnum but also his humanism and his historiography showed him that "positive" liberty, though attractive as a spiritual freedom, is narrow and coercive when vested in any small group of believers, and destroy both liberties for those who do not agree with the believers.

Despite optimistic moments in his own epoch, he soon realised that the day when all people, and all nations, share the same spirituality was a long, long way off. He drew the corollary, that freedom mattered last as well as first.

While many radicals advocate freedom only till they themselves win power, Milton advocated it whether in opposition or in power or in the internal "exile" of his last years. He was a more consistent, altruistic thinker than is often acknowledged.

Chapter 9

Milton and the Jacobean Church of England

If you put a straight stick into water at an angle, it appears to be bent where it meets the surface. Perhaps there is a similar explanation for some apparent inconsistencies between the early and the later Milton. For example, why is it that the author of elegiac verses praising the Bishops of Winchester and Ely in 1626 could fifteen years later write three tracts roundly denouncing episcopacy?

Something had changed, and I would suggest it was not just that the eighteen-year-old had matured; the church of his youth had been remarkably altered by 1641. (I am here partially differing with Nathaniel Henry, who minimizes these elegies as having little "ecclesiastical [or] religious significance.

But while all readers of Lycidas may know that Milton considered "our corrupted clergy" to be "in their height" in 1637, during the peak of Archbishop William Laud's ascendancy, they cannot be counted upon to be well informed about the Jacobean church in which Milton grew up to the age of seventeen.

For some time now historians have been discovering more precisely the nature of the Church of England in the time of James I, and revising some old views, but Milton scholarship seems not to have taken much notice. Just what difference did it make to the poet that he was raised in a church significantly distinct from the one Laud and Charles I tried to foster? This paper will delineate recent findings about the nature of the Jacobean church, including features which were not instantly transformed in 1625, and try to assess some of Milton's debts to that body. When I was an undergraduate and later (in the 1960s) a graduate student, ideas such as the following were current: Anglicans and puritans were thought of as two perfectly distinct, recognizable and coherent groups on the Jacobean religious scene, with no noticeable middle ground. Since puritans were by nature extreme, there could be no such thing as a moderate one.

Most puritans were separatists, or at any rate opponents of the national English church. Elizabethan and Jacobean puritanism was believed to have led steadily and inevitably to the revolution of the 1640s. Attackers of ritual and episcopacy, the puritans were also (except for Milton and a few others) ignorant, wrong-minded people who hated plays, and whose only effects on English culture were harmful. Under James, and especially under Archbishop George Abbot (so the story goes), the church suffered because of laxness toward the puritans.

Nevertheless, James hated the puritans and had nothing in common with them. Ritual was more important than doctrine for Anglicans of this time. The Church of England was halfway between Geneva and Rome in its doctrine, and thus an Anglican like John Donne can also usefully be called a High Anglican or Anglo-Catholic. The puritans, but not the Anglicans, were Calvinist. Doctrine and preaching were the especial concerns of the puritans, but not of the Anglicans.

The Anglicans in the Jacobean church were strongly influenced by Hooker, and the Laudians or Arminians were the most prominent group in the Jacobean church leadership. Ideas such as these, many of them originating from partisans of the seventeenth century like Peter Heylyn and from the nineteenth-century Oxford movement, have all been shown by recent historical writers to be either false or seriously questionable for the Jacobean Church of England, 1603-25.

Milton scholars of the last few decades generally do not assert them, and some acknowledge the thoroughly Protestant nature of the Jacobean church, but most simply ignore that church in writing about Milton. I have not been able to locate one book or article on Milton that refers to any of the writings of the historians Peter Lake or Kenneth Fincham, mentioned in my next paragraph.

Stephen Honeygosky, in Milton's House of God: The Invisible and Visible Church, breaks important new ground in asserting that Milton continues to believe in a visible church, but shows no awareness that Milton's high esteem for Calvin as one of the "most learned theologians" and "great leaders of the church" was probably shared by most leaders of the Jacobean church, or that Calvin should not simply be linked with the "English puritan tradition".

After decades during which historians have written many books about seventeenth-century puritans while generally neglecting the conformists (a term preferable to "Anglicans," which was not used till about 1635), writers such as Peter Lake and Kenneth Fincham have finally been paying detailed attention to the latter.

In so doing they are clarifying the nature of the Jacobean Church.According to the historical picture now emerging, scriptural doctrine (as in the moderate Calvinism of the Thirty-Nine Articles) continued to be the central, unifying force for the leadership of the church, as it had been in Elizabethan times.Peter Lake has described the dominant Calvinist piety of the Elizabethan English church as "word-centred" (focused on the Scripture and preaching)—a term that is just as apt for the Jacobean church as a whole.

Although Richard Hooker had sought to replace the existing piety with a sacrament-centred one, few Jacobean church leaders followed that initiative. Fincham reports that only about eight of James' sixty-six bishops could be counted as Arminian. People like Neile and Andrewes were in a tiny minority that rose to power only after 1625, with the backing of Charles I.

There is good evidence to show that John Donne, Dean of St. Paul's while Milton was at St. Paul's School, was not essentially a Laudian, but identified strongly with the rather Calvinist Jacobean Church. (Similarly, Christopher Hodgkins demonstrates that George Herbert was a "Calvinist..lower-church Episcopalian" who "kept to the 'middle way' of his boyhood church.") James I took a keen interest in church politics, and helped shape the distinctive quality of the Church of England in his time.

The report that at the Hampton Court Conference he threatened to "harry" the non-conforming puritans out of the land does not accurately reflect the extent to which James effectively made peace with moderate and conforming puritans. At Hampton Court he not only acceded to their request for a new translation of the Bible (a project in which puritans participated), but agreed with the puritans on a number of other matters, including the need to strengthen the church's preaching ministry.

According to Fincham and Lake, James set out to separate the moderates from the extremists in the church, and to welcome the former, even if they were still apprehensive about ritual or church government, provided they could see these matters as "things indifferent".

As a result James eventually "presided over a settled church from which the political radicalism of puritanism had been removed". Only two ministers are known to have been deprived for nonconformity from 1611 to 1625, and from 1611 to 1619 no publications against the liturgy or episcopacy issued from the English press.

In these circumstances moderate and conforming puritans could flourish and get on with what Peter Lake describes as their "real agenda"—not presbyterianism or liturgical reform, but the advancement of the spiritual life. The term "conforming puritan" might usefully describe even some bishops and archbishops; others, like Samuel Ward, John Preston (who was offered a bishopric but refused it), and Richard Sibbes became influential at the universities, as lecturers and/or heads of colleges.

Together with moderate conformists, they were at the centre of the English Protestant via media before Laud, which was located between the extremes of Rome and Amsterdam (not Geneva).It is no wonder that a young Milton could fully identify with his church, and intend to enter its ministry. We should notice that in Milton's youth there was no great divide between moderate conformists like John Donne and moderate or even fully conforming puritans. This is why Donne could well satisfy the benchers at Lincoln's Inn, where his predecessor and successor as reader in divinity were the moderate puritans Thomas Gataker and John Preston.

Donne's own father-in-law Sir George More, with whom he came to be on very good terms, was a puritan active in Parliament, and Donne voiced sentiments like More's when, within a year of James' Declaration of Sports, he critiqued the Declaration ironically in a sermon.

In 1623 the puritan Thomas Adams dedicated one of his works, a Paul's Cross sermon called The Barren Tree, "To the Reuerend and learned Doctor Donne, Dean of St. Pauls, together with the Prebend Residentiaries of the same Church, my very good Patrons in humble acknowledgement of your fauours".

A close friend of Donne's, Dr. Thomas Mountford, of the chapters at Westminster Abbey and St. Paul's Cathedral, repeatedly chose puritan lecturers for the parish church of which he was rector, St. Martin-in-the-Fields, beginning with Robert Hill.

Thomas Gataker, a long time friend of Richard Stock, also preached occasionally at St. Martin's, the London parish church of Magdalen Herbert and her family; later Milton's sister Anne Phillips attended here and maybe Milton himself, as his father had property in the parish.

Richard Stock, Milton's pastor as the rector of All Hallows, Bread Street, was not so much on the fringe as near the heart of his church. Stock may never have been called by what was then still a mocking epithet, "puritan," though he fits some modern definitions.

At St. John's College, Cambridge, he had been a favourite pupil of William Whitaker, one of whose Latin works he later translated. Although Harris Fletcher calls Whitaker "mildly antiprelatical," George Herbert hailed him as a "loyal warrior" for the Church, and Peter Lake takes him as an example of puritanism dissociated from presbyterianism or nonconformity—a puritanism marked instead by "insistence on the transformative effect of the word on the attitudes and behaviour of all true believers.

Stock accepted godly episcopacy: his Paul's Cross sermon of November 1606 was printed in 1609 with a dedication to "the Right Reverend Father in God, Iames, by Gods prouidence, Lord Bishop of Bathe, and Welles"—James Montague, one of the many Calvinist bishops - citing favour Stock had received from him both at Cambridge university and in the church.

In Stock's view Montague was "made ouerseer..for the furtherance of Gods glorie, the aduancement of Christs holie Gospell, [and] the comfort of his glorious spouse the Church".But the text of his sermon, Isaiah 9:14-16, warning of the judgment of God on religious leaders that cause the people to err, can be seen as anticipating puritan reaction in response to Laudian prelacy in later years.

Thomas Young, Milton's tutor for a few years before 1620, was unlike Stock a presbyterian, having protested in 1606 against the introduction of episcopacy in his native Scotland. However, holding first a benefice at Ware and later (1628) a post as vicar in Stowmarket, he was not a separatist like the Pilgrim Fathers, so that his leaving England in 1620 should not be associated with theirs, but was simply a search for more permanent and remunerative employment with the English church in Hamburg.

Young's continuance at Stowmarket until 1637 suggests that he was up to that time a conforming pastor, whose reactions against Laudian measures in the 1630s may have helped trigger the passage of protest in Lycidas.

Perhaps because modern readers are conscious of the English church's opposition to Roman CatholicismLaudians), we have trouble seeing or appreciating the relative breadth of the Jacobean church. Once there was agreement on essential doctrine, matters of ritual and polity were regarded as "things indifferent" on which the church could rule, but which it did not regard as essential to salvation. (Actually, James held that even some doctrines were "indifferent."

He himself had Calvinist views on predestination, but unlike many of his leading bishops did not think it essential that everyone should.) It was on such a basis that James extended some tolerance to puritans, and even to those of papist inclination willing to acknowledge his and the church's authority (Fincham and Lake 182-86). Milton, who praised James in his early poems, later faulted the king for vacillating in his attitude toward Roman Catholics.

Beginning in 1625 and even earlier, the Laudians sought to change the situation. They were unhappy with the tolerated variety in worship, which they considered disorder, and with the emphasis on preaching that most Jacobeans, including Donne, relished. The Laudians longed for a unity based not on the word, not on doctrine, but on uniformity of ritual. Also, they were notably more sacerdotal than most Jacobean church leaders. Kenneth Fincham classes the largest category of James' bishops as "preaching pastors," while the Arminians tended to be "custodians of order." The 1630s brought the greatest Laudian changes.

In 1633 Laud became Archbishop of Canterbury, and his bishops, with the approval and encouragement of the king, tried to force their own style of piety on a largely reluctant church. The treatment of George Herbert's book manuscripts in the 1630s gives an idea of the Laudian narrowness.

It was only at Nicholas Ferrar's insistence that The Temple was allowed to be printed complete with the lines suggesting that Religion would next flee to America, and in the late 1630s the Laudian censors refused to approve the publication of Herbert's The Country Parson, while puritans were trying to get it published without alterations (Doerksen, "'Too Good.'") The English middle way was being narrowed and shifted over to the side on which the Laudians had once formed a small minority group.

While in the Jacobean years and even later a civil war and executions of archbishop and king were unthinkable, let alone inevitable, it seems clear that the narrowness and insensitivity of some of the Laudian church authorities contributed significantly to making these things possible.

John Milton was well aware of what was going on in his national church. In the Jacobean era it was perfectly understandable that he should have been "destin'd of a child" to the service of the English church "by the intentions of my parents and friends [including, perhaps, Richard Stock].., and in mine own resolutions"; and of course the years of study in Cambridge were fully compatible with such a goal, but in the 1630s "perceaving what tyranny had invaded the Church," as he later says, Milton felt himself to be "Church-outed by the Prelate.

One should note that in the Jacobean years church government had ceased to be an issue, because most puritans felt that they could work in a system in which the bishops were their allies. Besides Stock there were examples like Richard Bernard, deprived for nonconformity in 1605, but reinstated a few years later, in spite of continued occasional nonconformity.

Bishop Montague, whom Stock had praised, deliberately invited Bernard into his diocese, where the latter became an eminent preacher and prolific writer of sermons. Bernard's The Faithfull Shepherd, republished in a "very much inlarged" edition in 1621, was intended to help "further young Diuines in the studie of Diuinitie" (title page), but was dedicated to "the Most Reverend Father in God, Tobie [Matthew], by the diuine prouidence, Lord Archbishop of Yorke," and in the dedication the archbishop was himself referred to as "a most faithfull Shepherd, A Patron to all faithfull Pastors".

Daniel Featley, a conformist chaplain to Archbishop Abbot, borrowed Bernard's title for a sermon at the consecration of the Bishops of Oxford, Bristol, and Chester in 1619, in which he cautioned them in language that recalls the strictures against "our corrupted Clergy" in Lycidas: "Feede not your selves but the flocke." "Lord-like pride complyeth not with the humility of Christs Ministers."

He also asked how a spiritual shepherd could "cure dimme and darke eyes, when himselfe was starke blinde". In 1617 Bernard challenged another bishop, Arthur Lake, to be vigilant: to "imitate the Good Shepherd and preach the gospel to his clergy, strengthening the diligent..and arousing the lethargic. The idle and profligate will be reformed with gentle discipline. The bishop will lead his flock through example, and protect orthodox doctrine from the barbs of Papists and Brownists alike." In Of Reformation, Milton's idea of a good "primitive" bishop includes humility, "incessant prayer, and preaching, continual watchings, and labours in his Ministery" — qualities of a kind that Fincham attributes to a number of leading Jacobean bishops.

But the Laudians, with their stress on sacerdotalism, alienated numbers of church people, and increasingly merited the distancing term "prelate," which smacks of wealth and power, rather than the shepherding more typical of their Jacobean predecessors. Thus Milton associates the Laudian bishop George Mountain with "the many- benefice-gaping mouth" and the "canary-sucking, and swan-eating palat" of a prelate.

Similarly in Lycidas there is a complaint about hirelings "that for their bellies' sake / Creep and intrude and climb into the fold." They are called "Blind mouths" [my emphasis] because they lack the vision which I suggest Milton had earlier caught from Stock and others, of the "faithful herdman's art," of what Fincham called the "preaching pastor."

If Milton now viewed the Church of England differently, it was not he who had changed so much as his church. What does Milton owe to the pre-Laudian Church of England? I want to propose seriously that Milton, like Donne, gains from the Jacobean church an impulse toward toleration in "things indifferent."

In recognizing Donne as an important voice for religious toleration in England, W.K. Jordan wrote that "his thought is to be linked with that of the moderates who subscribed to no party rather than with the main stream of Anglican theory" -Jordan, following the older views of the seventeenth-century church, could nevertheless see that Donne and the "moderates" were significantly different from Hooker and Laud.

Two of Donne's contemporaries Jordan cites as making significant contributions to the development of religious toleration are Richard Bernard and Richard Sibbes both moderate Calvinist puritans. Influenced by the old dichotomy of puritans versus "Anglicans," Jordan seems unaware of the extent to which Donne, Bernard, and Sibbes share Calvinist theology.

Of the latter he says:

Sibbes was thoroughly Calvinistic in his doctrinal views, but he strove throughout his life to preserve the unity of the Church and to formulate a moderate religious conception which would ensure tolerance and charity for all Christian men.

I would suggest that Donne, Bernard, and Sibbes received an impetus toward such attitudes from their church, the Jacobean Church of England. John Milton too grew up (to the age of seventeen) in that church, and it is there that he most likely received his first impressions of liberty and religious toleration. Although the Jacobean church was not centred on the liturgy, it used the Book of Common Prayer regularly if not rigorously.

Judith Maltby interestingly argues that a significant number of "Prayer Book protestants" during the 1630s "rather than forming a natural constituency for Laudianism,..helped to provide opposition to Laudian reforms". The youthful Milton, who might have bristled at a rigidly enforced church pattern, could absorb the Prayer Book's rhythms, its heavily scriptural phrasing. It thus makes good sense for Thomas Stroup to study Religious Rite and Ceremony in Milton's Poetry (1968).

Alexander Chambers demonstrates that "On the Morning of Christ's Nativity" "both crowns and recapitulates the [liturgical] tradition of which it is a part", and argues that the morning prayer of Adam and Eve in Paradise Lost, Book V, reflects Milton's response to a canticle for Morning Prayer, more than to directly biblical patterns.

Similarly, the setting of St. Paul's Cathedral no doubt inspired some of the closing lines in "Il Penseroso," which reflect a love for "the high embowèd roof, / With antique pillars massy proof, / And storied windows richly dight," along with "service high and anthems clear." If it had not been for the Laudian changes, perhaps Milton might have become known as the poet of the English church.

What has not been sufficiently noted (or at least stated) is that Milton, with Donne, Herbert, and others, owes a tremendous debt to a church which (though it did not neglect the biblical sacraments) was dominated by the Word.his was true of the English church as a whole (before the Laudian changes), not just the puritans within it.

Georgia Christopher appropriately draws attention to the links between Milton and the writings of Luther and Calvin in terms of their common "word-based piety," since Milton "shared their attitude toward sacred texts and their belief in a 'verbal" sacrament." But she does not recognize how pervasive such a piety was in the Church of England.

The Thirty- Nine Articles make the church's strongly biblical position clear, as Milton acknowledged in his 1673 tract Of True Religion:

With good and Religious Reason therefore all Protestant Churches with one consent, and particularly the Church of England in Her thirty nine Articles, Artic. 6th, 19th, 20th, 21st, and elsewhere, maintain..as [a] main Principle..of true Religion..that the Rule of true Religion is the Word of God only...

The English church position on this matter was not mere theory. Article XIX, defining the church, insists on the "pure Word of God preached", and in the church of James and in the experience of Donne and Milton biblical sermons were of the essence. To judge by printings, Bibles must also have been ubiquitous. More than that, along with Protestants generally, the English read the Bible as literary.

Calvin, trained as a humanist, published an edition of Seneca before embarking on a life in which he commented on almost all parts of the Bible, with many literary perceptions, as in his Sermons on Job, which went through four editions in English translation alone.

From Wyatt and Sidney on, most English poets in Reformation times tried their hand at vernacular verse translations of the Psalms. Donne praised such efforts by Philip and Mary Sidney in verse of his own, as well as giving his version of "The Lamentations of Jeremy"; and Milton's renderings of some Psalms are well known.

In the preface to the second book of The Reason of Church Government, where he speaks of his church-outing, Milton also shows his keen awareness of the literary genres of the Bible—Job as a brief epic, the Song of Solomon as "divine pastoral Drama," the "Apocalyps of Saint John" as "the majestick image of a high and stately Tragedy," and the "frequent songs" in the law and prophets "over all the kinds of Lyrick poesy..incomparable".

It was the Jacobean Church of England (in this respect the heir of Reformed Christianity more generally, and of the similarly word-centred Elizabethan Church, which we can associate with Spenser) that fostered some of the very best writers of biblically-inspired literature: the Donne of the Sermons, George Herbert,and (I claim here) John Milton.

Milton without the Reformation is unthinkable, and the Reformation with its scriptural emphasis was first mediated to him by his own pre-Laudian English church.

C.A. Patrides, still not aware of the degree of Jacobean Calvinism, nevertheless rightly turned to Donne, Herbert, and other Church of England writers to illuminate the biblical background for Milton and his age.Patrides could see a literary impact in these English church readings of scripture, and consequently claimed that "The creative form which Milton and Herbert and Donne [note the grouping] imposed on words appealed in the end to the prototypical activities of the creative Word" or the Bible, not so much a book of rules as a unique collection of fascinating stories and poems reflecting human experience and full of rich symbolism, gave these writers not only themes, but literary impulses.

If Donne had been preoccupied with external order as the Laudians were, his sermons would, I suggest, have lost much of their vitality; and much the same can be said for Herbert's poetry. Milton, not only in his prose writings, but in his most excellent poetry, has constant recourse to scripture.

Georgia Christopher argues that Milton's word-based theology, "properly considered,..helps to make his poetry simple, passionate, and even sensuous". Unlike Laud and his cohorts, we should be thankful that the Jacobean Church of England, which first nurtured Milton, was so word centred.

In his last published tract, Of True Religion, Milton wrote that while the Roman church "permits not her Laity to read the Bible in their own tongue: Our Church on the contrary hath proposd it to all men, and to this end translated it into English, with profitable Notes..that all sorts and degrees of men, not understanding the Original, may read it in their Mother Tongue".

By referring to the 1611 Authorized Version, and elsewhere in the same tract in detail to the Thirty-Nine Articles with their strongly biblical stance, as well as to the importance of preaching, Milton near the end of his life gave evidence of the stamp that the Jacobean church, "Our Church" as he says here, had placed upon him. In spite of, and perhaps because of the ways in which Milton and the church both changed in Laudian times, we need to recognize that stamp.

Chapter 10

Portrayal of Various Characters in Paradise Lost

SATAN

Probably the most famous quote about *Paradise Lost* is William Blake's statement that Milton was "of the Devil's party without knowing it." While Blake may have meant something other than what is generally understood from this quotation, the idea that Satan is the hero, or at least a type of hero, in *Paradise Lost* is widespread.

However, the progression, or, more precisely, regression, of Satan's character from Book I through Book X gives a much different and much clearer picture of Milton's attitude toward Satan.

Writers and critics of the Romantic era advanced the notion that Satan was a Promethean hero, pitting himself against an unjust God. Most of these writers based their ideas on the picture of Satan in the first two books of *Paradise Lost*. In those books, Satan rises off the lake of fire and delivers his heroic speech still challenging God. Satan tells the other rebels that they can make "a Heav'n of Hell, a Hell of Heav'n" and adds, "Better to reign in Hell than serve in Heav'n".

Satan also calls for and leads the grand council. Finally, he goes forth on his own to cross Chaos and find Earth. Without question, this picture of Satan makes him heroic in his initial introduction to the reader.

Besides his actions, Satan also appears heroic because the first two books focus on Hell and the fallen angels. The reader's introduction to the poem is through Satan's point of view. Milton, by beginning *in medias res* gives Satan the first scene in the poem, a fact that makes Satan the first empathetic character. Also, Milton's writing in these books, and his characterization of Satan, make the archfiend understandable and unforgettable.

These facts certainly make Satan the most interesting character in the poem—but they do not make him the hero. Because the reader hears Satan's version first, the reader is unaware of the exaggerations and outright lies that are parts of Satan's magnificent speeches. Moreover, the reader can easily overlook the fact that Milton states that, whatever powers and abilities the fallen angels have in Hell, those powers and abilities come from God, who could at any moment take them away.

In essence then, Milton's grand poetic style sets Satan up as heroic in Books I and II. The presentation of Satan makes him seem greater than he actually is and initially draws the reader to Satan's viewpoint. Further, because all of the other characters in the poem—Adam, Eve, God, the Son, the angels—are essentially types rather than characters, Milton spends more artistic energy on the development of Satan so that throughout the poem, Satan's character maintains the reader's interest and, perhaps, sympathy—at least to an extent.

No matter how brilliantly Milton created the character of Satan, the chief demon cannot be the hero of the poem. For Milton, Satan is the enemy who chooses to commit an act that goes against the basic laws of God, that challenges the very nature of the universe. Satan attempts to destroy the hierarchy of Heaven through his rebellion. Satan commits this act not because of the tyranny of God but because he wants what *he* wants rather than what God wants.

Satan is an egoist. His interests always turn on his personal desires. Unlike Adam, who discusses a multiplicity of subjects with Raphael, rarely mentioning his own desires, Satan sees everything in terms of what will happen to him. A true Promethean / Romantic hero has to rebel against an unjust tyranny in an attempt to right a wrong or help someone less fortunate. If Satan had been Prometheus, he would have stolen fire to warm himself, not to help Mankind.

Milton shows his own attitude toward Satan in the way the character degenerates or is degraded in the progression of the poem. Satan is magnificent, even admirable in Books I and II. By book IV, he is changed. In his soliloquy that starts Book IV, Satan declares that Hell is wherever he himself is. Away form his followers and allowed some introspection, Satan already reveals a more conflicted character.

Similarly, Satan's motives change as the story advances. At first, Satan wishes to continue the fight for freedom from God. Later his motive for continuing the fight becomes glory and renown. Next, the temptation of Adam and Eve is simply a way to disrupt God's plans. And, at the end, Satan seems to say that he has acted as he has to impress the other demons in Hell. This regression of motives shows quite a fall.

Satan also regresses or degenerates physically. Satan shifts shapes throughout the poem. These changes visually represent the degeneration of his character. First, he takes the form of a lesser angel, a cherub, when he speaks to Uriel. Next, he is a ravening cormorant in the tree of life--an animal but able to fly. Then he is a lion and a tiger—earth-bound beasts of prey, but magnificent. Finally, he is a toad and a snake. He becomes reptilian and disgusting. These shape changes graphically reveal how Satan's actions change him.

Even in his own shape, Satan degenerates. When Gabriel confronts Satan in Book V, none of the angels initially recognize Satan because his appearance is noticeably changed. Likewise, in Book X, when Satan once again sits on his throne in Hell, none of the earlier magnificence of his physical appearance is left. Now he looks like a drunken debauchee.

Though Satan is not heroic in *Paradise Lost*, he at times does border on tragedy. Ironically, he also borders on comedy. The comic element associated with Satan derives from the absurdity of his position.

As a rebel, he challenges an omnipotent foe, God, with power that is granted him by his foe. God simply toys with Satan in battle. Satan is, in fact, cartoonish when he and Belial gloat over the success of their infernal cannon in Book VI. Satan and Belial stand laughing at the disorder they have caused, but they are unaware of the mountains and boulders just about to land on their heads.

If all of *Paradise Lost* were on the level of the battle scene, the poem would be comic. But Satan's temptation of Adam and Eve moves the demon closer to tragedy. Satan's motives in destroying the human couple may be arguable, but the effect and its implications are not. Satan brings the humans down and causes their removal from Eden. In so doing, he also provides the way to salvation for those humans who choose freely to obey God.

However, Satan provides nothing for himself. Hell is where Satan is because he has no way to rejoin God. Unlike humanity, Satan and the other fallen angels have already sealed their fates. They live always with the knowledge of Hell.

In the end, Satan calls to mind the Macbeth of Shakespeare. Both characters are magnificent creations of evil. Both are heroic after a fashion, but both are doomed. Both are fatalistic about the afterlife. Satan knows that he must remain in Hell; Macbeth says that he would "jump the life to come," if he could kill Duncan with no consequence on Earth. Both characters are the driving force in their own works. And finally both create a kind of Hell; Macbeth's on Earth, Satan's in the universe.

GOD

Because God created the Son, the angels, Man, Heaven, Earth, and everything else, and since he is omniscient, Milton was faced with the difficulty of creating tension about what would happen since God already knew. This problem, of course, existed in one way or another in most Greek epics and tragedies so that the real question was in the presentation of a known set of incidents.

Milton approaches the problem of God's character by making him almost a chorus-like figure. God comments on scenes and actions, he explains what will happen and why, he gives the philosophical / theological basis for ideas like free will, but he does not truly participate in the action. God is aloof, almost emotionless. He embodies pure reason, and consequently his responses often seem cold. In the war in Heaven, God limits the power of the faithful angels and in the final moments sends only the Son to conquer the rebels. Yet his cosmic laugh at the presumption of Satan and his crew has a chilling effect.

If the reader had had any doubts about Satan's power against God, that laugh puts them to rest. God's unemotional reason is not without another side. God is also pure justice. He may see his plans for Man dashed by Satan's trickery, but through divine justice, he will put everything to right and conquer Satan. From evil, God will produce goodness. God gave Man free will. From Man's free will, sin and death came into the world, but God will see that goodness rules in the end.

THE SON

The merciful, compassionate side of God is presented in the Son, not referred to as Jesus because Jesus had not been born at this time in theological history. In Book III, God says that Adam and Eve will fall and must suffer death. However, death can be overcome for humans if someone in Heaven will sacrifice himself to death for Man.

The Son says that he will become human and die in order to defeat death. This act clearly defines the Son. He is powerful and brave, merciful, and willing to act to help Mankind. God's duty is to provide justice—the law has been declared. It is the Son who provides mercy to temper justice—the natural law.

The Son's power is also further revealed in Book VI when God decides to end the rebellion of the angels. God sends only the Son in a chariot against Satan and his hosts. The Son by himself is able to defeat the rebellious angels and cast them into Hell. Milton uses the Son as the acting hand of God's decisions.

God also uses the Son as the creator of Earth and the universe around it. Milton connects the Son closely to Mankind by making the Son the creator of the biblical account. Even though Milton refers to the Son as God in Book VII, it is, nonetheless, the Son who, with golden compasses, lays out the universe and creates Earth and Mankind. Once again, the Son carries out God's plan.

Finally, after the fall of Adam and Eve, the Son goes to Earth at God's request and passes judgment on the serpent, Adam, and Eve. Beyond telling the humans what their punishment will be, the Son also pities them and clothes them in skins. God seems to be almost the embodiment of ideas while the Son converts those ideas to actions.

At the end of *Paradise Lost*, Michael shows Adam a vision of Jesus, who is the Seed that will ultimately destroy Satan. This scene is the obvious close of the story. The Son, becoming human through Jesus, will live and die. Through resurrection from death, he will finally overcome Satan and save man from the results of the fall. If the reader finds God difficult to comprehend, he finds the Son more compassionate and merciful. Through both characters combined, Milton presents a complete picture of God.

ADAM

Before the fall, Adam is as nearly perfect a human being as can be imagined. He is physically attractive, mentally adept, and spiritually profound. He stands out in Eden as the apex of the hierarchical pyramid. Only Eve can compare to him, and she only in physical beauty.

The conversations between Adam and Eve before Book X are models of civilized discourse. These conversations are difficult to imagine as real, but they reflect the nature of the two humans. Adam's and humanity's values are reflected in his attitude, which is revealed through his speech—to Eve, to Raphael, and to God. In each instance when Adam speaks, he shows the proper relationship to the being with whom he converses.

While he is superior to Eve and inferior to Raphael and God, there is still no hint of haughtiness in his discussions with Eve or of subservience in his talks with the angel and God. Always Adam shows the proper respect and relationship in graceful speech and manners. When Adam sees Raphael's approach to Earth, he tells Eve, "go with speed, / And what thy stores contain, bring forth and pour / Abundance, fit to honour and receive / Our Heav'nly stranger". Eve replies, "Adam, earth's hallowed mould, / Of God inspir'd, small store will serve, where store, / All seasons, ripe for use hangs on the stalk". These words, which may seem overly formal, nonetheless reveal the relationship of Adam and Eve.

Adam is in charge, but his request for Eve to prepare a meal is not a dismissive command. Likewise, her response shows that she knows more about the food situation in Eden than Adam. This brief dialogue is a discussion between near equals who understand their responsibilities to each other and to the world. Adam's conversation with Raphael is similar and marked by the same tone.

Adam welcomes Raphael graciously but in a manner that acknowledges the superior standing of the angel. Further, Adam uses his time with the angel to learn about Heaven, about angels, about the war in Heaven, about creation, and about astronomy. Adam's curiosity and intellect are revealed. Likewise, Adam informs Raphael about Adam's and Eve's creation and about their relationship. Man and Angel have information for each other, and they present this information within the formalized structure that establishes their relationship.

After Adam's fall, his conversations with Eve become querulous. He blames her, and she him. It takes a *mea culpa* speech by Eve to rekindle Adam's love for his wife and to reestablish their proper relationship. Likewise, when Michael comes to Eden, the relationship between Man and Angel has changed. Michael is stern but compassionate.

He presents the vision of the future to Adam, but there is little, if any, give and take between the two. Adam and Raphael have a social meeting in which hierarchy is understood. Michael and Adam have a hierarchical meeting in which Michael talks and Adam listens.

If Adam has a flaw before the fall, it is uxoriousness. This term, which means "dotingly or irrationally fond of or submissive to one's wife," was applied to Adam early on in criticism of *Paradise Lost*. Adam tells Raphael that Eve's beauty affects him so much "that what she wills to do or say, / Seems wisest, virtuosest, discreetest, best; / All higher knowledge in her presence falls / Degraded". Even though Raphael warns Adam that this attitude toward Eve is improper and that Satan could use it to tempt the humans, Adam eats the fruit of the Tree of Knowledge precisely because he cannot bear to be without Eve.

As a near perfect human, Adam is ruled by reason. He immediately understands Eve's sin in eating the apple, but he willfully ignores his reason and eats because of his love and desire for her. Adam's uxorious attitude toward Eve, which perverts the hierarchy of Earth and Paradise, leads directly to his fall.

After the fall, Adam is prey to self-doubt, to anger and sullenness, and to self-pity. Ironically, Eve's love for him starts Adam on the path back to righteousness. Adam, after the fall, will never again be the old Adam, but he does recover his reason, he develops a new understanding of and love for Eve, and he sees the good that God will produce from his and Eve's sinful action. Adam goes from being the perfect human to becoming a good human.

EVE

Eve is a simpler character than Adam. She is created from Adam's rib as his helpmeet. While she is beautiful, wise, and able, she is superior to Adam only in her beauty. From the time of her creation, when she looks in the water and falls in love with her own reflection, Eve is linked to the flaw of vanity, and Satan as the serpent will use this defect against her. Before the fall, Eve is generally presented as submissive to Adam and, to some extent, dependent on him. Her reasoning powers are not as fully realized as his.

However, Milton in no way suggests a lack of intelligence on Eve's part. Eve listens to Raphael's description of the war in Heaven and the defeat of the rebellious angels. When the conversation turns to more abstract questions of creation and planetary motion at the start of Book VIII, Eve walks away to tend her Garden. Milton is quick to note, however, "Yet went she not, as not with such discourse / Delighted, or not capable of her ear / Of what was high: such pleasures she reserv'd, / Adam relating, she sole Auditress".

In other words, Eve is perfectly capable of comprehending the abstruse subject, but she prefers hearing the ideas from Adam alone. The implied idea here is that Eve understands her position in the hierarchical arrangement and leaves this conversation so that she will in no way usurp Adam's place with the angel.

Eve does have a tendency now and then to question Adam, but she does so in a rational, respectful manner. In Book IX, such questioning leads to temptation. Eve tell Adam at the start of Book IX that they can do more work if they work separately.

Adam knows that Eve is more likely to be tricked by Satan if she is alone and argues against separation. His love for Eve, though, allows him to be persuaded, and against his better judgment, he lets her go.

Most commentators see this action on Adam's part as another example of his uxoriousness; he yields to Eve's argument, not because her argument is better, but because he does not want to hurt her feelings. On the other hand, Eve wins the argument by knowingly using her advantages over Adam. Eve sets herself up for the fall and is not equal to the task of dealing with Satan by herself.

Eve yields to temptation through a combination of flattery (vanity) and sophistic argument by the serpent. Satan is happy to find Eve alone and acknowledges that Adam would be a much more difficult opponent. Satan knows Eve's weaknesses and plays on them. She is charmed by him and cannot detect the flaws in his arguments.

After she eats the fruit, Eve immediately changes. She begins to think of ways of becoming Adam's equal or perhaps his superior. But, fearful of losing Adam to another female creation, she decides that he must eat the fruit also. Adam does so but not because of Eve's arguments.

He eats willfully because he is unwilling to be parted from Eve. After the fall, Eve, like Adam, is acrimonious and depressed. However, her love for Adam initiates the regeneration of the pair. She apologizes, and her love causes a change in Adam; they can face the future together. Eve is also glorified by being told that her seed will eventually destroy Satan, though her position in relation to Adam is made clear when Michael puts her to sleep while he shows Adam the vision of the future.

Eve is certainly not a feminist heroine. Like so many characters in the epic, she has an assigned role in the hierarchy of the universe. Milton does not denigrate women through the character of Eve; he simply follows the thought of his time as to the role of women in society. Eve has as many important responsibilities as Adam, but in the hierarchy of the universe, she falls just below him.

Milton tells us that he is tackling the story told in Genesis of the Fall of Adam and the loss of the Garden of Eden. With it, Milton will also be exploring a cosmic battle in heaven between good and evil. Supernatural creatures, including Satan and the Judeo Christian God himself, will be mixing with humans and acting and reacting with humanlike feelings and emotions.

As in other poetic epics such as Homer's Iliad and Ulysses, the Popul Vuh, and Gilgamesh, Milton is actually attempting to describe the nature of man by reflecting on who his gods are and what his origins are. By demonstrating the nature of the beings who created mankind, Milton is presenting his, or his culture's, views on what good and evil mean, what mankind's relationship is with the Absolute, what man's destiny is as an individual and as a species.

The story, therefore, can be read as a simple narrative, with characters interacting with each other along a plot and various subplots. It can also, however, be extrapolated out to hold theological and religious messages, as well as political and social themes.

Milton introduces Book I with a simple summary of what his epic poem is about: the Fall of Adam and the loss of the

Garden of Eden. He tells us that his heavenly muse is the same as that of Moses, that is, the spirit that combines the absolute with the literary.

The voice is of a self-conscious narrator explaining his position. There is some background in the past tense, then suddenly the reader finds himself in the present tense on a fiery lake in hell. The quiet introduction, the backing into the story, then the verb change and plunge into the middle of the action, in medias res, creates a cinematic and exciting beginning.

On this lake we meet Satan, general and king of the fallen rebel angels. Milton's portrait of Satan has fascinated critics since Paradise Lost's publication, leading some in the Romantic period to claim that Satan is, in fact, the heroic protagonist of the whole work. Certainly Milton's depiction of Satan has greatly influenced the devil's image in Western art and literature since the book's publication.

The reader first meets a stunned Satan chained down to a fiery lake of hell, surrounded by his coconspirators. In this first chapter, the reason for his downfall is that he thought himself equal to God. Hell, however, has not taught him humility, and, in fact, strengthens his revolve to never bow to the Almighty (Interestingly, the word "God" is not used in the chapters dealing with Hell and Satan). Satan is often called a sympathetic character in Paradise Lost, despite being the source of all evil, and in the first chapter the reader is presented with some of Satan's frustration.

Satan tells his army that they were tricked, that it wasn't until they were at battle that God showed the true extent of his almightiness. If they had been shown this force previously, not only would the rebel angels not have declared war on heaven, but Satan, also, would never have presumed that he himself was better than God. Now they have been irreversibly punished for all eternity, but, rather than feel sorry for themselves or repent, Satan pushes his army to be strong, to make "a heaven of hell, a hell of heaven."

Hell reflecting heaven and, later, earth reflecting both, will be a common theme throughout the work. Satan chooses twelve close friends: all of them drawn from pagan mythology or from foreign kings in the Hebrew Bible: to echo and mimic Christ's twelve apostles. Satan's angels build a large a glorious temple and call a council, both of which will be echoed in heaven.

In fact, Satan uses the same architect as heaven, now called Mammon in hell. Many of the structures and symbols are similar. In heaven and hell there is a king and a military hierarchy of angels. In most cases, however, they the reverse of each other. In Book I, we are shown that the most prominent thing about hell is its darkness, whereas heaven is full of luminous light. As well, the fallen angels, previously glorious and beautiful, are now ugly and disfigured.

These mirror, and therefore reverse, images of heaven and hell also work on a theological level. The darkness of hell symbolizes the distance Satan and his army are from the luminous light and grace of God. Simultaneously, the rebel angels pulled away from God by their actions and are forced away by God himself, outside of all the blessings and glory that come with God's light and into the pain and suffering that comes with distance away from him.

The physical corruption and disfigurement that occurs to all the fallen angels is symbolic of the corruption which has occurred in their souls. Hell itself is described as a belching unhealthy body, whose "womb" will be torn open to expose the "ribs" of metal ore that are necessary to build Satan's temple. Natural occurrences in hell, such as the metaphor of the eclipsed sun, are symbols of natural, and therefore spiritual, decay.

Psychological motivations also work in reverse in hell. Hell is punishment for turning away from the Good, but instead of learning his lesson, Satan becomes more stubborn and more proud. While heaven is a place where all are turned toward the good and toward pleasing and obeying God, Satan makes hell a place turned away from God and turned deliberately toward displeasing him. Whereas before falling from heaven, Satan was only guilty of presuming to be greater than God (pride), now Satan has, in fact, become a creator himself. He has created evil: the direction away from God Other critics have examined the political implications of Milton's hell. Like Dante's hell, the characters and institutions in Milton's hell are often subtle references to political issues in Milton's day. The Temple of Satan, for example, has been thought to symbolize St. Peter's Cathedral in Rome, the "capitol" of Roman Catholicism and home of the Pope.

The comparison of the glory of hell to the light of an eclipsed sun was thought to be a veiled critique of the Sun King, King Charles, who reigned during Milton's time. A full understanding of the metaphors and images that Milton uses, however, would take more than a knowledge of his contemporary history or religious background.

Describing Satan's kingdom, Milton takes from a myriad of sources, including Greek mythology and epic poetry, Egyptian and Canaanite religious traditions, the Hebrew Bible and Mishnaic texts, the New Testament and apocryphal texts, the Church Fathers, popular legends, and other theological texts.

It should be noted that, in the epic tradition, Milton is using poetry to tell his story, following most prominently the style of Homer. The work, therefore, can also be examined through the lens of poetry with an eye toward rhythm and sound. In the first sentence, Milton uses an alliteration to conduct what is referred to as a double discourse: "Of man's first disobedience, and the fruit of that forbidden tree..."

Not only does the repeated "f" sound add to the aesthetic of the sentence, it connects the "f" words to present a different idea than the sentence itself is presenting. In this case, "first..fruits" are "forbidden." This double discourse, literally two sentences spoken at the same time, is repeated throughout Milton.

SIGNIFICANCE OF SATAN IN MILTON'S PARADISE LOST

There have been many different interpretations of John Milton's epic, Paradise Lost. Milton's purpose in writing the epic was to explain the biblical story of Adam and Eve.

Although the epic is similar to the Bible story in many ways, Milton's character structure differs from that of the Bible's version. Through-out the epic Milton describes the characters in the way he believes they are. In book II of Paradise Lost, Milton portrays Satan as a rebel who exhibits certain heroic qualities, but who turns out not to be a hero.

Milton's introduction of Satan shows the reader how significant Satan is to Paradise Lost. He uses Satan's heroic qualities to his followers, and his ability to corrupt to show the thin line between good and evil. Satan was one of the highest angels in Heaven and was know as Lucifer, meaning, light bearer.

This shows he was once a good angel. Milton makes the reader see him as a leader and a strong influence to all in his presence. He best describes Satan's ways when stating, "His pride/ had cast him out from Heaven, with all his host. / Of rebel angels, by whose aspiring/ To set himself in glory above his peers" (Milton Book I). Satan's pride was the main reason that God banned him from heaven. Satan always tried to be number one and a leader, instead of following in God's shadow. He would of lived a life in Paradise forever, but he had to follow his feelings as he states, "Better to reign in Hell than serve in Heaven". This shows how strongly he felt about not being above everybody else.

Milton uses many events like the ones listed above to encourage the reader to view Satan as a hero. "Satan is described to be the brightest and most important angel". These traits of Satan show how one might recognize Satan as the second in power right below God, who was the highest power of all. Before Satan decides to give up what he has and to rebel against God, he was one of the wisest and most beautiful of all the angels in heaven.

Although Satan was beautiful, the most important trait that makes him fit into the hero category is that he was the most powerful angel in heaven. This helps him greatly in his rebellion, because the other angels would look up to him.

Satan's rebellion leads us to another one of his most noticeable skills. This would be his ability to give speeches.

With this ability, Satan is able to persuade others to follow him in his rebellion. When Satan says, "to govern, not to serve" he emphasizes liberty and encourages the other angels in heaven to all join him and his rebellion. Milton uses the whole rebellion scene, when put together with the battle in heaven, ends up being one-eighth of Paradise Lost, to show heroic qualities in Satan.

Devoting this much time to a certain scene, Milton makes it clear how important Satan is in his eyes. Satan gives many speeches throughout the epic. Although, the speeches are very long and thorough, they are also very persuasive at the same time. Satan was able to persuade "one-third of all the angels in heaven" to join with him in his rebellion.

Satan would give speeches, that would raise the attention of his followers and make them feel more confident in him.

To suffer, as to do,
Our strength is equal; nor the law unjust
That so ordains. This was at first resolved,
If we were wise, against so great a foe
Contending, and so doubtful what might fall.

In this fraction of Satan's speech, Milton shows how skilled Satan is in his choice of words. Also, this shows why the others look up to Satan as their leader, as Hamilton says, "Satan is seen as a prince of Hell, as Well as commoner and matchless chief". After gaining followers, Satan is ready for battle against God. The most observable trait given to Satan is his excellence in battle.

"In the forefront of the battle, where we expect him, is Milton's Satan, the great rebel of Paradise Lost". Hamilton also introduces the idea of an underdog, describing Satan as a person fighting against an inferior power, with extreme odds against a victory for his side. In the scenes around the battle in heaven, Milton shows how Satan is viewed as a leader by the other fallen angels.

There are other speeches of war in the epic that arouse the reader. One of the most significant is after Satan has made a meeting in the new Capitol of Hell, Pandemonium. "To have built Heaven high towers; Nor did he scape By all his engines but was headlong sent With industrious crew to build in Hell". Following the rapid building, all the fallen angels gather for their meeting asking shall it be war or peace.

"Their rising all at one was as the sound Of thunder heard remote. Towards him they bend With awful reverence prone, and as a god". When his followers cheer Satan on, the reader notices how much he likes the attention. This is another sign of how Milton shows the significant role that Satan's pride plays in his decisions. In many different encounters Satan lets his pride interfere with his actions.

In doing this, Satan begins to worry only about himself and the opinions his followers hold of him. Satan continues with the speech saying, "Should we again provoke Our Stronger, some worse way his wrath may find To our destruction".

This speech seems to be one of Satan's highest moments in the eyes of his followers. They are all willing to cooperate with Satan, and Satan loves being in charge of his followers. "Satan except, none higher sat, with grave Aspect he rose and in rising seemed a pillar of state".

Now that Satan has reached the peek of his greatness, he must start to decline in his heroic ways.

The first sign is after his speech,
I should be much for open war, O peers,
As not behind in hate, if what was urged,
Main reason to persuade immediate war,
Did not dissuade me most,

This speech shows how Satan seems ready to battle with God, but after his flight to heaven we see him in a different view with respect to the following citation. "Satan, with thoughts inflamed of highest design, Puts on swift wings, and towards the gates of hell Explores his solitary flight. In these lines, Satan seems to be overwhelmed with thoughts of how he is going to confront God. Satan is still viewed as a hero to his followers due to the way he goes to face God alone, "Satan their chief, undertakes alone the voyage, is honored and applauded". Although, Milton shows the reader this side of Satan to make them think before assuming that Satan is the hero of the epic. Even with the "heroic qualities" Satan is given, one does not have to think of him as a "hero".

This speech foreshadows a future speech of Satan that places enough evidence against Satan being a hero. The time for Satan to have to confront God has come and Satan states,

Ye powers
And spirits of this nethermost abyss,
Chaos and ancient Night, I come no spy
With purpose to explore or to disturb
The secrets of your realm; but, by constraint
Wandering this darksome dessert, as my way
Lies through your spacious empire up to light,

He is not as "bold" as he was in the first of the epic, but "he has sank to low cunning". Milton begins to show the reader these traits to acknowledge the truths of Satan. With these facts, one can see how Satan is not a hero, but only a character with so much "reliance on power" that he has many heroic qualities.

Satan can very well be described as a hero in the start of this great epic, but Milton changes the view of Satan drastically as the epic continues. Satan is really and egoistic coward that let his "pride lead to ingratitude towards God" from the beginning of the epic.

Although Satan is a great warrior and can give wonderful speeches, he seems to be hypocritical of what he tells his followers he believes and what he really does. An example of this is when we are first introduced to Satan. Satan and the other fallen angels are in hell and Satan tells the others to not be frightened, when he is frightened as well.

The character of Satan "deteriorates" greatly through the epic. Satan is viewed as a great warrior and then as time passes, his own followers begin to doubt him. "Milton has his brilliant hero advance to be met and repulsed, first verbally, and then in arms". This explains how the two most heroic qualities, that Milton uses to describe Satan as a rebellious hero, were diminished and Milton's Satan is not a hero after all.

The argument over who is the true protagonist of Paradise Lost, has been brewing for centuries. One would gather that Milton, a Puritan, would have no problem casting God as the hero, and Satan as the antagonist. But looking back in history, Milton saw that most epic heroes had conflicts that prevented them from accomplishing their goals. God and his Son have no conflict, and Adam's story doesn't really begin until the Fall of Man. Therefore, Milton was forced to select Satan as the hero of Paradise Lost because he adheres to the guidelines of epic poetry set by Homer, Virgil and others.

There many examples of how Milton uses and edits the tradition of these previous epics in the formation of the Devil as a hero. One of the most basic examples of heroism in epic poetry is the exhortation of the leader to his followers. In The Odyssey, Homer lets Odysseus give a speech that would convince anyone they could survive the journey to the Strait of Messina, Then we die with our eyes open, if we are going to die, or know what death we baffle if we can.

After passing the Sirens, the ship approaches the Strait, and the crew sees the twin terrors of Scylla and Charybdis, they are mortified. Odysseus again lifts their spirits with this speech, Garcia Friends, have we ever been in danger before this? More fearsome, is it now, than when the Cyclops penned us in his cave?

What power he had! Did I not keep my nerve, and use my wits to find a way out for us? ... Heads up, lads! We must now obey orders as I give them. Here Odysseus shows the true ability of a hero to lead in the face of adversity. Of course Odysseus had the assurance that he would survive the journey and his crew will not, but that does not stop him from leading them. In Paradise Lost, this device is used in the opening scene. After suffering a major defeat at the hands of the Almighty and his angels, Satan awakens in a lake of fire.

He first speaks to Beelzebub, his second in command, telling him, All is not lost, the unconquerable Will, and study of revenge, immortal hate, and courage never to submit or yield: and what else is not to be overcome?... Since by Fate the strength of Gods and Empyreal substance cannot fail, Since though experience of this great event in Arms not worse, in foresight much advance's, We may with more successful hope resolve to wage by force or guile eternal War irreconcilable, to our grand Foe, who now triumphs, and in th'excess of joy sole reigning holds the Tyranny of Heav'n. Beelzebub, perhaps showing signs of little faith in his leader (like Odysseus' crew), raises some important questions.

What if he our Conqueror, (whom I now of force believe Almighty, since no less than such could have overpowered such force as ours) have Garcia left us this our spirit and strength entire strongly to suffer and support our pains, that we may so suffice his vengeful ire, or do him mightier service as his thralls by right of War, whate'er his business be, here in the heart of Hell to work in Fire, Or to do his errands in the gloomy Deep; What can it then avail though yet we feel Strength undiminisht, or eternal being to undergo eternal punishment? Satan, as any good leader would, quickly allays his companion's fear with more speech.

During the speech, Satan casts doubts about God's supremacy and boldly states that they are better off where they are, Here at least we shall be free... Here we may reign secure...Better to reign in Hell, than serve in Heaven. Beelzebub is taken aback by Satan's words and awakens all of the fallen angels. Once Satan has their attention, he rouses these fallen angels with another speech, asking How such united force of Gods, how such stood like these, could ever know repulse?

For who can yet believe, though after loss, that all these puissant Legions, whose exile hath emptied Heav'n, shall fail to re-ascend self-raised, and repossess their native seat. Finally, at the end his speech, Satan sets them all on their course of conflict, Peace is despaired, for who can think of Submission? War then,

War open or understood, must be resolved. The fallen angels respond with a rowdy confirmation, waving their swords in the and hurling defiance at Heaven. Milton has given you Satan in the tradition of the epic hero.

Even though he knows Satan is not the good-guy, he does possess some of the qualities of a hero. Garcia 4 He is the pinnacle of the assembled crew, hailed even by enemies as the strongest of the lot. All the angels face a bad situation (exile in

Hell) and yet Satan exhorts them all with a speech. He recounts how they survived some bad encounters in the past, and then says they will survive their present predicament. His speech also spurns the angels into some positive action.

The action of war against God sets a task out in front of Satan. This quest allows Satan to fulfill another quintessential element of the epic hero.

In almost every epic ever written the hero has to overcome obstacles that stand in their way to complete their daunting task. In The Odyssey, Odysseus is away from his home 20 years, 10 fighting the Trojan War and another 10 years trying desperately to get back home. Odysseus quest or journey is to travel against the will of Poseidon to get back home to Ithaca.

The invocation of the muses, describes most but not all of the trials and tribulations of Odysseus. Tell me the story of a man skilled in all ways of contending the wanderer, harried for years on end after he plundered the stronghold of Troy. He saw the townlands and learned the minds of many distant men, and weathered many bitter nights and days in his deep heart at sea, while he fought only to save his life, to bring his shipmates home.

But not by will or valor could he save them... Odysseus' obstacles can be traced back to a mistake he made when he blinded Polyphemos and let his pride get the best of him, announcing to the Cyclops his real name. This allowed Poseidon to enact Polyphemos' wrath on Odysseus, vowing that he Garcia would never see his home again.

But Odysseus does conquer those obstacles and finally makes it home. Satan can be said to have the same flaw as Odysseus. He, in part, is the cause of his own demise. Had Satan served God willfully, the war never would have raged in Heaven, and Satan and his Army never would've been thrown in the fiery pits of Hell.

However, without that action Satan would not be a hero. His being in Hell leads to him realize his purpose, to corrupt the new type of being God has created on Earth. Satan's journey can be said to be some of Milton's most original piece of writing, because nobody had ever written about Satan's journey so intricately as Milton. To quote Isabel MacCaffrey, The voyage of Books II and III is Milton's greatest original creation.

There was precedent for the journey motif in epic tradition, but no real parallel to a voyage by Satan in the Christian literature on which Milton drew. Unlike most epic heroes, Satan does not necessarily come out on top at the end of his journey/quest. This is where many are quick to judge and point out that since Satan losses, he can not be an epic hero. Milton intended for Satan to lose, after all, the epic is based on the Bible and is meant to justify the ways of God to man. Milton was merely explaining that Satan both won and lost.

He won in the hero sense by completing his task of corrupting Adam & Eve, which allowed Sin and Death to enter the world. But he lost in more ways than one. One of Milton's central themes is that God knows what Garcia 6 Satan will do before he actually does it.

This is where Milton's poetic side and his religious side clash. It creates a hypocritical division because Milton wants to show that God is All-Knowing (Satan is just hunk of mass with no free will) and that Satan is our epic hero (Satan is head the rebel angels).

Satan also loses because of the fact that due to his trickery he would be a snake forever)The Son was going to come down to earth and die to save Adam & Eve, so that Satan's action would be eliminated. Break down Paradise Lost to it bare bones, removing all religious overtones, and you have yourself an epic poem, plain and simple.

The hero of this poem is a man named Satan who is banished for challenging the leadership of the clan. This man Satan makes a vow to destroy or corrupt anything created by the clan. This Satan was resourceful, making the best of what he had, very little, and accomplishing his goal. Satan may just be the nonconformist who couldn't abide by what was considered normal. In any case one must show their admiration for Satan in his unwillingness to serve in Heaven, and then in the way he accepted his resulting role in Hell.

Milton does address the issue of loyalty; but does he succeed in clarifying Genesis? "To explain the ways of God to men" Milton loftily proclaims his goal in writing Paradise Lost.

He will, he asserts, clarify many ambiguities of the Bible itself. Thereby begins one of the greatest epic poems in literary history – and the war of the sexes is raised to new heights. Milton claims to be the mouthpiece of God. If so, God was quite the rhetorician, not to mention misogynist. A being of absolute reason, he fails to understand how his reasonless creations can be devoid of allegiance to his person. A strict and orderly God, he brings a case against his own brain-children, and thus condemns himself.

Allegiance is a key issue in untying the political knot fastened in Paradise Lost. Allegiance between creator and created, between king and subject, between man and woman. Adam and Eve owe God allegiance for their lives. Genesis doesn't address this; the idea is implicit in the text. In Genesis, we are led to believe that God wished for his creations to be faithful and obedient in accordance with his wishes.

Milton, in personifying God and the first human beings, takes this concept one step further. In bringing God down to man through the vehicle of the epic poem, Milton attributes to God the capacity for reason. God does not act arbitrarily: each action is planned with a specific end in mind.

Loyalty is important because it can be used, in the field of reason, to prove innocence. Innocent beings have no understanding of inferiority, power, or debt; and therefore no grasp of even the necessity for loyalty. Milton's God is a God of reason – but his creations, Milton asserts, were wholly innocent. The question, then, that Genesis poses and Milton addresses is: Can God expects to be faithfully obeyed by his innocent creations when those creations, by their very innocence, have no comprehension of allegiance?

Milton is not only anthropomorphizing God, he invests his God character with his own personal religious ideology. A far cry from the Old Testament God of fire and wrath, Milton's God is orderly. God looks for "proof that they could have given sincere, for true allegiance, constant faith, or love" from his creations. Herein lies the paradox: God looks for what he has not instilled. Men do not have a knowledge of good and evil, as God's angels do. It is strongly implied that this knowledge is required to recognize power and the idea of a creator.

Milton, unwittingly or no, seems to draw the conclusion that, if men were only possessed of the concept of allegiance in their state of innocence (a paradox as we now understand humankind and the state of innocence) the fall from grace would have been avoided altogether.

How can God call the Fall of mankind the fault of mankind when Eve, tempted by Satan, is not possessed of adequate knowledge to form a "right" decision? For faith in power and a comprehension of truth, experience and knowledge are in some degree necessary.

Eve: "for contemplation he and valor formed, for softness her and sweet attractive grace, him for God only, and her for God in him". Are Adam and Eve made of the same stuff? Is Adam capable of forming judgment and understanding God, while Eve is relegated to the task of understanding Adam? Adam was made in God's image, Eve in Adam's.

By Milton's own assertions concerning the valor and strength of character Adam displays is Eve vindicated of the sin of the Fall from grace. Adam knows that God is a superior being and is to be obeyed. "O woman, best are all things as the will of God ordained them", Adam tells Eve, long before their Fall.

Eve has only spoken directly to God once before the temptation of the serpent. All of her information is second-hand, through Adam. Milton's Eve is much like the proper Stuart lady, prior, of course, to the Interregnum years when the world was turned upside down.

When Eve, swayed easily by Satan because of her lack of allegiance or faith, eats a piece of the fruit of the tree of knowledge of good and evil, she decides to offer a piece to Adam because he is her deity. All good things for Eve, we are told, come through Adam, even the word of God.

Why shouldn't she make a sacrificial offering of this

wondrous fruit to him? Adam's allegiance here shows itself to be misplaced: he is more loyal to Eve than to God. He is furious with Eve for disobeying God, and yet he disobeys himself in order that Eve should not die alone: "against his better knowledge, not deceived, but fondly overcome with female charms".

Adam holds the Eve, God's "gift", perhaps even his power over Eve, higher than God and his faith to God. Adam, in his conversation with angels, displays inherent faith in the power of God before eating the forbidden fruit. Eve is pure innocence (and therefore gullibility) until she converses with the angel Michael after having partaken of the fruit.

Thus, although Milton does address the issue of loyalty, he does not succeed in clarifying Genesis. He merely further obscures the point, if point there ever was, in his attempts to ratify his own religious and societal ideals. During the Interregnum, who was not recreating God and man? Paradise Lost is filled with paradox and contradiction.

For example, why does Milton agree with the biblical assertion that Adam and Eve are innocent, and then bestow certain advantages, such as loyalty, faith, and integrity, upon Adam? Innocent beings cannot have a knowledge of right and wrong, and yet Adam and Eve comprehend the angel Raphael when he warns them of evil in the Garden of Eden.

Writing in an era when nothing was sacred, when every man was reinventing himself in the new model of government and political philosophy, Milton's Paradise is filled with the turmoil of Milton's world. Shifting loyalties, intrigue and espionage infiltrated the highest circles of court life. Among the peasantry, women were beginning to take an active role in mechanic preaching, Digging and Leveling. Milton himself penned a pamphlet advocating "loose" behaviour in young women as the key to later marital bliss.

Only three generations earlier, the Church of England was born, torn from Henry VIII to Mary to Elizabeth, and plunging the kingdom into civil war and turmoil. Who owes allegiance to whom? If the King is God, and the people of England Adam and Eve, on whom is the stain of the Charles I's blood? On the

King, Milton answers, pointing to his God of paradox, arbitrary law, and unreasonable reason.

GOD, SATAN, AND THE LITERARY IMAGINATION IN PARADISE LOST

While one can also examine these portrayals from an historical, biographical, or theological point of view, what I am most interested in is how these two characters hold up as literary creations and how they mirror one another in terms of identity and the perceptual concepts of self-definition.

Such concepts are commonplace in contemporary literature, but Milton's attention to the interiority of these characters prefigures both the rise of the novel in Western literature and the Modernist movement, which was intrigued with the characterization of the psyche. Milton's intention, just as Lewis and Fish have claimed, to explain God and, for that matter, Satan, involves examining the identities of both these characters.

A facile interpretation of the differences between Milton's God and Satan would be one that follows Christian beliefs: God is the personification of Good; Satan is the personification of Evil. But if one sees Milton's interpretations through this lens, then his portrayal of these two characters might give one pause.

The interiority Milton supplies to Satan, his anger, psychological pain, and complexity give him an empathetic edge.Nineteenth century Romantic poets such as Blake considered him a romantic hero, which makes sense when one compares Milton's Satan with such literary creations as Emily Bronte's Heathcliff in Wuthering Heights. Milton's rendition of God, on the other hand, as noted by such critics as Empson, seems to reveal a contemptuous nature. His God is petty and self-absorbed.

In Book 3, when God appears for the first time in the text, he seems more interested in exonerating himself for Satan's rebellion and Man's fall:

As if Predestination over-rul'd
Thir will, dispos'd by absolute Decree

Or high foreknowledge; they themselves decreed
Thir own revolt, not I: if I foreknew,
Foreknowledge had no influence on their fault,
Which had no less prov'd certain unforeknown

God chooses to hold no responsibility for Satan's descent, which was predicated by his own free will. As with certain Deists who believed that God created the creation and the universe but stepped back from it, Milton's God is likewise uninvolved. Yet, there are similarities between God and Satan that make them fascinating literary creations.

What I mean by literary creations is simply that Milton has endowed God and Satan with characteristics that make them both active participants in the plot. Paradise Lost begins with an act of betrayal: God's exaltation of his Son. While Milton portrays this as an innocent act that is only perverted in Satan's mind, thus bringing forth Sin and Death into the world with his jealous thoughts, God's act nonetheless sets the story in motion.

Milton's choice in beginning his poem in this way is a curious one, since God's exaltation is purely his literary creation. There is no mention of this in the Bible nor other Christian tracts, such as Milton's own De Doctrina.

In fact, "Milton seems to have invented it in order to have an unexplained divine decree leading to the fall of the angels analogous to that which led to the Fall of Man, so as to reinforce the parallel between earth and heaven". Milton may also have chosen to begin the poem this way to make his character more empathetic, thus providing a villain who carries gravitas in the story's actions.

As John Carey writes in his literary criticism of Milton's work: "A black Satan would raise the question of how God had created him and would, besides, remove the possibility of temptation".

A Satan, though wracked with jealousy, paranoia, delusions of grandeur, and who is driven to rebellion, might be more understood if his actions were preceded by an act of betrayal. By understanding, in fact, empathizing with Satan's rejection, the reader is thus able to comprehend why Adam could so easily choose sin, especially since "he had of [God]/ All he could have" (Milton 1883). Satan becomes more than an iconographic theological figure but a villain in the true literary sense.

Milton's portrayal of God's "betrayal" and Satan's rebellion somewhat parallels Cain and Abel, in which one son is given God's grace while the other is rejected. Yet, in that parable, it is clear that God's preference is based on merit. There is no such indication in Paradise Lost. While, in Milton's case, merit is based on one's ability to embrace God's glory (and God's Son is described in this way), there is no reason to believe that Satan did not also merit such consideration.

In fact, Satan's descent into Hell is preceded by his jealous thoughts in response to God's exaltation of his Son, when Satan reaches Hell's gates and meets Sin and Death. Sin describes to Satan her birth at the "Assembly" in Heaven, in which Satan and his devils conspire against God. Sin springs forth from Satan's head.

An incestuous act between Satan and his daughter thus leads to the birth of Death. Therefore, Satan's act of rebellion leads to his fall and his calling forth Sin and Death into the world. Yet, this all occurs only after God's first act of "betrayal." One is left to assume then that Satan always had it in him.

But this assumption inevitably leads to God's own foreknowledge. If God created Satan, and gave him the free will to choose sin, then God must have foreseen Satan's reaction when he exalted his Son. In Milton's interpretation, God very much resembles King Lear. Like Lear, who conveys his ultimate loyalty to whichever daughter who expresses her flattery to him, God exalts his Son, whose later sacrifice to save Man after his fall from grace is as flattering an act a son can offer to his father.

Lear's act leads to tragedy, and thus the same follows in Paradise Lost. The tragedy, the fall of Adam and Eve, is brought about by the thoughtless parent. If God's love is unconditional, then Milton's choice in having God exalt his Son makes no sense theologically, but makes perfect sense as a literary device. God's act forces Satan to action, which, in turn, leads to Satan giving "birth" to Sin and Death and the downfall of Man.

Milton provides both Satan and God with mirror traits that thrust the plot forward on its inevitable course. Both use revenge as a means to settle debts with one another. Satan's use of revenge is, nonetheless, self-serving, while God's form of revenge is based on morality. Yet, neither are willing to compromise or come to any understanding of hurt feelings that are brought up by God's thoughtless and Satan's treasonous acts. They are very much within the tradition of literary characters whose traits form the tension that is necessary to create story.

Milton, drawing that tension between Good and Evil, makes it impossible for either of his characters to bridge the gap. The relationship between Satan and God is therefore differentiated from the relationship between God and Man, who, although earns God's punishment, is still open for redemption.

While Man is created in God's likeness, perhaps God and Satan are too close in similarity for any promise of redemption to occur. Carey writes, "Vindictiveness, anger, and a passion for self-aggrandizement are three characteristics that bind Milton's God to his Satan. Heaven's morality is one of vengeance as well as Hell's".

Both characters are aware of or obsessed with their own self-importance. God's response to Satan's treason and Man's fall are less about the actual sins themselves but about how the sin reflects on him. This is revealed in God's need to exonerate himself for their faults.

As with most Christian beliefs, as well as in Milton's Paradise Lost, God created all "Ethereal Powers and Spirits" with the will to choose grace or sin. Yet, Milton's God cannot find "pleasure" from any obedience owed him by his creations unless it serves no other purpose but him. Therefore, Satan's actions, as equally self-aggrandizing, are treasonous because they challenge God's own sense of self. Since God is the personification of Good, then he very well cannot inspire the kind of evil Satan represents. God's punishment of Satan and Man act a means to differentiate them from God's own self-image.

Likewise, Satan's descent into Hell challenges his own sense of self-importance: "what can be worse/Than to dwell here, driv'n out from bliss, condemn'd/In this abhorred deep to utter woe;". It is interesting to note here that Satan's chief complaint is to be "driv'n out from bliss, condemn'd" by God for his actions. While Satan's treasonous act deserved some response from God, Satan speaks out from an utter lack of awareness about the seriousness of his own actions.

He seems more surprised that God should respond in such a manner. Satan sounds more like a prodigal child who is nonetheless shocked by its parents' lack of love. In this case, bliss is defined by God's grace and love. Now, that Satan is driven from "bliss," and condemned to "this abhorred deep to utter woe," he is lacking any real identity except one that has been forced on him by God. And yet, Satan's fall becomes the means for Satan to develop a sense of identity that is his own creation.

As with any child, Satan needs God for self- identification and importance. As he states to his daughter Sin:

But what owe I to his commands above
Who hates me, and hath hither trust me down
Into this gloom of Tartarus profound,
To sit in hateful Office here confin'd,
Inhabitant of Heav'n, and heav'nly-born,
Here in perpetual agony and pain...

Satan's self-identification with being an "Inhabitant of Heav'n" and "heav'nly born" offers a glimpse into his own psychic turmoil at being invalidated by God's punishment. In other words, because Satan's actions were undeserving of his perch in Heaven, he now must dwell in an environment that suits his true nature, and yet it is the very banishment that causes Satan's crisis of identity. His need for God's love and validation, evidenced in his jealousy over God's exaltation of his son, is as much a self-identifying factor as God's need for his creation's obedience.

Satan can only be obedient to God if God returns with an unconditional love that molds Satan's own sense of self. Without it, a rejected Satan embraces a new identity predicated on becoming God's opposite: the personification of Evil. And yet, Satan's new identity could only have come into being by God's own need for self-aggrandisement, his own desire for his "glory to excel." Another aspect in which these mirror images become apparent is how both Satan and God form a trinity.

God, Son, and the Holy Ghost is a well-known iconography in Christianity. But Milton creates a trinity of evil which revolves around Satan, Sin, and Death. It is through their help that Satan is able to escape from Hell and travel to Earth where he intends to dwell with his minions.

This trinity, again, identifies Satan as evil, and differentiates him from God. And, yet, ironically, Sin and Death spring to life only through Satan's jealousy. Milton suggests that the first sin is jealousy (or, in this case, lack of faith in God's love), but in many Christian tracts, God is described as a jealous God, one whose wrath knows no bounds when he is rejected.

This is apparent in his response to Satan's treason: "Man therefore shall find grace,/The other none". While Man, an innocent, is tempted by an outside source into rejecting God, and is, therefore, still worthy of redemption, Satan falls of his own temptations, i.e., his own jealousies and desires for self-identification ("The first sort by third own suggestion fell,/Self-tempted, self-depraved", and therefore, is forever shut off from any redeeming values in God's eyes. Here, God and Satan operate from similar traits: both are given to jealous and grudging behaviors that lead them to acts of vengeance.

These dual images become the thrust that pushes the narrative forward. Each character is, in effect, responding to the other in a dysfunctional relationship that is so common in modern-day literature. One cannot exist without the other because each plays a role in shaping the other's identity. While the similarities between these two characters are many, it is this one difference which creates the real tension that forms the crux of the story.

What is fascinating is how those similarities create a deeper understanding of the psychological aspects of Milton's work. The heart of Paradise Lost is about the loss of love and acceptance, two aspects of human nature that has been the driving force of literature for centuries.

It is important to note that Paradise Lost is a literary work of art. While many critical analyses have been made about how Milton's own religious and political beliefs inspired the work, his poem has the shape and the force of a true work of fiction and his fully realized renditions of both God and Satan fully bear that out.

USAGE OF SYMBOLS IN PARADISE LOST

MILTON'S UNIVERSE

The universe, including Heaven and Hell, that Milton imagines in Paradise Lost was much more familiar to his original audience than to today's readers. Today the heliocentric view of the solar system and many more, at times baffling, theories about the universe and its creation are accepted without question.

In seventeenth-century England, the debate between the geocentric view of the universe, proposed by the ancient Roman astronomer, Ptolemy, and the heliocentric view, advocated by Copernicus, Kepler, Brahe, Galileo, and others was still fiercely debated.

Through the years, critics have argued confidently about Milton's view of this debate, though these same critics have often been in disagreement concerning which side Milton accepted. Evidence exists that Milton might have met Galileo. Milton mentions Galileo's telescope in the poem (V, 262–62). But, when Adam asks Raphael whether the Earth is stationary with the rest of the universe circling it or whether the Earth circles the sun along with the other planets, Raphael (and Milton) equivocates, leaving Milton's own views unstated.

Of course, the geocentric / heliocentric debate is but one small part of the cosmos that Milton presents in Paradise Lost. In general terms, Milton describes a universe with Heaven at the top, Hell at the bottom, and Chaos in between. Earth dangles on a golden chain dropped from Heaven, and, by the end of the epic, a bridge connects Hell to Earth. To grasp the significance of this view of the universe, one must examine each part separately and compare the fictional / theological construct with the scientific knowledge of Milton's day.

HEAVEN

At the top of the universe is Heaven. It is inhabited by God and those angels who did not rebel against him. The primary quality of Heaven is light. God is pure light of such quality that the angels must observe him through a cloud. The angels themselves are also a type of stunning, pure light but not comparable to the light of God because they give off colors. Raphael is described as being made of "colors dipt in Heaven" (283) in Book V. Milton's source for this Heaven of light is the first command of God in Genesis: "Let there be light, and there was light."

The name Milton uses for this light-filled Heaven is the Empyrean, which for classical authors was the indestructible realm of light or fire. Thus, when the war in Heaven occurs, it is between beings who are indestructible. God says that the rebellious angels can be annihilated, but exactly what he means is never clear. With that one exception, however, everything associated with Heaven or the Empyrean is eternal and indestructible.

Within Heaven, God sits at the top of a mountain on his eternal throne. He is shrouded in a cloudy mist because of the quality and intensity of the light he emanates. The Son is at his side. In orthodox Protestant theology, they are two parts of a tripartite whole—the Holy Spirit being the third. Each of these characters represents an aspect of God. God is the Father; pure reason and intellect, perfect unemotional justice. The Son is the more merciful side. He demonstrates pity, mercy, sacrifice, and hope. (The Holy Spirit is mentioned only in the prologues as the true Urania, Milton's muse.) In Milton's personal view, the Son and God are not the same. God created the Son who is so close to God that any distinction is imperceptible, even to angelic sensibilities. Theologically then, Milton was a Unitarian, though he never develops this viewpoint in Paradise Lost.

Below God and the Son are the angels. Traditional Christian thought grouped angels into nine hierarchical categories. The traditional Christian categories and hierarchies of angels were Seraphim, Cherubim, Thrones, Dominations or Dominions, Virtues, Powers, Principalities, Archangels, and Angels.

Milton mentions all of these groups in Paradise Lost, but he does not adhere strictly to the hierarchies. Each of these classifications was called a choir. Each group of three choirs starting at the top with Seraphim, Cherubim, and Thrones had specific functions in relation to God.

It is readily apparent that Milton does not follow this arrangement of angels in his depiction of Heaven. The important angels—Michael, Raphael, Gabriel—are called archangels and certainly seem to be those closest to God. Further, when Satan approaches the archangel Uriel on the sun in Book III, he disguises himself as a cherubim, a "stripling Cherub", obviously of lesser rank than Uriel. Moreover, Satan addresses Uriel as a "Seraph", which is a confusion of two highly separated categories.

Milton's attitude toward the angels is at best hazy. Most of the time, he seems to follow the ancient Hebrew tradition that classified all angels as either angels or archangels, with the archangels being the more important and the closest to God. However, Milton also mentions all the other categories in several places.

In the end, the only real conclusion is that with angels, as with so many other aspects of Paradise Lost, Milton follows his own ideas while maintaining at least the semblance of the traditional Christian doctrine and emphasizing the hierarchy. He acknowledges the hierarchy of angels but arranges it to suit his own views.

HELL

Hell in Paradise Lost is the antithesis of Heaven. In a sense,

Hell is an ironic parody of Heaven. Hell for Milton is literally the underworld. Heaven is the zenith of the universe, then there is the great gulf of Chaos and Night, and finally, at the bottom, underneath everything, is Hell.

The phrase associated with Milton's Hell that has occasioned much discussion is the statement that Hell, "As one great furnace flamed, yet from those flames / No light, but rather, darkness visible". The idea of flames that do give off light and darkness that is visible has troubled some commentators over the years.

But, while one may grant that the phrase "darkness visible" is oxymoronic, it is also meaningful. Heaven, which is pure light, is also pure goodness. Hell is the opposite, pure evil and pure darkness, in fact a darkness so pure that it is visible, a contrasting quality to the blinding light of Heaven.

At first, Hell seems like Dante's place of miserable torment. The fallen angels wake, lying on a lake of fire, surrounded by sulfurous fumes. However, this first image of Hell is soon replaced by a second. The demons build a capital, Pandemonium, with a palace and a throne for Satan, contrasting with God's throne in Heaven.

The demons also have contests, sing, and debate, so that Hell begins to seem more like Dante's Limbo, not such bad place except that it is apart from God. Both these images are aspects of Hell for Milton; it is a place of punishment and also a place where demons live in a manner that ironically imitates Heaven. The difference is that the demons' games, songs, and debates are all corrupt and have no true end unlike the absolute beauty and truth of Heaven.

Milton will also introduce a third Hell, an inner, psychological Hell. At the start of Book IV, Satan has a soliloquy in which he concludes, "Which way I fly is Hell; myself am Hell". This inner Hell is as much a part of Milton's universe as the physical lake of fire. In fact, for Milton, the inner turmoil that makes anywhere Satan is into Hell is probably the foremost Hell. Hell as a spiritual state that cannot be avoided is worse than any particular place.

In the physical Hell, though, the demons form a hierarchy

of sorts. Milton lists no classifications of demons, but obviously some are more important that others. The demons who speak at the council are the most important and ironically match the archangels associated with God.

Beelzebub, Belial, Moloch, and Mammon are the chief demons under Satan. Besides these four demons who speak at the great council, Milton catalogs over a dozen more. Some of the names are familiar; some not. Osiris, Isis, perhaps Baal and Astaroth are recognizable names; Rimnon, Thammuz, Chemos, Dagon, and a number of others are known primarily by scholars.

Milton has taken the names of numerous pagan gods who were worshiped by tribes that opposed the Israelites and made them into fallen angels, now demons. For an audience closer to the Bible and biblical literature than a modern one, all of these names resonated with meaning. Milton's point is that the pagan gods were once angels who, in corrupted form, became the false gods of those nations that opposed the Chosen People. The purpose behind the cataloging of demons in Hell and the hierarchy of angels in Heaven is not made clear by Milton, but the two groups are obviously comparable and intended to be so. Similarly, the different aspects of Hell are usually set up in an ironic contrast with a counterpoint in Heaven.

The hierarchy of Hell is not a real arrangement based on superiority and inferiority. Satan has taken control, but in actuality all the fallen angels are essentially the same, a point made clear when they are all turned into snakes and both their importance in the universe and their degrees in Hell vanish. In Heaven, the hierarchy is real; in Hell, a sham.

CHAOS

At the top of Milton's universe is Heaven with God on his throne; at the bottom of this universe is Hell, with Satan on his throne. In between the two is Chaos with his consort Night. Chaos and Night are depicted as characters, but they are actually personifications of the great unorganized chasm that separates Heaven from Hell.

For Milton, relying on earlier writers and thinkers, Chaos

was the formless void that existed before creation. It was the abyss, the darkness, and the mighty wind out of which God created first Heaven and, later, Earth.

Chaos also physically demonstrates the profound width of the gap between Heaven and Hell. Not only is Hell at the bottom of the universe in Milton's design, it is at the bottom of an almost limitless and unimaginably disordered space. Milton describes Chaos as "Eternal Anarchy" (II, 896) and a "wild Abyss" (II, 917). He adds that it is "The Womb of nature, and perhaps her Grave, / Of neither Sea, nor Shore, nor Air, nor Fire, / But all these in their pregnant causes mixt / Confusedly, and which thus must ever fight" (II, 911–914).

In Paradise Lost, Satan has to journey across Chaos to find Earth. This journey is long and arduous and is one of the accomplishments of Satan that makes him seem heroic. In Book II, Satan, with no clear idea of where he is going or how to get there, sets out across Chaos, intent on finding God's new creation. If the reader forgets Satan's motive, to corrupt and destroy, then Satan becomes the heroic individual, pitting himself against the universe.

EARTH

The Earth that is depicted in Paradise Lost is different from the Earth we know today. Milton describes Earth as a creation by God after the rebellion of Satan and his followers. Raphael tells Adam that God created Earth through the Son to keep Satan from feeling pride that he had "dispeopl'd Heav'n". Earth and Man were created so that Man, through trial, could reach the state of the angels, and Earth could become a part of Heaven.

To that end, the Son creates not only Earth but also the heavens surrounding Earth, and all that lives on Earth. All of these, he suspends from Heaven on a golden chain. The great image in Paradise Lost is of the Son, a celestial architect with a golden compass, plotting out the universe in which Earth will exist.

After its creation, Earth, like Heaven and Hell, has a hierarchical arrangement. Also like Heaven and Hell, this arrangement is understated and vague. On Earth, Paradise—the Garden of Eden—is the paramount place. The hill from which Adam receives his vision of the future from Michael is apparently, though this is not stated, the highest place on Earth. So when Adam and Eve are banished from the Garden, they leave the perfect place on Earth and enter a world that is both flawed and unknown.

On Earth, Adam is the superior being. He was created first, and Eve was created from his rib. Adam is also the paradigmatic Man, the pattern for all who will come later; likewise Eve is the pattern for all women. But, in relation to each other, Adam is superior both in intellect and ability.

Eve is more beautiful, but she has been created as a slightly inferior helpmeet to Adam. Together the two humans are superior to all other living creatures on Earth. Raphael's speech beginning at line 469 in Book V makes it clear that all of the creatures of Earth can be arranged in hierarchical order. The idea that the entire universe is hierarchical was basic to all thought in the seventeenth century. The first serious expressions of the equality of man were still over a century away.

The position of Earth in Milton's universe also reflects a hierarchical arrangement. Heaven is the top of the universe; Hell, the bottom. Earth is attached to Heaven by a golden chain. Had Adam and Eve not fallen, there is a sense that at least metaphorically the chain would have slowly pulled Earth up to Heaven so the two places could merge. The fall changed the nature of the original plan.

The fall, however, did not change the connection of Earth to Heaven. The chain remains, although at the end of Paradise Lost, a wide bridge across Chaos connects Hell to Earth. Man must either find the difficult way up the chain or stroll across the wide causeway to Hell. The easier pathway is obvious.

The final aspect of Earth in Milton's universe is its position in relation to the scientific knowledge of the day. As noted, Milton was well aware of the scientific theories of his time. He certainly knew the Copernican heliocentric theories and probably accepted them.

As with so many specifics in Paradise Lost, though,

Milton's description of Earth does not reveal his personal views of the geocentric / heliocentric controversy. The chain that attaches Earth to Heaven attaches not only Earth but also the heavens that surround Earth. The universe humans see in the night sky is only a small part, removed by God from the gigantic Chaos which surrounds Earth.

Adam's question concerning whether the chain connects to Earth with the sun and stars rotating around the planet or whether the chain attaches in some other way so that Earth rotates around the sun is never answered. Raphael simply says that some questions are better left unanswered, and that God laughs at Man's attempts to understand how he made the universe.

Milton's refusal to give a straight answer to the geocentric / heliocentric debate may have a better rationale behind it than simple bet hedging. Milton consciously wrote Paradise Lost for the ages. He saw it as the great Christian epic following in the tradition of Homer, Virgil, Dante, and Tasso. The scientific questions concerning the universe were questions still hotly debated in Milton's time.

If Milton had had Raphael explain exactly what God had done, and then, at some later date, that explanation was shown to be false, a serious flaw would exist in Paradise Lost—God would be incorrect. By having Raphael equivocate on the answer, Milton allows God to be eternally correct. God knows how he created the universe and how the solar system works, but he does not share that information with Man in Paradise Lost.

In the end, Milton's cosmos is one of the great imaginary cosmographies of Western literature. Almost as many depictions of Milton's cosmos exist as do of Dante's Hell, Purgatory, and Heaven. It is a fictional world that presumes to represent the real world. As such, it is an achievement that is almost as impressive as the epic for which it was created.

BINARY RELATIONSHIPS CONNECT SEPARATE CONCEPTUAL IDEAS IN PARADISE LOST

The construction of "authorship" in the poem exists as a

good example of just such a relationship. This theme incorporates two very different ideas in the poem, and is central to the understanding of issues concerning the creation and use of power. The attention Milton gives to each character, and their specific personality, allows us to interpret their actions as consciously chosen deeds within the larger framework of the poem.

Great detail is given to the idea of "creation". Beyond that of the creation of the world in Book I, there are many instances where the act of creation itself becomes an act of endowing power on some object or person. The most obvious example would be the creation of Adam and Eve by God. By creating the pair, God, desires them to glorify His ways through their praises and deeds. He gives them enough power over their destiny to choose to worship Him as the Almighty.

The fact that they have free will is important to God because they choose to give Him praise despite any outside temptation. There is one obvious drawback to this kind of power. They chose to follow Satan's beguiling words. The fact that they had the free will to follow Satan's words meant that their decision was cosmically more important because it was arrived at through conscious thought.

We can see this idea of power demonstrated throughout Paradise Lost. The dual relationship between the beneficial act of bestowing power at the time of creation and the negative side of the free will to use that power freely, shows up within every character.

Instances of creation appear in every book, and can be associated with every character. Some of the first appearances of the word "author" are connected with the idea of creation. In Book III, the throngs of assembled angels say, "Eternal King, the Author of all being/Fountain of light, thyself invisible/ ...".Here God is portrayed as the great originator of everything in all of creation. To be the "author" of something is to be the creator, much the same way as Milton himself is creating the world of the poem.

In virtually every instance the act of "authoring", is associated with images of primacy and legitimacy. The ultimate act of creation, that of shaping the physical world itself, brings about another reference to this idea. As the story of the creation is retold, God is called the,"Author and end of all things,..."

In reference to God, the word author is used, to describe the timelessness of God's rule. He authored the world by creating it, and will be there to see it end. God looks over the world as a literal father does over his own children. But, as the poem shows us, one of His children went bad. Satan, the other main power in the book, also shares references to the act of authoring.

In very similar phrasing to the description of God's authorship, the fallen angel's personality is described as:

...Satan, and in part proposed: for whence,
But from the author of all ill could spring
So deep a malice, to confound the race
Of mankind in one root, and earth with hell
To mingle and involve, done all to spite
The great Creator?..

This passage links the creative power of Satan to the abounding evil within his character. It is not because of this evilness alone that humankind is destined to Sin and Death. It is through the way in which Satan has created himself, that he can hold so much power over the rest of God's creation. In this passage, Satan is shown as an author which has the ability to create a hell of the very Paradise which is earth.

The creative power of God destined this being to commit sins of ultimate evil, and at the same time has little apparent power to control it. The very root, or fundamental quality of mankind, can be affected by the power of evil in such a way as to drive it away from the divine goodness of God.

In a very real way, Satan can be compared to the epitome of creation. Though evil, his entire purpose in the universe is to create actions and ideas which go against the established order of cosmic harmony. His existence symbolizes the separation of the stagnant from the explosive. God in this poem seems to be somewhat quiet and exclusive until He is upset or bothered by some force.

Satan's only existence is to prod the form of God until something happens. Although the poem calls him evil, Satan could be merely a figure of the act or need of creation within an apparently inflexible system. Such a force would be called evil, but would, in a sense, only be trying to write for itself a different kind of role. Satan's creativity does not only exist within his own little sphere. He is the father of both Sin and Death, which guard the gates of Hell. As he wings his way up to the realm of earth, he encounters them, holding the gates of Hell closed to all who would get out.

Sin recognizes Satan first as her father and says," Thou art my father, thou my author, thou/My being gav'st me; whom should I obey/But thee, whom follow?...".Through Satan, the principal assailants of mankind, after the Fall, are brought into the world. This passage explains that the act of creation implies some sort of servitude, or at the very least, some type of gratitude.

In every example, whether from God or Satan, the act which brings something new into the world is essentially good. Sin is grateful for her birth, just as Adam is thankful to God for breathing life into him at the time of his creation. Even the great war in heaven is an example of the way in which a good value is assigned to the creation of something new.

Satan approaches Michael, both garbed in full battle armor, and Michael says:

" 'Author of evil, unknown till thy revolt,
Unnamed in heav'n, now plenteous, as thou seest
These acts of hateful strife, hateful to all
...how hast thou disturbed
Heav'n's blessed peace, and into nature brought
Misery, uncreated till the crime
Of thy rebellion!'"

This passage says two very important things. The presence of evil in heaven was not noticed by any (except God) until it boiled over and became the great war. This points to the fact that the roots of evil are so intrinsically intertwined within the fallen angels' souls so as to be undetectable even to their brethren. The evil inside Satan manifested itself, according to

Michael's speech, by creating a new force in heaven, namely, Misery. Earlier we find out that the rebellion of Satan causes his daughter, Sin, to break out of his head and enter the created world. In many ways, this is a fight against the established order created by God. Satan is fighting for a right to be master over his own existence. Before this gets into imagery depicting the fight for a "democratic heaven", we can say that the poem itself is trying to build a framework for interpreting the "ways of God to men."

By making or fashioning something, the creator endows that object with a certain measure of agency in the world. This arises from the dynamic between the creative forces of the individual, and the final material result of the labour. Whether originating from Satan or from God, creation in Paradise Lost is accompanied by issues concerning free will.

No matter how anything is supposed to behave within the poem, something interferes with the designs of man, Satan, and (though He is omniscient) to some extent, God. God's original design for mankind is corrupted by Satan. The hopes of Adam and Eve are foiled by the plot of Satan.

The Fall is upturned by the redemption of man through the Son. The great movers of the poem have their plans canceled by each other. Importantly, all the action which we see within the plot of the poem revolves around this point. The architecture of creation, in any form, drives the action of both the characters in the narrative, and generates meaning for the reader. After the Fall, Satan is visited by his offspring, Sin and Death. Sin says,"O Parent, these are thy magnific deeds,/Thy trophies, which thou view'st as not thine own,/ Thou art their author and prime architect:...". This passage exemplifies the connection between the power given by the accomplishment of creation, here the creation of evil in Paradise, and the legitimizing force of that act upon the created.

Here, the fallen angel has won the humans for his own, forever bringing them to corruption in God's eyes. Though Satan did not originally create the humans, he did make them intrinsically real by bringing them to know Knowledge in its pure form. Sin shows Satan building, like an architect, Adam and Eve from inconsequential beings to the level of reality itself. No longer will they be mindless servants to a higher power, now they have the capability to choose what they wish to believe in, exercising their own free will. God, also, gives this gift to Adam, but in a different way. The ways in which God creates in Paradise Lost focus mainly on acts of physical creation.

Adam tells Raphael about his own memory of his first hours:

Said mildly,'Author of all this thou seest
Above, or round about thee or beneath.
This paradise I give thee, count it thine
To till and keep, and of the fruit to eat:...

God, similar to His actions in other parts of the poem, gives something to the human(s). He tries to be a nice deity and says that the humans can have this neat garden, and may eat all they want of the nice food they might find therein. In some ways, the gift "given" by Satan becomes more beneficial to mankind than God's gift of some juicy pieces of fruit. While God concerns himself with the granting of material possessions: the garden, the food, and the universe itself (you know, little stuff), the arch-fiend gives the intangible gifts of independent thought.

What he offers is the chance to become truly self-willed creatures who are free to choose their own path. After the initial temptation, the humans become their own agents within Creation. Satan creates creatures which are from the mold of God, but have a will that exists almost outside of Divine influence. Throughout Paradise Lost, the act of authorship can be likened to the main economic commodity of the primal world. The creative process is the force through which action occurs within the poem. Milton repeats again and again, the idea that to create something is to legitimize it. The passages talking about both God and Satan give them a sense of power over the things they create.

This power has an opposite side to it, however. The binary which resides within the concept of "authorship" endows the creative process with a more spontaneous characteristic than might have been previously obvious. Milton emphasizes through the actions of the principal characters that a higher type of power is endowed within a fashioned object, one which the creator has virtually no control over.

An example of this would be, in living creatures, the element of free will God assigns to Adam and Eve. Even physical reality has this vital component. The Tree of Knowledge within the Garden must exist in order for the world of reality to have any legitimacy or worth. Meaning arises, for Milton, in the act of creating, or authorship.

In a larger sense, the entire poem symbolizes an act of creation on the part of Milton. Taking the role of the "author", Milton wields a kind of power over the creation of the poem. It becomes his choice, in the end, on what parts to create, and which to omit. The binary exists here also, as we look to the ways in which this text has influenced many generations of poets, scholars, and thinkers.

The power of Paradise Lost can be traced far past the lifetime of Milton. The very fact that people today still regard this as one of the great poetical texts of all time, points to the life the text has, independent of its author.

In any truly masterful work, whether in art, or music, or writing, the creative process spawns a unique result which takes on a life of its own. Each main actor within Paradise Lost is part of a process which results in the creation of something entirely original into the greater scheme of the universe. Every time this happens, a piece of the creator goes into the new object, endowing it with life, and power. In this way, we can see that the fundamental structures of power at work in Milton's universe depend on each other in order for any of them to incorporate any meaning.

Chapter 11

Reflections on Milton and Ariosto

We used to have a good piece of literary gossip about Milton and his supposed scribbles in a 1591 edition of Sir John Harington's translation of Ariosto. William Riley Parker, the great biographer of Milton, transmitted and endorsed the rumor. According to Parker, sometime around the year 1642, awaiting the return of his errant wife Mary Powell, Milton "had reread Sir John Harington's translation of Ariosto's Orlando Furioso".

This sounds too good to be true. We would have Milton, awaiting the return of his estranged wife, perhaps reading Canto 28 over and over. Parker is referring to a marginal note in a copy of the 1591 edition of Harington, which he thought "almost certainly in Milton's hand".

The note, actually to be found at the end of Canto 46, reads "Questo libro due volte Io letto, Sept. 21. 1642". I have always wanted to believe that this book belonged to Milton and was written in it by him, but that bit in Italian had always seemed a bit touristy to me — why Italian, why that canto, and why should Milton boast about reading a book twice?

John Shawcross, in 1963, denied that the spelling or the handwriting was Milton's. Working independently, Sotheby's Peter Beal also listed the marginalia among "undoubtedly spurious" attributions. Parker's gossip, as a consequence, should be disbelieved, though the same misinformation remains enshrined in the Columbia Milton and the Yale Milton, and critics are still citing it as truth; Mary Ann Radzinowicz, for example, does so.

Some mystery remains: the book, that 1591 copy of Ariosto

in which Milton was supposed to have written, has disappeared so far as I know. Maurice Kelley saw it. The Reverend H. A. D. Surridge apparently bought it and reported on it in 1938 (Parker 861, 884), but no one knows anything of Surridge.

When Gordon Campbell and Peter Beal went separately looking for the book, Campbell could not locate it. Beal reports that it is "privately owned in England." With the witnesses of Shawcross and Beal, though, we can be assured that the hand in the margin was not Milton's.

As if this weren't confusing enough, Milton certainly did read the poet he called "Ariosto of Ferrara" (Of Reformation, and in Of Reformation he himself translated two four-line sequences from Canto 34, from the English knight Astolfo's slightly sacrilegious voyage to the moon, where the lunatics who have lost their wits reside, where Astolfo is guided by St. John the Evangelist.

Milton's translation is very close to that of Sir John Harington, in the two four-line passages from which he chooses to quote. So we can conclude that Milton did indeed read Ariosto's Orlando Furioso, probably in the original but certainly in Harington's famous folio. Thanks to John Shawcross and to Peter Beal, however, we know he did not scribble in that 1591 book.

Milton's comments in Of Reformation (dated May 1641) reveal his critical perspective on Ariosto. In bringing St. John to the Moon, Ariosto is culpable: "he feigns," says Milton, laconically. Upon arriving at the episode dealing with Astolfo on the moon, Milton writes, a reader has to be "following the scope of his [Ariosto's] Poem in a difficult knot" (560).

Ariosto, perhaps because he is taking a man to the moon as well as defaming the sanctitude of St. John, is considered to be feigning as a writer and composing knotty poetry or a knotty plot.

Milton always uses the word feign pejoratively — the same way he uses the word fable as a verb — to put down writers who do not admit eternal Christian truths, whether they are the unenlightened ancient poets like Ovid, or modern Roman

Catholic, romantic epicists like Ariosto. Pagans and Papists look alike. Either the plot or the poetry itself of Orlando Furioso, Milton implies, is in a "knot." The more polite word that many modern critics use for Ariosto's intricate plotting is tapestry (Wiggins). Milton seems to be on to something critically with that knot image, and he does not appear to use it in a complimentary way: a few pages later in Of Reformation he contrasts the "sobre, plain, and unaffected stile of the Scriptures" with the "knotty Africanisms, the pamper'd metafors; the intricat, and involv'd sentences of the Fathers;...".

Milton apparently did not like tapestry plots or knotty styles. We can add up the epithet "of Ferrara," the "feign" reference, and the "difficult knot" to indicate that Milton knew something of Ariosto's biography and possibly about his connection with the Este family in Ferrara (by 1641 Milton had been to Italy and come back); that he was highly suspicious of an Italian romantic epic's attempt to take an English knight to the moon; and that he considered Ariosto's plotting to be "knotty."

In 1642, when he published Reason of Church Government, Milton was still thinking of Ariosto, and the famous unobeyed injunction of Pietro Bembo to Ariosto that he should write in Latin rather than in his native tongue.Milton expressed his opinion about his choice to write poetry in English, borrowing from Harington's life of Ariosto:

For which cause, and not only for that I knew it would be hard to arrive at the second rank among the Latines, I apply'd my selfe to that resolution which Ariosto follow'd against the perswasions of Bembo, to fix all the industry and art I could unite to the adorning of my native tongue;...

Milton is certainly following Harington's "Life of Ariosto," included as an appendix to his translation of Orlando Furioso, very closely: when Bembo would have disswaded him [Ariosto] from writing Italian, alledging that he should winne more praise by writing Latine, his answere was that he had rather be one of the principal and chiefe

Thuscan writers then scarce the second or third among the Latines, adding that he found his humour (his Genius, he called it) best inclining to it. Milton is making an implicit comparison between himself, as native vernacular poet writing beautifully in London English, and Ariosto, who made the same choice to write in the choicest Italian, the Tuscan dialect also used by Dante and Boiardo (at least in Berni's refacimento).

Though Milton seems to have had a youthful infatuation with the poetry of Ariosto, Boiardo, Vida, DuBartas (through Sylvester), Sidney, Spenser, and Shakespeare, he seems to have rejected the poetic styles and the subject matter of almost all of their works by the time he wrote Paradise Lost. But Tasso is not in this list.

His epic theory gave Milton the underpinning for his own sage and serious epic poetry, and Jerusalem Delivered was an example of serious elegance and eloquence — even of hidden allegory — that he could not ignore. But why was Ariosto to be relegated to the status of the writer of episodes that needed to be parodied, satirized (see Kantra), and discarded as part of the "tinsel trappings" that had, for Milton, infested romantic epic, causing him to reject King Arthur and the Matter of Britain as a subject and to choose instead the timeless and placeless history of Adam and Eve?

Following a method derived from Clark Hulse in his recent book, I would like to carry a tradition of illustration from Ariosto to Harington to Milton, in the posthumous 1688 folio edition of Paradise Lost, in order to indicate what Milton would have kept and what he would have rejected of Ariosto's method of constructing an epic. Two panels of illustrations, the first from the infamous Canto 28 in Harington's translation, show Harington's typical, lovable, "dirty" tricks.

Being something of a professional rogue and mischief-maker, Harington took Ariosto's illustration to Canto 28 and caused three obscene panels to be added to it, scenes of copulation that one hardly notices until one looks closely. Neither Milton nor his illustrators would think of posing Adam and Eve in this way.

Although they are naked and make love, neither Milton nor his illustrators would let Adam and Eve's nudity in their love-making become prurient. Milton dropped what he considered to be trivial or titillative. His Adam and Eve do not carve their names on trees, nor is Eve a flirtatious bolter like Angelica. The comedy in Paradise Lost is heavy by comparison with that in the Orlando Furioso — it exists, as Tasso said it should, in the heavier forms of sarcasm or dark humour holding evil up to ridicule and scorn.

There is very little of what appears to be gratuitous humour in Paradise Lost, perhaps some in that elephant who writhes his lithe proboscis to make Adam and Eve laugh, and perhaps some in the situation of Adam telling God why He doesn't need a mate, while Adam does. In thinking for thirty years or so about Ariosto and Milton — with or without believing that Milton made marginal comments in a specific edition of Harington's translation — I keep returning to what Milton in his argument to book 3 first labeled the Limbo of Vanity.

So on this windie Sea of Land, the Fiend
Walk'd up and down alone bent on his prey,
Alone, for other Creature in this place
Living or liveless to be found was none,
None yet, but store hereafter from the earth
Up hither like Aereal vapours flew
Of all things transitorie and vain, when Sin
With vanity had filld the works of men:
Both all things vain, and all who in vain things
Built thir fond hopes of Glorie or lasting fame,
Or happiness in this or th' other life;
All who have thir reward on Earth, the fruits
Of painful Superstition and blind Zeal,
Naught seeking but the praise of men, here find
Fit retribution, emptie as thir deeds;
All th' unaccomplisht works of Natures hand,
Abortive, monstrous, or unkindly mixt,
Dissolvd on Earth, fleet hither, and in vain,
Till final dissolution, wander here,
Not in the neighbouring Moon, as some have dreamd;
Those argent Fields more likely habitants,
Translated Saints, or middle Spirits hold
Betwixt th' Angelical and Human kinde:

Hither of ill-joynd Sons and Daughters born
First from the ancient World those Giants came
With many a vain exploit, though then renownd:

What Ariosto had done with his moon inhabited by lost wits, Milton deliberately distorts into anti-Roman Catholic propaganda. Milton seems to be correcting Ariosto's moral misconceptions about what sorts of odd beings might be inhabiting worlds other than ours. The Limbo of Vanity is a parody of Ariosto's Moon of Lost Wits. Just as Milton's illustrators would change Harington's innocent prurience to serious cyclical depiction of the activities of Adam and Eve, Milton makes Ariosto serious and uses his own version of Ariosto's moon-wandering with which to make sardonic satire.

Milton rises up against Italian religion and Italian false-hearted literature, to some extent betraying friends in Italy that he had kept contact with at least into the late 1640s. To set the record straight, however, Milton never told his Italian friends such as Carlo Dati that he would not betray them on religious grounds.

The satire in the Limbo of Vanity narration in Paradise Lost is unique in the epic. It is obviously satire, it is propaganda, and it is out of place—except that it is in a Satanic setting, at a point in the epic when Satan is chaotically sailing through the air towards Earth. It associates the Roman Catholic Church that Milton had observed in action in 1638 with indulgences, relics, icons, abuses, much as Chaucer's depiction of the Summoner and Pardoner does.

It makes the reader laugh abusively at the prospect of all those precious relics floating in air. When I think, often, of what Milton might have received from Ariosto — his equal in brilliance and poetic control — I keep returning to the Moon of Lost Wits and the Limbo of Vanity. What Milton did to Ariosto's voyage is similar to Harington's manipulation of Ariosto's illustration: he took it away from Ariosto, put it into his own pocket, altered it, and corrected Ariosto's irreverence toward his own Roman Catholic religion with his, Milton's own, sardonic seriousness about his version of protestantism.

Chapter 12

Milton's Religious Views

Modern criticism of Paradise Lost has taken many different views of Milton's ideas in the poem. One problem is that Paradise Lost is almost militantly Christian in an age that now seeks out diverse viewpoints and admires the man who stands forth against the accepted view. Milton's religious views reflect the time in which he lived and the church to which he belonged. He was not always completely orthodox in his ideas, but he was devout. His purpose or theme in Paradise Lost is relatively easy to see, if not to accept.

Milton begins Paradise Lost by saying that he will sing, "Of Man's First Disobedience" (I, 1) so that he can "assert Eternal Providence, / And justify the ways of God to men" (I, 25–26). The purpose or theme of Paradise Lost then is religious and has three parts: 1) disobedience, 2) Eternal Providence, and 3) justification of God to men.

Frequently, discussions of Paradise Lost centre on the latter of these three to the exclusion of the first two. And, just as frequently, readers and those casually acquainted with Paradise Lost misunderstand what Milton means by the word justify, assuming that Milton is rather arrogantly asserting that God's actions and motives seem so arbitrary that they require vindication and explanation.

However, Milton's idea of justification is not as arrogant as many readers think. Milton does not use the word justification in its modern sense of proving that an action is or was proper. Such a reading of justify would mean that Milton is taking it upon himself to explain the propriety of God's actions—a presumptuous undertaking when one is dealing with any deity. Rather, Milton uses justify in the sense of showing the justice that underlies an action. Milton wishes to show that the fall, death, and salvation are all acts of a just God. To understand the theme of Paradise Lost then, a reader does not have to accept Milton's ideas as a vindication of God's actions; rather the reader needs to understand the idea of justice that lies behind the actions.

DISOBEDIENCE

The first part of Milton's argument hinges on the word disobedience and its opposite, obedience. The universe that Milton imagined with Heaven at the top, Hell at the bottom, and Earth in between is a hierarchical place. God literally sits on a throne at the top of Heaven. Angels are arranged in groups according to their proximity to God. On Earth, Adam is superior to Eve; humans rule over animals. Even in Hell, Satan sits on a throne, higher than the other demons.

This hierarchical arrangement by Milton is not simply happenstance. The worldview of the Middle Ages, Renaissance, and Restoration was that all of creation was arranged in various hierarchies.

The proper way of the world was for inferiors to obey superiors because superiors were, well, superior. A king was king not because he was chosen but because he was superior to his subjects. It was, therefore, not just proper to obey the king; it was morally required. Conversely, if the king proved unfit or not superior to his subjects, it was morally improper to obey him and revolution could be justified.

God, being God, was by definition superior to every other thing in the universe and should always be obeyed. In Paradise Lost, God places one prohibition on Adam and Eve—not to eat from the Tree of Knowledge. The prohibition is not so much a matter of the fruit of the tree as it is obeying God's ordinance. The proper running of the universe requires the obedience of inferiors to their superiors. By not obeying God's rule, Adam and Eve bring calamity into their lives and the lives of all mankind.

The significance of obedience to superiors is not just a

matter of Adam and Eve and the Tree of Knowledge; it is a major subject throughout the poem. Satan's rebellion because of jealousy is the first great act of disobedience and commences all that happens in the epic.

When Abdiel stands up to Satan in Book V, Abdiel says that God created the angels "in their bright degrees" and adds "His laws our laws". Abdiel's point is that Satan's rebellion because of the Son is wrong because Satan is disobeying a decree of his obvious superior. Satan has no answer to this point except sophistic rigmarole. Further instances of the crucial importance of both hierarchy and obedience occur in both large and small matters. The deference with which Adam greets Raphael shows the human accepting his position in regard to the angel.

The image is one of the proper manners between inferior and superior. Eve's normal attitude toward Adam reflects the same relationship. The crucial moment in the poem results from disobedience and a breakdown of hierarchy. Eve argues with Adam about whether they should work together or apart, and Adam gives in to her. The problem here lies with both humans. Eve should not argue with her superior, Adam, but likewise, Adam, should not yield his authority to his inferior, Eve.

When Eve eats the fruit, one of her first thoughts is that the fruit "may render me more equal" (IX, 823) to which she quickly adds, "for inferior who is free?" Her reasoning, from Milton's point of view, is incorrect. Freedom comes precisely from recognizing one's place in the grand scheme and obeying the dictates of that position. By disobeying God, Eve has gained neither equality nor freedom; she has instead lost Paradise and brought sin and death into the world.

Likewise, when Adam also eats the fruit, he disobeys God. Further, he disobeys by knowingly putting Eve ahead of God. Disobedience and disruption of the correct order result in sin and death. Finally, in the last two books of the epic, Milton shows example after example of people who ignore the responsibilities they have and try to either raise themselves above God or disobey God's commands. The result is always the same—destruction. The first part of Milton's purpose in Paradise Lost then is to show that disobedience leads to a breakdown of hierarchical or social order with disastrous consequences.

Some have argued that Milton puts himself in a contradictory position in Paradise Lost, since he supported the overthrow of Charles I. In his political writings, Milton makes it clear that obeying an inferior is equally as bad as disobeying a superior. In the case of a king, the people must determine if the king is truly their superior or not. Thus, Milton justifies his position toward Charles and toward God.

ETERNAL PROVIDENCE

Milton's theme in Paradise Lost, however, does not end with the idea of disobedience. Milton says that he will also "assert Eternal Providence." If Man had never disobeyed God, death would never have entered the world and Man would have become a kind of lesser angel. Because Adam and Eve gave in to temptation and disobeyed God, they provided the opportunity for God to show love, mercy, and grace so that ultimately the fall produces a greater good than would have happened otherwise. This is the argument about the fall called felix culpa or "happy fault."

The general reasoning is that God created Man after the rebellion of Satan. His stated purpose is to show Satan that the rebellious angels will not be missed, that God can create new beings as he sees fit. God gives Man a free will, but at the same time, God being God, knows what Man will do because of free will. Over and over in Paradise Lost, God says that Man has free will, that God knows Man will yield to Satan's temptation, but that he (God) is not the cause of that yielding; He simply knows that it will occur.

This point is theologically tricky. In many ways, it makes God seem like a cosmic prig. He knows what Man will do, but he does nothing to stop him because somehow that would be against the rules. He could send Raphael with a more explicit warning; he could tell Gabriel and the other guards where Satan will enter Eden; he could seal Satan up in Hell immediately. He could do a number of things to prevent the fall, but he does nothing.

From the standpoint of fictional drama, a reader may be correct in faulting God for the fall of Adam and Eve. From a theological / philosophical standpoint, God must not act. If Man truly has free will, he must be allowed to exercise it. Because of free will then, Adam and Eve disobey God and pervert the natural hierarchy. Death is the result, and Death could be the end of the story if Paradise Lost were a tragedy.

JUSTIFICATION OF GOD'S WAYS

Eternal Providence moves the story to a different level. Death must come into the world, but the Son steps forward with the offer to sacrifice himself to Death in order to defeat Death. Through the Son, God is able to temper divine justice with mercy, grace, and salvation. Without the fall, this divine love would never have been demonstrated. Because Adam and Eve disobeyed God, mercy, grace, and salvation occur through God's love, and all Mankind, by obeying God, can achieve salvation. The fall actually produces a new and higher love from God to Man.

This idea then is the final point of Milton's theme—the sacrifice of the Son which overcomes Death gives Man the chance to achieve salvation even though, through the sin of Adam and Eve, all men are sinful. As Adam says, "O goodness infinite, goodness immense! / That all this good of evil shall produce, / And evil turn to good" (XII, 469–471). The fall of Man, then, turns evil into good, and that fact shows the justice of God's actions, or in Milton's terms, "justifies the ways of God to men."

Chapter 13

T.S. Eliot on John Milton

Eliot praised Milton in "A Note on the Verse of John Milton" (Martz 12–18): "[W]hat he could do well he did better than anyone else has ever done." Then Eliot added, "Milton's poetry could only be an influence for the worse, upon any poet whatever." The general thrust of Eliot's criticism is that Milton's purposely adopted grand style is both so difficult to accomplish and so complicated (in places) to understand that it causes a deterioration in the poetic style of those who are influenced by it and cannot meet its demands. "In fact," said Eliot, "it was an influence against which we still have to struggle."

Eliot's prime example is from Book V as Satan addresses his followers concerning the Son:

Thrones, Dominations, Princedoms, Virtues, Powers,
If these magnific Titles yet remain
Not merely titular, since by Decree
Another now hath to himself ingross't
All Power, and us eclipst under the name
Of King anointed, for whom all this haste
Of midnight march, and hurried meeting here,
This only to consult how we may best
With what may be devis'd of honors new
Receive him coming to receive from us
Knee-tribute yet unpaid, prostration vile,
Too much to one, but double how endur'd,
To one and to his image now proclaim'd? (V, 772-784).

That Satan's point here is obscured by the language cannot be denied. Most readers are probably unaware that a question is being asked until they see the question mark at the end of the passage. The meaning here can be puzzled out, but it is difficult to call such writing good, let alone great. Many readers, from put-upon high schoolers to experienced scholars took Eliot's criticism to heart.

Often, they overlooked the fact that Eliot did not suggest that Milton was a bad poet; rather he suggested that the grand style could lead to bad poetry, particularly by the many who used Milton's style as the paradigm of great English poetry.

Defenders of Milton quickly appeared to answer Eliot. C. S. Lewis, in his work A Preface to Paradise Lost, and Christopher Ricks in Milton's Grand Style both mounted vigorous defenses of Milton's style. Lewis in particular argued that Milton needed this particular style for a "secondary epic," his term for an epic meant to be read rather than the "primary epic," which was presented orally in a formal setting and meant to be heard. Lewis' basic point was that the grand style provided the formality of setting that the secondary epic, by the nature of its composition, lost.

Both Lewis and Ricks offered numerous counter examples to show that Milton's style was sublime. Certainly, aside from Shakespeare, no other writer in English could manipulate the language as Milton did. His justly famous description of Mulciber falling soars:

from Morn
To Noon he fell, from Noon to dewy Eve,
A Summer's day; and with the setting Sun
Dropt from the Zenith like a falling Star (I, 742–745).

Or consider the pathos, poignancy, and hopefulness that fill the last few lines of the epic:

Some natural tears they dropped, but wiped them soon;
The world was all before them, where to choose
Their place of rest, and Providence their guide.
They hand in hand, with wand'ring steps and slow,
Through Eden took their solitary way. (XII, 645–650)

However, the questions about Milton's style cannot be answered by playing a game of bad line versus good line. The answer to the question posed by Eliot and opposed by Lewis and Ricks is of such a subjective nature that it can never be truly settled. Arguments about Milton's style will persist just as they do about the styles of Henry James, Jane Austen, even James Joyce. One man's sublimity is another's conundrum.

What can be accomplished is a clear description regarding what Milton's grand style consists of and how he made use of it in the poem. With this information, the reader can at least have an objective foundation on which to base his subjective opinion.

ALLUSIONS AND VOCABULARY

The first aspect of the grand style that most readers notice is the number of allusions and references, many of which seem obscure, along with the arcane and archaic vocabulary. In just the first few lines of the poem references to "Oreb", "That Shepherd", "chosen seed", "Siloa's Brook", and "Aonian Mount" occur. The purpose of the references is to extend the reader's understanding through comparison.

Most readers will know some of the references, but few will know all. The question thus arises whether Milton achieves his effect or its opposite. Further, words such as "Adamantine", "durst" "Compeer", "Sovran" and many others, both more and less familiar, add an imposing tone to the work. Paradise Lost was not written for an uneducated audience, but in many editions the explanatory notes are almost as long as the text.

SENTENCE CONSTRUCTION

Besides the references and vocabulary, Milton also tends to use Latinate constructions. English is a syntactical language using word order in sentences to produce sense. Latin, in contrast, is an inflected language in which endings on words indicate the words' functions within a sentence, thereby making word order less important. Latin verbs, for example, often come at the end of the sentence or a direct object may precede the subject.

In Paradise Lost, Milton seems purposely to strive for atypical English syntactical patterns. He almost never writes in simple sentences. Partly, this type of inverted, at times convoluted, syntax is necessary for the poetics, to maintain the correct meter, but at other times the odd syntax itself seems to be Milton's stylistic goal.

In this passage from Book VIII, the exact meaning of the words is elusive because of the Latinate syntax:

soft oppression seis'd
My droused sense, untroubl'd though I thought
I then was passing to my former state
Insensible, and forthwith to dissolve (VIII, 291–296).

Lewis, and others who admire the grand style, argue that in passages such as this, the precise meaning matters less than the impressionistic effect, that the images of drowsing, insensibility, and dissolution occurring in order show the breakdown of a conscious mind, in this case Adam's, as God produces a dream vision for him. Certainly this passage, as difficult to understand literally as it is, is not bad writing. The reader understands what Adam is experiencing. However, in the hands of lesser talents than Milton, such writing becomes nonsense.

EXTENDED SIMILES

Another aspect of Milton's style is the extended simile. The use of epic similes goes back to Homer in the Iliad and Odyssey, but Milton uses more similes and with more detail. A Miltonic simile can easily become the subject of an essay, perhaps a book. Milton's similes run a gamut from those that seem forced (the comparison of Satan's arrival in Eden to the smell of fish to those that are perfect (Eden compared to the field where Proserpine gathered flowers.

But, in all cases, a critical exploration of the simile reveals depths of unexpected meaning about the objects or persons being compared. Once again, Milton achieves a purpose with his highly involved language and similes. The ability to do this seems almost unique to Milton, a man of immense learning and great poetic ability.

REPEATED IMAGES

Besides extended similes, Milton also traces a number of

images throughout the poem. One of the most apparent is the image of the maze or labyrinth. Over and over in the poem, there are mentions of mazes—like the tangled curls of Eve's hair—which finally culminate with the serpent confronting Eve on a "Circular base of rising folds, that tow'r'd / Fold above fold a surging maze" (IX, 498–499). Other images also run throughout the poem as a kind of tour de force of imagination and organization. Each image opens up new possibilities for understanding Milton's ideas.

No doubt, particular aspects of Milton's style could be presented at great length, but these are sufficient. Milton intended to write in "a grand style." That style took the form of numerous references and allusions, complex vocabulary, complicated grammatical constructions, and extended similes and images.

In consciously doing these things, Milton devised a means of giving the written epic the bardic grandeur of the original recited epic. In so doing, he created an artificial style that very few writers could hope to emulate though many tried. As with the unique styles of William Faulkner and James Joyce, Milton's style is inimitable, and those who try to copy it sometimes give the original a bad name.

Milton's style is certainly his own. Elements of it can be criticized, but in terms of his accomplishment in Paradise Lost, it is difficult to see how such a work could be better written in some other style. Milton defined the style of the English epic and, in a real sense, with that style, ended the genre. After Milton and Paradise Lost, the English epic ends.

To which Genre *Paradise Lost belongs?*In his Preface to Paradise Lost, C. S. Lewis wrote, "Every poem can be considered in two ways — as what the poet has to say, and as a thing which he makes. From the one point of view it is an expression of opinions and emotions; from the other, it is an organization of words which exists to produce a particular kind of patterned experience in the readers").

Genre, therefore, is important not only as a mode of framing a story, but also as a model that produces expectations in readers. In Book 2 of The Reason of Church Government,

Milton declares his desire to write a great work that will serve to glorify England as earlier poets had glorified their native lands and cultures: "what the greatest and choycest wits of Athens, Rome, or modern Italy, and those Hebrews of old did for their country, I in my proportion with this over and above of being a Christian, might doe for mine").

He declares his intention to write in English rather than another language such as Latin, and then ponders what genre to adopt: epic, tragic, or lyric. These three genres of poetry have existed since ancient Greece, and by Milton's time they carried with them a set of connotations and expectations that most educated people recognized.

Milton's concern about which genre to choose, therefore, was not simply a matter of seeking the perfect medium for his story, but the anxiety of a writer seeking to place himself within a centuries-old poetic tradition.

In deciding to write an epic, Milton consciously places himself in the tradition of prior epic writers, such as the ancients Homer and Virgil, and the Medieval and Renaissance poets Dante, Tasso, Ariosto, and Spenser. By doing this, he raises specific sets of expectations both for himself and for readers.

Formally, Paradise Lost contains many classical and Renaissance epic conceits: it begins in medias res; it concerns heavenly and earthly beings and the interactions between them; it uses conventions such as epic similes, catalogues of people and places, and invocations to a muse; and it contains themes common to epics, such as war, nationalism, empire, and stories of origin.

Milton's range of variations on epic conventions contribute to Paradise Lost's stunning effects. Unlike classics such as the Iliad and the Aeneid, Paradise Lost has no easily identified hero. The most Achilles-like character in the poem is Satan, whom Milton surrounds with "epic matter and motivations, epic genre conventions, and constant allusions to specific passages in famous heroic poems".

Critics and writers such as William Blake and Percy Bysshe Shelley believed Satan to be the hero of Paradise Lost.

Yet the problems inherent in viewing Satan as a hero have led modern critics to reject this idea. As Lewalski writes, "by measuring Satan against the heroic standards, we become conscious of the inadequacy and fragility of all the heroic virtues celebrated in literature, of the susceptibility of them all to demonic perversion"

Another possibility for the hero of *Paradise Lost* is the Son of God, but although he is an important force in the poem, the story is not ultimately about him. The most likely possibility, therefore, is Adam. Adam resembles Aeneas in many respects: he is the father of a new race, responsible for founding civilization on earth. But unlike Aeneas, Adam's primary heroic act is not heroic at all: it is the first act of disobedience. The heroism celebrated in Book 9 as "Patience and Heroic Martyrdom" stands in stark contrast to traditional epic heroism.

Is Adam's disobedience an indictment of traditional heroism? If the quiet Adam is the true hero of *Paradise Lost*, and Satan with all his heroic oratory is not, then Milton is simultaneously entering into a dialogue with previous works about the nature of heroism, reconfiguring the old model, and effectively redefining notions of heroism for his seventeenth-century English Protestant audience. The hero is not the only epic tradition to be reconfigured in *Paradise Lost*; the poem also plays on readers' expectations about epic form.

Although it most resembles an epic, *Paradise Lost* contains elements of many other genres: there are elements of lyric poetry, including the pastoral mode, as in the descriptions of Paradise, the conversations between the unfallen Adam and Eve, and their joyful prayers to God in the Garden.

(There is an aubade, a type of symposium, and examples of georgic verse. There are also elements of tragedy, as in Book 9 when Milton, preparing his readers for the fall, writes, "I now must change / Those Notes to Tragic," and continues throughout the book to employ tragic conventions, as when he apostrophizes Eve (and describes the earth's response to the eating of the fruit.

Throughout the poem Milton makes use of soliloquy,

another tragic convention. And even the ten-book structure of the 1667 edition, according to John Leonard, "might owe something to English tragedy, forming five dramatic acts of two books each". In fact, Milton's first attempts to write the story of man's fall took the form of a tragedy that he later rejected in favor of epic.

Scott Elledge writes that Milton favored tragedy because of its "affective and curative powers," which are no less present in *Paradise Lost* than in his more formal tragedy, *Samson Agonistes*. As Barbara Lewalski writes, the incorporation of multiple genres into the poem invites us "to identify certain patterns and certain poems as subtexts for portions of Milton's poem, and then to attend to the completion or transformation of those allusive patterns as the poem proceeds".

"Things invisible to mortal sight": Milton's God

Unlike the gods and goddesses of classical epics, whose desires and disagreements often mirror those of humans, Milton's God is invisible and omnipresent, a being who cannot be considered an individual so much as an existence. Milton's underlying claim in *Paradise Lost* is that he has been inspired by his heavenly muse with knowledge of things unknowable to fallen humans.

His dilemma of how to describe God to the reader resembles the archangel Raphael's dilemma of how to "relate / To human sense th'invisible exploits" of the angels in Heaven. Like Raphael, Milton solves the problem by expressing the infinite in terms of the tangible by portraying God as if he were an individual, when he is really something much greater. Therefore, although Milton credits God with speech and with enough form that the Son can sit "on his right," everything relating to God in *Paradise Lost* should be understood as a kind of metaphor, a device used to place the divine in human terms.

Perhaps because of the contradictions inherent in the attribution of human characteristics to a divine being, Milton's portrayal of God has been a frequent subject of debate among scholars and critics. Milton presents God as a harsh and uncompromising judge over his subjects, hardly the figure one would expect a poet to present whose goal is to "justifie the wayes of God to men". C.S. Lewis explains the aversion that readers often feel towards Milton's God by blaming the modern reader: "Many of those who say they dislike Milton's God only mean that they dislike God: infinite sovereignty, by its very nature, includes wrath also".

But Milton seems to be doing more than merely portraying the Christian God; he is, according to William Empson, "struggling to make his God appear less wicked than the traditional Christian one".

Perhaps this is why Milton's God often appears on the defensive, explaining again and again that his foreknowledge of the fall has nothing to do with fate: Adam and Eve fall of their own free will, not because God in any way decreed it. This defensive tone is hardly becoming in an omnipotent deity, yet Milton needs to use it in order to justify God; hence the endless potential for contradiction in Milton's presentation of God (and those of many seventeenth-century writers as well).

Empson and other critics also bring into question God's justice. The Romantic poet Percy Bysshe Shelley writes that Milton "alleged no superiority of moral virtue to his God over his Devil". Empson agrees, writing that God's "apparently arbitrary harshness is intended to test us with baffling moral problems", such as why a hierarchy is necessary in Heaven at all, or why God would establish a complex arrangement of demonic and angelic guards to prevent an adversary from traveling from Hell to Eden, only to call them off "as soon as [they] look like succeeding".

One can explain these problems by recalling that God does not simply want absolute obedience in his subjects, he wants the obedience of free beings. In his own words, "Not free, what proof could they have given sincere / Of true allegiance, constant Faith or Love.". Yet at times, God's complexities do make him difficult to find trustworthy, while Satan's seemingly logical challenges to his authority are quite appealing.

William Blake found Milton's depiction of God so far inferior to his depiction of Satan that he considered Milton to be an unwitting Satanist (Flannagan, *The Riverside Milton*).

There seems to be good evidence for it: God's language is "flat, uncolored, unmetaphorical," compared with Satan's vivid and inspiring rhetoric.

But Stanley Fish presents a different theory: his thesis is that Milton deliberately lets Satan seduce not only Adam and Eve, but the reader as well. Fish writes, "The reading experience becomes the felt measure of man's loss" as the reader is first seduced by Satan's powerful and impressive logic, then slowly realizes that the logic is in fact twisted and nonsensical (*Surprised by Sin*. The reader emerges from the experience renewed with a greater sense of faith, which is the ultimate goal of the poem.

If we are not to trust Satan at all, however, then what should we make of Satan's enlightened questioning of God's authority? When contemplating the ascendancy of the Son, Satan says, "Who can in reason then or right assume / Monarchie over such as live by right / His equals, if in power and splendor less / In freedome equal?". This argument in favor of equality and against monarchy would strike a familiar note among seventeenth-century readers who had so recently experienced the English Civil War.

Milton had been a supporter of Cromwell and had strongly advocated the execution of Charles I in. Satan's doubts about God's authority seem based in republican values — values that Milton believed in and promoted through his writing — yet Milton consciously undermines those values by placing them in Satan's mouth.

Paraphrasing Blair Worden, Lewalski writes that perhaps "Satan's rhetoric of republicanism signals Milton's profound disillusion with his own party and with political discourse generally".But Lewalski herself thinks differently, pointing out the great difference between God's natural eminence and the "Stuart ideology of divine kingship" that created idols out of monarchs in the seventeenth century.

She writes, "By demonstrating that there can be no possible parallel between earthly kings and divine kingship [Milton] flatly denies the familiar royalist analogies: God and King Charles, Satan and the Puritan rebels". Satan's doubts about God are unfounded and sinful, not because they are inherently evil, but because God is a true monarch whose authority should never be questioned.

MILTON'S REDEFINITION OF MARRIAGE

John Milton's epic of theology and politics, heaven, hell, creation, free will, and redemption features a human relationship at its centre. Paradise is lost after Adam chooses to disobey God, choosing, in Milton's imagination, Eve instead. Milton's Adam exclaims to Eve: "How can I live without thee, how forgoe / Thy sweet Converse and Love so dearly joyn'd" (*PL* 9.908-9).

In response to this choice, the Son demands: "Was shee thy God" (*PL* 10.145)? Why and how Milton chose to tell this story of human love challenging God's claim to unquestioning human obedience reveals the domestic sphere's emerging centrality to seventeenth century society and the extent to which theology mapped the course of its development.

In Genesis, the story of Adam and Eve's fall is told in a single line: "she took of the fruit thereof, and did eat, and gave also unto her husband with her; and he did eat" (Genesis 3:6). In *Paradise Lost,* Adam eats the fruit of knowledge two hundred fourteen lines after Eve. Milton imagines an intervening mental strife unequalled in the history of the world as Adam comes to choose love and death over rational knowledge of God.

The story is no longer one of disobedience, but man's disobedience of God in favor of a human relationship. Critics argue that Milton struggles to define the ideal human relationship even as he views such bonds as inherently human flaws that distance the individual from God. The Adam of Genesis sins against God after Eve gives him the apple; the Adam of *Paradise Lost* sins against God not because of what Eve gives him, but because of what he needs of her.

The passages depicting Adam and Eve's marriage have long been used as "the key to unlocking Milton's attitudes toward gender and sexuality" (*One Flesh, One Heart* 266), but recent critical analysis suggests a greater "complexity of these issues in Milton's works" (*One Flesh, One Heart* 266). Gregory

Chaplin argues that *Paradise Lost* is remarkable as a "stageâ where [Milton] has the opportunity to depict his ideal union" (*One Flesh, One Heart* 291), which is "a merger of Neoplatonic friendship and Christian marriage" (*One Flesh, One Heart* 291).

Thomas Luxon elaborates on this theme when he states in *Single Imperfection* that Milton's "project" is "to redefine heteroerotic marriage using the terms and principles of classical friendship, and then to promote this newly dignified version of marriage as the originary human relation and, therefore, the bedrock of social and political culture in Protestant Christendom" (*Single Imperfection* 1-2). Both critics view Milton's theology as inseparable from his understanding of human relationships.

Milton began theorizing in print about marriage with the publication of *The Doctrine and Discipline of Divorce* (*DDD*) in 1643. His argument was inspired both by personal experience and by extensive reading. His wife, Mary Powell, had returned to her father's household after less than two months of marriage in 1642; Milton was left alone with neither a spouse nor any prospect of remarriage.

In addressing his loneliness, Milton argued "that the chief end God intended in marriage was the cheerfull conversation of man with woman'". Luxon argues that Milton tried to " redefine marriage as principally a conversation" in order to diminish the division between marriage and friendship. With this new emphasis, Milton illustrates a shift of focus from marriage for procreation and physical necessity and toward relationships that satisfy the desire for classical friendship and intellectual fulfillment.

Critics map these intermingled themes of marriage and friendship further in *Paradise Lost* and use them to follow Adam's development of human understanding culminating in the Fall. The newly created Adam desires any fit companion and laments "In solitude / What happiness, who can enjoy alone?" (*PL*8.364-5).

Thomas Luxon observes that Adam, unlike God, is incomplete without companionship, and this "single imperfection" (*PL* 8.423), unless it is overcome, will occasion mankind's downfall (*Single Imperfection* 107), as the need for companionship will obstruct the rational choice to prefer obedience to God above other necessities.

However, Luxon objects such a "fusion never succeeded and that Milton's attempt to reimagine marriage as a heteroerotic version of the classical homoerotic ideal resulted instead in a very uneasy and temporizing supersession of friendship by marriage" (*Single Imperfection*. Luxon explains this conclusion by asserting: "Milton withholds from his marriage theories the linchpin of classical and humanist friendship doctrine — equality".

Adam's progression from loneliness, to inseparable devotion to a single partner, to his choice of Eve over God, is a theme that Milton develops throughout his major poetic works. In *Samson Agonistes*, Milton's Samson "divorces his wife and resumes an intimacy, however vague, with God" (*Single Imperfection*).

In *Paradise Regain'd*, the Son develops theory into praxis as he "draws strength from solitude and emerges alone but not lonely, a man who has transformed the single imperfection' of loneliness into the site of recovered manliness, liberty and godliness" (*Single Imperfection*). As Luxon traces man's flaw through this series, he finds: "the Milton who desired citizenship in the kingdom of heaven wound up imagining his perfect man as solitary" (*Single Imperfection*.

Milton considers absence of carnal lust as one of the special attributes of prelapsarian marriage, but friendship alone cannot satisfy all of man's desires, despite the necessity of conversation. James Grantham Turner offers another explanation of this relationship in *One Flesh: Paradisal Marriage and Sexual Relations in the Age of Milton*: "Milton's ideal of married love should not therefore be thought of as a social drive or as a higher form of friendship, but as a private bonding of male and female suffused with erotic energy" (*One Flesh* 207).

Although Chaplin and Luxon argue that Milton will not "leave marriage as one sort of relationship (for utility and perhaps pleasure) and friendship another Milton wants marriage *itself* to be redefined as a friendship of virtue" (*Single Imperfection*, original emphasis), Milton also suggests that the ideal relationship requires the special bond offered by marriage: one person existing solely for another.

Thus, while Adam condemns Eve's actions, he seeks no other companion: "Should God create another Eve, and I/ Another Rib afford yet loss of thee / Would never from my heart and from thy State / Mine never shall be parted, bliss or woe" (*PL* 9.911-16).

After the fall, however, lust quickly perverts the pure assertion of devotion and the wish for satisfying and instructive conversation: as "that false Fruit" Carnal desire enflaming" (*PL* 9.1011-13). The fatal flaw left an opening for the more dangerous human carnal desires that would distort human relationships. In emphasizing the value of conversation, and other examples drawn from classical friendship, Milton suggests a way to recreate the purity and fulfillment of the original marriage in a postlapsarian world.

"Radiant image of his Glory": The Son

In some respects the Son of God more closely resembles a classical epic hero than any other figure in *Paradise Lost*: like many classical heroes he is a king, a great statesman, and a military champion.

Also like those figures he is at once both glorious and vulnerable, glorious in his godliness, goodness, and military prowess, and vulnerable in the promise of his future humanity and suffering as the incarnate Christ. Roy Flannagan writes that the Son "does do things that epic heroes do, as when He volunteers for the most dangerous of duties (confronting Satan and, later, sacrificing Himself for the sin of humankind)".

But Milton's goal in *Paradise Lost* is not simply to create a classical epic with a traditional hero: as Lewalski writes, "the fundamental concern" of *Paradise Lost* is not heroism in the classical sense, but "a poem-long exploration and redefinition of heroes and heroism". Fish agrees, writing, "In effect, the reader comes to understand heroism by repeatedly adjusting his idea of what makes one hero heroic".

Milton himself writes that *Paradise Lost* is about something different than "fabl'd Knights / In Battels feign'd," but rather, "Patience and Heroic Martyrdom," or quiet persistence in the face of adversity.

This new definition of heroism is uniquely Christian, and leads to the conclusion that Milton's epic is essentially a Christian one. The new heroism, like the old, is most embodied by the Son in *Paradise Lost,* but the Son's role as a hero becomes more complex when it is combined with Milton's intent to express the Christian faith.

The Son in *Paradise Lost* is called the Son because he is not the historical figure Jesus, nor is he the risen Christ: he is the Son of God — a God-figure who sits at the right hand of the Father. Milton distinguishes between God the Father and God the Son by implying that the Father is invisible and ineffable, while Son is the Father "Substantially express'd".

While the Father exists in the "pure Empyrean" throughout the epic, the Son as his substantial expression descends to Earth to judge Adam and Eve after the fall, and it is of course the Son who eventually will take human form in order to redeem mankind.

But the Son is not only an expression of the Father: Milton creates an identity for him that is far more complex than that when he addresses the issues of the Son's begetting and status in Heaven, issues that were controversial in Milton's time and have led many critics to speculate about Milton's own personal theology.

Chronologically, the very first scene that Milton describes in *Paradise Lost* occurs when "As yet this world was not," when God announces to the angels that he has begotten the Son (*PL* 5.577). God says, "This day have I begot whom I declare / My onely Son your Head I him appoint" (*PL* 5.603-4, 606). This declaration is the occasion of Satan's rebellion and the start of the War in Heaven, the result of which is the expulsion of one third of the angels from Heaven, and, ultimately, God's creation of Eden.

But what has God really done in this scene? The Nicene Creed states that the Son was "born of the Father before all ages." Milton, however, echoing Psalm 2:7, uses the phrase "this day," as if God had begotten the Son in actual time. This idea threatens the Christian belief in the holy trinity: how can the Son be a begotten being — begotten in time after the angels — and yet be God? Moreover, why, if the Son is of the same essence as the Father (as Christian orthodoxy proclaims), does he obey him as if the Father were a superior being?

Like Adam and Eve, the Son has his own free will, choosing freely to obey the Father: he says, "Father Eternal, thine is to decree, / Mine both in Heav'n and Earth to do thy will / Supream". These are not the words of an equal. And is the Son even of the same essence as the Father? At one point the Father tells the Son, "Into thee such Vertue and Grace / Immense I have transfus'd, that all may know / In Heav'n and Hell thy Power above compare".

If the Son were of the same essence as the Father, why would the Father need to transfuse virtue and grace into him? The Son seems to have his own being separate from the Father, as in Book 3 when he "takes the part of Mercy more than Justice in that he appeals to his father's sense of compassion," and finally, when he volunteers freely to die for man's sins (. Is Milton, then, describing a trinity in which the Father and Son are not of the same essence and not equal?

One way to explain the begetting of the Son in Book 5 is by "distinguishing between the existence of the divine Logos or Word, which had been in existence "in the beginning" and which had created everything, including the angels, and the recognition of the Word as Son at this later point in time". When God is saying that he has "begotten" the Son, therefore, he is not saying that he has created him, because the Son already existed as the Word; he is instead acknowledging the Son as the "Messiah King anointed". But this still does not explain the way that the Son can be read as a lower being than the Father.

During the seventeenth century in England there was much discussion about aspects of Protestant theology, in which debates about the doctrine of the trinity "rapidly took the religious centre stage". According to John P. Rumrich, "at least eight antitrinitarian heretics were burned at the stake from 1548 to 1612". One of the most prominent antitrinitarian sects was Arianism, named after the fourth-century Bishop Arius, who preached against the trinity.

Rumrich discusses why disbelief in the trinity "provoked authorities as no other heresy could," and explains, "Perhaps the impulse toward demystification expressed in Arianism was dimly perceived as a threat to the ideological basis of monarchical power".

Many intellectuals, including Isaac Newton and John Locke, believed in Arianism, and now scholars are generally agreed that Milton did as well. Much of the basis for this belief is derived from Milton's theological treatise *On Christian Doctrine,* in which Milton relied solely on the text of the Bible to formulate his ideas, even at the risk of denying commonly accepted Church doctrine.

He discusses the trinity at length, using biblical quotations to demonstrate that "the Father and the Son are certainly not one in essence," and that "the Father is greater than the Son in all things". Milton's beliefs about the relationship between the Father and Son, therefore, may have led him to describe in *Paradise Lost* a Son who is neither of the Father's essence nor equal in status to the Father. Do Milton's beliefs about the nature of the trinity, then, affect his literary work even to the extent of molding the literary character of the Son to fit his beliefs?

As W. B. Hunter writes, Milton's "central purpose in writing the poem was this justification [of God] with its concomitant theology. His means were literary, indeed, but his artistry was handmaiden to his theology, not the other way around". Recent doubts regarding the authorship of On Christian Doctrine, however, have necessitated a reconsideration of Milton's theology and the relationship between it and *Paradise Lost.*

In the introduction to their book *Bright Essence,* Hunter, C. A. Patrides, and J. H. Adamson go so far as to reject Milton's Arianism completely and reconsider the role of the Son in *Paradise Lost*. They write, "we have discovered a new Milton for whom the Son is of fundamental importance in the act of creation, the revelation of the Godhead within history, and the salvation of man" (vii). Perhaps the Son is a hero after all.

"Contemplation of Created Things": Knowledge in *Paradise Lost*

In his treatise *Of Education* Milton writes, "The end then of Learning is to repair the ruines of our first Parents by regaining to know God aright, and out of that knowledge to love him". Themes of knowledge and education play important roles in *Paradise Lost*, which, according to Lewalski, is "preeminently a poem about knowing and choosing". The dominance of these themes comes from the fact that Milton is writing about the first humans on earth, humans who have no history and no way of knowing the world except through God's inspiration.

When Raphael comes to earth in Book 5, he explains to Adam the difference between human knowledge, which is attained through discourse, and angelic knowledge, which is attained through intuition. He says that the two types of knowledge differ "but in degree, of kind the same," suggesting that if humans remain obedient they will eventually attain intuitive knowledge.

He is eager to explain to Adam the story of the war in Heaven and the creation of earth, but he stops when Adam asks about the nature of the universe. He tells Adam, "Solicit not thy thoughts with matters hid, / Leave them to God above, him serve and feare".

At this point Milton is suggesting that the goal of knowledge is not to know everything in the universe, but to increase our "appreciation of God's goodness" and ultimately increase our faith. Interestingly, Eve — perhaps demonstrating intuitive knowledge of the kind Adam has yet to attain — chooses the moment directly preceding Raphael's comment to move out of hearing of the conversation.

This act "represents in dramatic terms the same lesson Raphael has tried to make clear: Creation is to be both enjoyed and understood as a sign of God; to examine it critically is to forget man's place in it" Similarly, Milton has Raphael say,

"Knowledge is as food, and "needs no less / Her Temperance over Appetite". Just as we should be temperate with food, we must discriminate between different kinds of knowledge, avoiding that which will move us away from God.

This brings us to the Tree of Knowledge of Good and Evil. Milton emphasizes that the importance of the Tree lies less in the knowledge it brings than in its function as "The only sign of our obedience". Nevertheless, the Tree raises questions about the different types of knowledge that exist before and after the fall. When Adam and Eve eat the fruit, they lose the capacity to attain intuitive knowledge.

Instead, according to Leonard, they "gain knowledge of the darkness into which creation falls when it is deprived of God's goodness".

Because they are more removed from God, they cannot learn in the same way they once did. When the angel Michael comes to earth to tell Adam about the future, he begins by giving him visions, but eventually must stop and narrate the rest because he perceives Adam's "mortal sight to faile". The fallen Adam has less access to an understanding of God and Heaven than the unfallen one, and Michael must be more careful than Raphael to relate his tale in an understandable way.

Ira Clark writes, "Repeatedly, *Paradise Lost*'s narrators declare their problems of telling caused by problems of knowing". These problems exist between God and the angels, between angels and humans, between Adam and Eve, and finally, between the poem and the reader.

As Clark explains, the fallen reader has no way to understand Paradise, let alone Heaven and Hell, and Milton's method of describing them involve metaphors, similes, and negatives. But if the fallen reader cannot know Paradise, does it then follow that the unfallen Adam and Eve cannot know evil?

Many critics, including Michael Lieb, argue that the significance of God's command not to eat the fruit lies in its very ambiguity: if Adam and Eve do not understand evil or death, the consequences of eating the fruit, their only reason to obey God is their faith, which should be reason enough. But Clark disagrees, writing that the climax of the work "depends on Eve and Adam's having a competent sense of knowledge".

These opposing views are wrapped up in Milton's depiction of a Paradise in which Adam and Eve have instant knowledge of everything they can name, and are simultaneously too pure to know unhappiness or recognize evil when they see it.

Chapter 14

The Fall of Man in Eve Speaks and Paradise Lost

Over the course of time, there have been many interpretations of man's fall from grace, as told by the Bible. Among the literary interpretations are those of John Milton's Paradise Lost and the American poet Louis Untermeyer's "Eve Speaks." John Milton's epic poem deals with the entire story of man's fall from grace, including background for Satan's motives. Louis Untermeyer's "Eve Speaks" was written about Eve's thoughts, many years after she was forced to leave Eden.

While both poems are derived from the same biblical root, they offer different interpretations of man's fall through Eve's motives, her attitude toward Adam, and her attitude toward her sin. In Paradise Lost, Eve was tricked by Satan, who assumed the form of a serpent, into eating from the Tree of Knowledge.

Satan had whispered into her ear when she was asleep, and when he spoke to her later, he used his cunning to mislead her:

He ended, and his words replete with guile
Into her heart too easy entrance won.
Fixed on the fruit she gazed, which to behold
Might tempt alone, and in her ears the sound
Yet rung of his persuasive words, impregned
With reason, to her seeming, and with truth.

Louis Untermeyer's interpretation of Eve's motives in "Eve Speaks", were very different in their implications. He suggests that Eve was not tricked by Satan, but instead she made a conscious decision to eat the forbidden fruit. Eve thought that man was created for more than living in Paradise; She was seeking for a greater world: The thought that there was something more than joy, Beyond perfection, greater than singing peace And tranquil happiness, vexed all my hours.

Eve reached these conclusions through the traits that she perceived in Adam. He was strong and had a brain designed to "dream and mould". According to Eve, he was designed for "fiercer things and lustier worlds". Another glaring dissimilarity between the two poems was the in which Eve perceived Adam.

Milton's Eve felt inferior to Adam; When Eve was trying to decide whether or not to share the apple with Adam, one of her reasons for not sharing was so that she could be his equal, if not his superior. After she gave the apple to Adam, her demeanor turned even more submissive. This was in agreement with the traditional 17th century view of women.

Louis Untermeyer gave Eve a more domineering position; In "Eve Speaks", Eve acts for the good of Adam and does what she believes is the best for him. There were no subservient thoughts in Eve's mind; Instead, she was actually attempting to attain divine like knowledge for herself and Adam: "..answer God with God's own words and deeds." The final major difference between Paradise Lost and Louis Untermeyer's "Eve

Speaks", was Adam and Eve's attitude toward their "mortal sin". In Paradise Lost, Adam andEve where extremely ashamed of their actions.

Adam was especially ashamed of their sin:
Bad fruit of knowledge, if this be to know,
Which leaves us naked thus, of honour void,
Of innocence, of faith, of purity,
Our wonted ornaments now soiled and stained.

As Adam and Eve left Eden, they wept for the loss of their innocence, but were hopeful for their new lives. Louis Untermeyer, however, showed that Eve was not at all ashamed of her actions. Eve felt that she made the proper decision to eat the apple, and for this reason she was not afraid of God's wrath. Eve thought that they had lost little when they were thrown from Eden, yet gained much, for they had gained knowledge, "the force and shaper of the world."

The different interpretations of the same biblical story may be a result of the large time span between the stories. Milton's Paradise Lost was written in a more religious time in which the fall of man would seem to be a great sin. During Louis Untermeyer's time, worldly knowledge was seen as more important than the more spiritual ideas of the past.

Despite their differences, both poems present the biblical story through a more human point of view.

PUBLICATION HISTORY OF PARADISE LOST

One can learn a great deal from the gap between when Milton wrote *Paradise Lost* and when it finally went to press. As David Kastan notes in his helpful introduction, "it had been finished at least two years" before Samuel Simmons finally published it in 1667. Between completion and publication, the political instability of the period conspired to delay the release of *Paradise Lost.* In a practical sense, the second Anglo-Dutch war of 1665 caused a paper shortage.

The confusion and fear after the plague and fire of London added to the turbulence of the period. Altogether, this created an unfavorable environment for controversial literature (see Nicholas von Maltzahn's article, "The First Reception of *Paradise Lost*").

Eventually, of course, Milton did seek a printer. It is uncertain why he chose Samuel Simmons, an obscure stationer, to print *Paradise Lost*. Kastan speculates that the stationer's proximity to Milton's home was a factor, especially since Simmons's presses were among the few unharmed by the Great Fire.

He also speculates that "perhaps it was family loyalty," as Simmons's father had printed several of Milton's prose works. Kastan notes that Simmons had a reputation for printing "seditious books;" this may have drawn Milton to Simmons. Their business relationship was remarkable, as Kastan details it, in that "the surviving contract is the earliest between a writer and publisher that has come to light, and Simmons, at least to later generations, has been often criticized for taking advantage of the blind and disgraced Milton." However, their agreement was likely typical for the period.

In order to protect his copyright to *Paradise Lost*, Milton had to apply to have the poem licensed. "That Milton or his bookseller even sought the license," writes von Maltzahn, "shows the gravity of the poet's situation in the Resoration". Both von Maltzahn and Kastan detail the objections of Thomas Tomkins, the licenser and chaplain to the Archbishop of Canterbury. Milton's anti-monarchist themes, combined with his reputation as a proponent of regicide, made Tomkins seeks to deny the poem license.

But in 1667 with the government in retreat, and licensers under pressure, the focus in controlling the press needed narrowing to those who raised more present fears and encouraged sedition. If Milton by reputation might be expected to "make [the people] to fear," it was at the same time plain that *Paradise Lost* was of a different order from the licensers' usual fare.

Thus, despite his issues with the subversive nature of the poem, and lines 1.594-99 in particular, Tomkins licensed the poem. The first edition of *Paradise Lost* was published in 1667. "What has long been recognized is that the poem sold slowly and that different title pages were issued both to reflect changes in bookselling arrangements and to encourage new sales" (Kastan).

Major changes to the first edition, however, did not occur until the 1668 printing, which added fourteen pages. In this printing, Milton added the introductory "arguments" for each book; these were compiled at the beginning of the poem, since the type was not re-set. This printing also included a letter from Simmons to the "Courteous Reader;" in fact, this printing is the first in which Simmons' name appears. At last, in 1669, Milton's contract was fulfilled when the first 1,300 copies were sold.

In 1674, Simmons printed the second edition of *Paradise Lost*, which featured significant changes. Books seven and ten were each divided into two books, moving the total number of books from ten to twelve. This may have been because books seven and ten were exceptionally long, but twelve books also suggests a half-epic.

Whereas the first edition was a quarto, the second is an octavo. It is not ruled, and does not feature line numbers. However, the arguments appear before their respective books, and the printing includes two poems and a portrait of the poet. Kastan remarks that "in general, the edition is less welcoming than the first.

It is, however, better printed than 1667, probably from the fact that it is set seemingly from a corrected copy of the first edition rather than from a manuscript." What is remarkable here, as Kastan claims, is that Milton, due to his relationship with Simmons, seems to have had a hand in the publication process: "Sometime in the summer of 1674, Milton's *Paradise Lost* appeared in print essentially in the form the poet had come to imagine it." Just how much aesthetic control a blind poet could exercise over the printing of his poem is a topic for speculation.

"What if the Sun / Be Centre to the World": Cosmology in *Paradise Lost*

Nothing less than the creation and ordering of the universe defines the scope of *Paradise Lost*. The epic explores its cosmological theme in theoretical discussions between Adam and Raphael and in the narrator's descriptions and metaphors. Further, Milton imagines Satan surveying the universe in an expedition of discovery through a new world in his fall from Heaven and his passage through Chaos to Earth. Adam tries to understand the earth's physical place in the universe and its associated ontological and theological value as the home of man.

He wonders aloud about "this Earth a spot, a grain,/ An Atom, with the Firmament compar'd/ And all her numbered Starrs, that seem to rowl /Spaces incomprehensible" (*PL* 8.17-21). Milton asks us to imagine the first man struggling with many of the same questions a Renaissance thinker, contemplating new models of the universe, must have considered. In response to the theory that everything revolves around the sun and not the earth, philosophers were forced to question the importance of man's role in the universal order. Raphael, responding to Adam's concerns, suggests there is no reason "bodies bright and greater should not serve / The less not bright, nor Heav'n such journies run / Earth sitting still" (*PL* 8.87-9).

Yet, the poem does not answer all such questions directly, and scholars often find it difficult to determine Milton's attitude toward science. In these debates, it is helpful to remember that Milton was not a scientist but a theorist. He did not contribute to scientific knowledge so much as to an understanding of what new scientific ideas might mean to traditional Christian cosmology. He meditates on this in a conditional modes, as does Raphael in his description of the universe: "What if the Sun/ Be Centre to the World" (*PL* 8.122-3).

In the mid-sixteenth century, Nicolaus Copernicus and his followers, most notably Johannes Kepler and Galileo Galilei, disturbed the entire Christian world by proposing a heliocentric model of the universe that displaced the earth, and by extension humanity, from the centre. As the Reformation progressed, resulting theological debates acquired political importance and Milton, as a politically conscious theologian, addressed these issues in *Paradise Lost*.

Critics debate the extent of Milton's interest in the advancement of science. Catherine Gimelli Martin notes that many find "his cosmology stands on the wrong side of the great scientific revolution initiated by Copernicus, furthered by Galileo, and completed by Newton" ("What If the Sun Be Centre" 233).

However, Martin argues that classifying Milton as scientifically backward is a mistake resulting from our modern society: "we too easily forget that during this formative period, no â€˜advancement of learning,' scientific or otherwise, could yet be conceived as succeeding apart from the requisite disclaimers about the folly of seeking superhuman knowledge and the proper assurances of humility before heights of Divine

Wisdom" (Martin 231-2). Modern readers tend to treat scientific knowledge as inevitably progressive and therefore expect in Milton an appreciation of our modern scientific values and knowledge.

As a rationalist, Milton must have admired the new sciences but, as a classicist and a Christian theologian, he had not yet placed scientific knowledge ahead of piety or biblical knowledge.

William Poole notes the danger of seeing in Milton an advanced scientific philosopher and warns: "we should be extremely wary forcing Milton into clothes he does not fit" ("Milton and Science: A Caveat" 18). However, within the middle ground, scholars agree with Martin that Milton appreciated the value of scientific thought and development, although he may have doubted the reach of this branch of human knowledge.

Cosmology appears in *Paradise Lost* through direct scientific references, incorporation of new scientific theories into various characters' worldviews, and warnings against seeking beyond the limits of human knowledge. Martin observes: "Galileo or his telescope is approvingly cited on five separate occasions in Milton's epic (the only contemporary reference to appear at all)" (Martin 238). These instances illustrate that such scientific discovery can be a means of comprehending God's glory and "Almightie works" (*PL* 7.112), as Raphael says to Adam: "what thou canst attain, which best may serve / To glorifie the Maker, and inferr / Thee also happier, shall not be withheld" (*PL* 7.115-7).

Other scholars note that Milton's theories of social order in *Paradise Lost* echo scientific thought. In *The Matter of Revolution*, John Rogers contends that Milton's work explores the extent of the vitalist scientific movement that argued for "the infusion of all material substance with the power of reason" (*The Matter of Revolution*).

Rogers finds this theory at work in Milton's understanding of creation and his ordering of the universe, as well as in human systems of society and government. Rather than relegating humanity to the periphery with the earth in the heliocentric model, Rogers suggests "Milton decentralizes divinity, representing an action logically prior to the decentralizations of the state" (*The Matter of Revolution*). Thus, Milton uses new scientific theories of order to inform his consideration of issues such as politics and free will in his epic poem.

While scientific arguments, such as a heliocentric universe, offer positive contributions to his revolutionary political theory, Milton hesitates before the theological ramifications. A decentralized universe or one centered on something other than man, created in God's image"requires each object to behave predictably and suitably within the larger scheme, "each in thir several active Sphears assign'd"). If this pattern fails, chaos will result.

As Rogers notes: "Satan, in Book Two, promises Chaos that he will work to return to its original chaotic state the belated imposition of creation. The possibility of a chaotic resurgence has no meaningful role in the poem's cosmology, but its expression voices Milton's fear, perhaps not so unsound, of an ever-encroaching political chaos". In the wake of the English Civil War, anarchy was too tangibly the political counterpart of this return to chaos.

Thus, Milton depicts the anxiety resulting from new and often unwelcome discoveries and theories, as Raphael cautions: "God to remove his wayes from human sense,/ Plac'd Heav'n from Earth so farr, that earthly sight, / If it presume, might err in things too high,/ and no advantage gain". Scholars currently seem to be in agreement that Milton was aware of scientific developments and their implications.

Whether we can understand Milton's philosophy in terms of scientific theory, or even know Milton's conception of the extent of appropriate human knowledge, has yet to be determined. Although Adam may be "led on, yet sinless, with desire to know/ What neerer might concern him", Raphael's warning to him concludes: "Sollicit not thy thoughts with matters hid, / Leave them to God above, him serve and feare..Heav'n is for thee too high / To know what passes there; be lowlie wise".

What knowledge glorifies God and what knowledge too great for human understanding"threatens the very systems it seeks to explain? Milton was likely still uncertain about this issue as he sent Adam and Eve forth from Eden: "High in Front advanc't,/ The brandisht Sword of God before them blaz'd/ Fierce as a Comet".

HUMANISM IN DANTE AND MILTON

Humanism had a profound impact on European society during the Renaissance. This movement transformed the thinking processes of many Europeans, altering the way these people viewed themselves, their lives, and their place in the world. Literature written around the time of the Renaissance displays humanism's influence on the European social order. Dante Alighieri, a prominent Florentine writer, completed his Inferno around 1314.

Although Dante lived before the widespread proliferation of humanism and humanistic writings, his style exhibits many precursors, if not aspects, of later humanistic thought. The aftereffects of humanism are apparent in the writings of John Milton, an English writer whose works were greatly influenced by the tumultuous political climate of seventeenth century England.

Whereas Dante's Inferno displays many qualities to be emphasized by humanism, Milton's Paradise Lost, published in 1667, demonstrates the culmination of the effect humanism has had on his society. The writings of both men are products of the respective times in which they were written; Milton wrote almost three and a half centuries after Dante, and he lived in a different society in which Dante lived. Despite these differences, both the Inferno and Paradise Lost display aspects found in humanism, although they may convey these aspects to the reader very differently.

In order to understand how humanism pervades the themes and descriptions found within the Inferno and Paradise Lost, one must first grasp the concept of humanism. Humanism, literally "the study of man", can be defined as an awakening of the self. Humanism emphasized both the study of the classics and the "liberating arts", arts that liberate the mind. The study of moral philosophy, history, grammar, rhetoric, and poetry allowed humanists to broaden their minds, become more worldly, and more individualized. Whereas before the Renaissance, Europeans had defined themselves as part of the collective, humanists began to define themselves as individuals.

Whereas the Medieval thinkers had embraced the teachings of the Church, humanists distanced themselves from the Church by their intense study of the classics and the liberal arts. As a result, humanists concentrated their efforts towards improving their life on earth as well as improving their position in the afterlife.

The liberation of one's mind through studying, coupled with the humanist's precedence of life over afterlife, allowed for the humanist to take control of his own life, rather than to submit to the pre-Renaissance view that one is a pawn in the hands of more powerful forces.

Both Dante's Inferno and Milton's Paradise Lost display most of these aspects of humanism in some form and at some point during their progression. Throughout the Inferno, Dante meets a wide range of characters, all with different personalities. Many of these characters are those with whom Dante's was once acquainted. Dante's decision to put his contemporaries in Hell reflects humanism, since he respects both his friends and enemies as individuals.

All of these characters have their own distinct personalities, and Dante makes them stand out from the collective group of their fellow sinners. Dante isolates characters such as Capaneus, Ser Brunetto Latino, and Bertrand De Born. Dante describes the powerful figure Farinata Degli Uberti as if "he seemed to hold all of Hell in disrespect,". Dante could have easily walked through Hell, simply describing the punishments of each specified group of sinners. Dante's choice to isolate members of a specific group as individuals displays his humanistic process of thinking.

In the Inferno, Dante introduces many characters; in the first two books of Paradise Lost, Milton only introduces a handful of characters. Dante briefly and concisely fleshes his characters out, while Milton illustrates his characters with great detail, paying close attention to their particular traits and attributes which identify them as individuals. Milton identifies many of the main characters as part of one singular group, the fallen angels, similar to the way Dante identifies the individual sinners he meets with their respective sins.

However, Milton places a much greater emphasis on the individual, and how each individual character differs. The use of contrast to individualize characters is most easily recognized during the speeches of Moloch and Belial in Book II of Paradise Lost. Moloch appears extremely rash and reckless, advocating for open war against Heaven.

Immediately following Moloch's speech, Belial tries to persuade the fallen angels not to recommence the war with Heaven. Moloch's speech is rather short and filled with emotion; Belial's speech is long, calm, devious, and persuasive. The speeches of these characters offer the reader a very detailed view of these two individual characters. Milton's juxtaposition of these completely different characters further identifies each of them as individuals, rather than as members of the fallen angel collective.

Although both the Inferno and Paradise Lost display humanism in the form of individualism, each work is a product of the period in which it was produced. Milton's Paradise Lost was written during the Baroque period, a movement of extremes, so Milton fleshes out his characters with great, almost extreme detail. The late medieval era and early Renaissance shaped Dante's Inferno; the Inferno was written before humanism had its momentous impact on the vast majority of intellectuals.

As a result of this, Dante does not describe his characters in as great detail as Milton describes his characters, but Dante still individualizes his characters by isolating them from the rest of the sinners. Not only did humanism emphasize individualism, but humanism also emphasized the importance and esteem of Classical Civilization and literature. Both the Inferno and Paradise Lost can be considered humanist works simply because they attempt to mimic the epic style of the great Greek and Roman poets.

The invocation of a Muse, a distinct characteristic of classical epics, is present in both the Inferno and Paradise Lost. Milton invokes the "Heav'enly Muse" in his opening sentence, while Dante buries his invocation, "O Muses! O High Genius! Be my aid! / O Memory, recorder of the vision, / here shall your true nobility be displayed," in lines 7-9 of Book II.

Both Dante and Milton anticipated their works to become modern epics in the style of Homer and Vergil; Dante hoped his Divine Comedy would be considered the greatest Italian epic, whereas Milton intended for his Paradise Lost to become the greatest English epic. One distinct difference between the Inferno and Paradise Lost occurs in the role of Classical characters and allusions present.

In the Inferno, many characters in Classical mythology play significant roles in the progression of the story. Such characters include Minos, Charon, the Harpies, and Geryon. No characters in Greek or Roman mythology play a significant role in Books I and II of Paradise Lost. Milton may have chosen to forsake such characters primarily because Paradise Lost is a story about "Man's First Disobedience".

According to Christianity, no characters found in Classical myths play any part in the corruption of mankind; thus, Milton has no need to include any prominent characters of Classical myths in his epic. One can easily misinterpret Milton's neglect to include any characters of Classical mythology in his epic as a sign that humanism is not present in Paradise Lost. However, it should be noted that even though the characters in Paradise Lost may not be of a Classical origin, the individualism that these characters display reflects the effect humanism has had on Milton.

Strangely enough, both the Inferno and Paradise Lost were not written in Latin. If these two compositions were written in Latin, this overt mimicry of the Classical epic would ooze humanism. However, both works were written in the vernacular. This can be explained by the fact that the Inferno was written just prior to the humanistic movement, and that

Paradise Lost was written during the Baroque period, considerably after the high-tide of the humanistic movement. If both works had been written during the middle of the fifteenth century, at the pinnacle of humanism's influence, they may well have been written in Latin.

Both Dante's Inferno and Milton's Paradise Lost exhibit many aspects of humanism. The most recognizable of these aspects include the emphasis Dante and Milton give to selected individuals, rather than to a collective group. Throughout the Inferno, Dante briefly isolates several characters, giving them individual traits and attributes.

Throughout Books I and II of Paradise Lost, Milton fleshes out in great detail a small number of characters. Milton individualizes and describes characters in greater detail than Dante because Milton writes much later than Dante, and humanism has had over two hundred years to pervade Milton's society. Whereas Dante's Inferno anticipates humanism, Milton's Paradise Lost displays the effect humanism has had on European culture.

HUMAN NATURE IN REPUBLICAN TRADITION AND PARADISE LOST

Many critics and historians have recently come to agree that Milton's late poetry and prose are, among other things, expressions of his "republicanism." Though this term is used to mean different things, its meaning in this context is commonly taken to include a commitment to a way of thinking about politics that is displayed by figures in what, in light of the work of historians of political thought such as J. G. A. Pocock, Blair Worden, and Quentin Skinner, we now think of as the republican tradition of political thought.

That is to say that the case for Milton's republicanism commonly includes the proposition that, to one extent or another, Milton's thinking about politics conforms in important ways with the thinking of one or more figures in a tradition of thought running from Aristotle, through ancient Romans such as Sallust, Cicero, Livy, and Seneca, and up through Renaissance Italians such as Bruni and Machiavelli.

Though scholars of republican political thought seldom see it as a philosophy of human nature, many recognise that an understanding of human nature serves as a crucial premise of arguments concerning forms of government, liberty, history, and virtue which are more commonly thought of as the essentials of this tradition. J. G. A. Pocock, for example, emphasises that republican tradition is grounded in a vision of man as "the *zoon politikon* whose nature was to rule, to act, to make decisions" and who thus found his fulfilment in citizenship.

Quentin Skinner claims that the negative theory of civil liberty he sees at the heart of republican tradition is grounded in a rejection of Aristotle's understanding of human nature as something that has specific ends or purposes (1990). Machiavelli's restatement of this theory of liberty is, moreover, grounded in "his generally pessimistic view of human nature, his view that it is wisest to regard our tendency to act corruptly as ineliminable".

Taking issue with Skinner, Paul Rahe argues that "the classical republican argument, articulated by Aristotle and Cicero on the basis of their observation of Greek and Roman practice, was grounded in the conviction that the distinctive human feature is man's capacity for moral and political rationality." On the basis of this claim, he goes on to insist that Machiavelli must be differentiated from the classical republicans, both Greek and Roman, on grounds that he rejects this understanding of what man is.

Though there is considerable disagreement amongst historians of political thought over what the republican view of human nature is, there is thus strong agreement that a view on this issue is a major premise in republican argumentation about politics.

One thing a comprehensive argument for the view that Milton is aligned with the tradition of republican political thought would have to do, then, is to identify the republican understanding/s of human nature, and then show that Milton's portrayal of human nature conforms with it/them. The case for Milton's republicanism as it currently stands does not do this. That it *could* not reasonably do so becomes clear if we compare how three of the major figures in republican tradition–a Greek, a Roman, and an Italian—envision human nature with how Milton does this in his major poem, *Paradise Lost* (1667).

Over the course of this comparison, it will also become clear that because Milton differs from the republicans on this issue, he also differs from them on other major issues. On the basis of these observations, we will be able to see that the current account of Milton's republicanism (at least when it comes to his epic) is simplistic, and thereby work towards a more refined account of how this poet is related to republicanism understood as a tradition of political thought. In the *Nicomachean Ethics,*

Aristotle understands human nature to be a "composite nature" made up of body and soul, where the soul has an irrational and a rational element. The irrational element consists of a "nutritive" or "vegetative" element and an "appetitive" element, and the rational element consists of a "scientific" (or as some translations have it, "theoretical" or "speculative") element and a "calculative" or "practical" element. By virtue of the scientific element, "we contemplate the kind of things whose originative causes are invariable," while by virtue of the calculative element "we contemplate variable things".

There are two main kinds of virtues of the soul which are defined in terms of the standing of its various elements and how they are related to each other: the virtues of character (which Aristotle sometimes also calls the moral or practical virtues) and the virtues of intellect.

The moral virtues are those virtues Aristotle emphasises in his discussion of the virtues of citizenship: courage, justice, pride, temperance, and liberality. He understands these moral virtues as virtues of the appetitive, desiring part of the soul which, though part of the irrational part of the soul and though sometimes resisting and opposing rational principle, yet shares in rational principle "insofar as it listens to and obeys it".

Aristotle describes these moral virtues as "states of

character," where a state of character (*hexis*) is that "in virtue of which we stand well or badly with reference to" passions such as fear and anger, where to stand badly in reference to a passion is to feel it too weakly or too strongly, and where to stand well with reference to a passion is to "feel it moderately.

Though we are adapted by nature to receive these states of character which constitute the moral virtues, though we have a potential or capacity (*dynamis*) for them, we do not possess or come to possess them by nature; we acquire them mainly by way of the repeated performance of those particular actions to which the moral virtues would dispose us. Thus, "the virtues we get by first exercising them, as also happens in the case of the arts as well.

For the things we have to learn before we can do them, we learn by doing them, e.g. men become builders by building and lyre-players by playing the lyre; so too we become just by doing just acts, temperate by doing temperate acts, brave by doing brave acts". Since the repeated performance of actions of a particular kind is habitual action or produces a habit within us, "moral virtue comes about as a result of habit". Once we have these moral virtues, not only are we *disposed* to act in accordance with them–to act temperately, liberally, courageously, justly—but we also desire to do so and take pleasure in doing so.

But however strongly disposed we may feel by virtue of our virtues to perform a particular action, they never simply cause us to perform that action, and we still must always *choose* to perform an action in order to act virtuously. This choosing or choice (*prohairesis*) that for Aristotle is an essential element of morally virtuous action is, as Nederman puts it, "the outcome of desire and intellect acting together in order to achieve an end".

So crucial a capacity is this for Aristotle that he at one point identifies man with it: "choice is either desiderative reason or ratiocinative desire, and such an origin of action is a man". In the first book of the *Nicomachean Ethics,* Aristotle also identifies what, for human nature, constitutes "the chief good," that for the sake of which men act. He calls it "happiness" (*eudaimonia*), and explains what this is by identifying "the function (*ergon*) of man" on the basis of his perception of "what is peculiar to man". Observing that whereas man shares with plants and animals the life of nutrition, growth, and perception, only he has "the element that has a rational principle," Aristotle infers that the function of man is "an activity of soul which follows or implies" this principle.

Given that i) this is the function of man, ii) the function of a good man is to perform this function well and, iii) those actions are well performed when performed in accordance with a particular excellence or virtue, Aristotle feels he can reasonably provide a more comprehensive definition of happiness or human good: "human good turns out to be activity of soul in accordance with virtue, and if there are more than one virtue, in accordance with the best and most complete".

Since he has identified the particular activity of soul which is to be well performed (i.e. performed in accordance with the virtues that are proper to the soul) as one that follows or implies the rational principle, Aristotle is here claiming that the good life consists in the excellent exercise of rational principle.

It is because "the activity of the practical virtues..[which] is exhibited in political or military affairs" is in accordance with part of the rational principle in us that it can count as a fulfilment of the function or work of mankind and qualify as a happy life. But the political life may also qualify as the means by which the human animal may fulfill specific innate and natural impulses, and reach its full development or end (*telos*).

For, in an extraordinarily controversial passage at the opening of the *Politics,* Aristotle also defines man as a "political animal" (*zoon politikon*) that forms political societies in order to satisfy "the bare needs of life" but that continues to exist in them "for the sake of the good life". In so doing, he seems to mean, as Keyt argues, "that nature endows man with a latent capacity for civic virtue (*politike arete*) and an impulse to live in a polis," and that man *needs* to exist within political societies in order to fulfill this impulse and achieve happiness.

As we have seen, however, the rational principle is bipartite: besides the calculative or practical reason which, having the virtue of practical wisdom, enters into good deliberation and choice of those actions which are in accordance with the moral virtues, there is scientific reason. The particular virtues proper to scientific reason, those states of scientific reason which permit it to function well, are philosophical wisdom (*sophia*), intuitive knowledge, and scientific knowledge.

The objects of scientific reason, those things about which one contemplates, are necessary, eternal, invariable things, such as the gods and the heavenly bodies. For Aristotle, not only is scientific reason, as a *faculty* or *element*, better than and superior to calculative reason, but its *virtues* are superior to those of calculative reason, and its *objects* are superior to those of calculative reason.

It would seem to follow that the *activity* of scientific reason—contemplation (*theoria*) —is superior to that of calculative reason (which includes deliberation) and that contemplation would be closer to the life of happiness than political activity. And, in the final book of the *Nicomachean Ethics*, Aristotle does indeed argue that contemplation is "superior to that which is the exercise of the other kind of virtue" (i.e. the political life which is the exercise of moral, practical virtue) and is, indeed, "perfect happiness".

However, nowhere in the *Politics* does Aristotle so explicitly and comprehensively subordinate the life of the citizen and statesman (lived in accordance with the moral virtues) to the life of the philosopher (lived in accordance with the moral virtues and the virtues of both scientific and speculative reason) as he does in the celebrated passage in Book X of the *Nicomachean Ethics*.

Indeed, the explicit discussion of the relation between the two lives at the opening of Book VII of the *Politics* is inconclusive. Moreover, in the *Nicomachean Ethics*, Aristotle still claims that "man is born for citizenship" and that "man is a political creature and one whose nature is to live with others". In Books VIII and IX, he emphasises that these others must include friends, for "the supremely happy man will need [virtuous] friends". And even in Book X, there is some question as to the appropriateness and feasibility of the life of contemplation for humans: while it may be proper for the gods, the life of contemplation is "too high for man" and "our nature is not self-sufficient for the purpose of contemplation".

As he presents what he refers to as "our philosophy of human nature" over the course of the *Politics* and the *Nicomachean Ethics,* Aristotle is thus ambivalent, if not simply inconsistent, on precisely how the contemplative life and the political life are related to each other, human nature, and happiness, and this is one reason why there has been such extensive controversy over his treatment of this issue.

But it is at least clear that, while sometimes wanting to grant some kind of priority to the contemplative life, Aristotle sees both the political life and the contemplative life as forms of human action that are in accordance with the best part of man's composite nature—reason. As such, both qualify as fulfilments of the function man have by nature and as forms of the happy life, though the political life will perhaps be happy only "in a secondary degree".

In his major philosophical writings, Cicero, too, presents an account of human nature which serves as the foundation for many of his propositions about human fulfilment and the political life. In *The Laws,* for example, he deduces "the nature of justice" from his account of "the nature of man" according to which only man shares the capacity to reason with the gods, and only he is therefore a member of that "single community shared by gods and men" which is subject to the law of nature.

Because Cicero understands all humans to be endowed with reason which allows them to recognise and obey this natural law which is the criterion of justice for both gods and men, he feels that we all have a particular purpose in life: "we are born for justice".

By this he means that "we have been made by nature to share justice amongst ourselves and to impart it to one another," and that "we are born to join a fellowship of citizens". Though, as Nederman observes, Cicero sometimes speaks of this capacity to form and join in fellowships as something that is rather passive which requires "an external stimulus," such as a wise orator, "to awaken and invigorate it", Cicero also indicates that human nature has an inborn desire and impulse to exercise reason and to behave in a way which is consistent with it and natural law: in the opening of the remaining pages of *The Republic*, for example, he claims that "nature has given to mankind such a compulsion to do good, and such a desire to defend the well-being of the community, that this force prevails over all the temptations of pleasure and ease".

"We are led by a powerful urge," he writes as he continues to recommend the political life, "to increase the wealth of the human race; we are keen to make men's lives safer and richer by our policies and efforts; we are spurred on by nature herself to fulfill this purpose". In addition to this, men have a "sense of shame–that dread, as it were, of justified rebuke which nature has imparted to man".

Cicero thus postulates the purpose or end of human nature on the basis of his observation of both a capacity to reason which is peculiar to humans, and a powerful inborn desire and urge in man to exercise that capacity through the formation of communities and the administration of justice within them. Finally, Cicero also makes clear in these works that at the heart of this political activity are forms of speech and eloquence.

Given that mankind is born for justice, where this means being born with powerful urges to exercise reason through speech in order to administer justice within a human community, it follows that mankind can fulfill itself and live the good life only by being a member of and participating in some kind of community.

Since "all are held together by a natural goodwill and kindliness and also by a fellowship in justice", since every human is really a "citizen of the whole world as though it were a single city", it might seem that humans do not really need to be members of any more limited political communities, such as man-made states, in order to fulfill themselves. But Cicero claims that participation in this universal community of all rational agents which is under the law of nature is insufficient to satisfy the human socio-political instinct. As he says in *The Republic,* human beings also have an "innate desire" to form communities bound by legal consent and community of interest.

In order to fulfill themselves, men must therefore participate in smaller communities bound by laws of their own making, but where these laws still conform with the law of nature which is the natural criterion of all justice. As Scipio puts it later in the dialogue, "the good life is impossible without a good state; and there is no greater blessing than a well-ordered state". And it is because this is the case that Cicero also commonly claims that of all forms of community, our country should have the first place in our affections.

Creating and administering a state is not only the means of fulfilling our natural impulses and achieving the good life, but also the means of pleasing the gods and achieving eternal happiness in the after-life. Early in *The Republic,* Cicero claims that there is no "occupation which brings human excellence closer to divine power than founding new states and preserving those already founded".

In so doing, he differs sharply from Aristotle who in the final book of the *Nicomachean Ethics* identifies contemplation as that activity which brings humans closest to the gods. Scipio's adoptive grandfather, Scipio Africanus the elder, further distances the work from Aristotle when he appears to Scipio in a dream and informs him that "for everyone who has saved and served his country and helped it to grow, a sure place is set aside in heaven where he may enjoy a life of eternal bliss".

Doing what it was born to do, then, the human animal not only fulfills its nature and achieves the good life, but also assures its soul of eternal bliss once it has "escaped from the fetters of the body as though from prison". On the other hand, those who fail to act politically deny their nature, fail to fulfill themselves, and suffer various forms of punishment. Cicero thus does not share the vision of man, occasionally affirmed by Aristotle, as an animal that achieves perfect happiness only in contemplation. Because Cicero ranks the political life above the contemplative life, Cicero, as Nederman observes, is more emphatic concerning the importance of the exercise of speech in the form of eloquence than Aristotle is (*Medieval Aristotelianism*).

While Aristotle explicitly asserts the importance of speech to the life of the statesman, there would appear to be little place for it in the contemplative life. And he seems to be more skeptical than Cicero is concerning the power of "arguments" to make people virtuous. There is, in addition, nothing in Aristotle's ethical and political writings approximating Cicero's view that one of the reasons living the life of the statesman and citizen is valuable and important is that it is a means of achieving bliss in the afterlife.

These important differences should not, however, prevent us from seeing how the Greek and the Roman agree on basic issues. Both assert that the human animal has a composite nature (of body and soul), though Cicero's dualistic interpretation of it differs from Aristotle's. Both see reason as a crucial element of the soul, an element which sets it apart from the animals.

Both assert that humans, by virtue of their nature, have special abilities to reason and to speak, and inborn urges to exercise those abilities within socio-political communities. Both define the end or purpose of human nature in terms of the exercise and development of these inborn abilities and urges, and both understand human flourishing and perfection in terms of the achievement of this end.

Both think of human virtue basically in terms of the rule of reason over passion and appetite, and both see virtue understood in this way as a precondition of human fulfilment. Though both see human nature as being moved by an impulse to live as members of a political society, they tend not to see the virtue that is required to do this well as being natural, but as something that must be instilled and sustained through education and civil law.

Both think of statesmanship as, if not *the,* than at least *a* principal way humans may exercise their reason, live the life of virtue, and fulfil the purposes they have by nature. Though in the preface to the *Discourses* Machiavelli confesses to be "filled with astonishment and grief" by the fact that "the highly virtuous actions" performed by the ancients are now shunned and that "of the virtue of bygone days there remains no trace," he nevertheless commonly asserts that humanity has remained the same over time, as has the general order of things in which it exists.

Near the end of the work, for example, he agrees with those prudent men who claim that "men have, and always have had, the same passions, whence it necessarily comes about that the same effects are produced". The indication here that Machiavelli is inclined to think of the unchanging human agent mainly in terms of passion and desire is confirmed throughout the work by explicit descriptions of how man by nature desires, and descriptions of both men and women being driven and motived by the passions of love, fear, and envy, and the desires to rule (which he sometimes calls "ambition") and to seek vengeance. On occasion he explicitly equates these passions and desires with "the force of nature" which cannot be resisted.

Machiavelli sometimes associates these passions and desires which are inherent to human nature with vice and corruption and immoral, blameworthy, wicked, and dishonourable conduct. Thus, he refers to men who, "less virtuous" than Themistocles, "let themselves be swayed by their desires and their passions" and urges all legislators "to be all the more ready to restrain human appetites and to deprive them of all hope of doing wrong with impunity".

And on a number of occasions he strongly urges that those unchanging passions and desires which constitute human nature lead to a kind of "mental blindness" which prevent men from seeing things as they are and following courses of action which would allow them to achieve their goals.

That Machiavelli understands human nature in terms of passion and desire and often associates them with evil and failure, has lead Rahe and others to find an Augustinian strain in his writing. And Machiavelli does indeed claim that "in constituting and legislating for a commonwealth it needs be taken for granted that all men are wicked and that they will always give vent to the malignity that is in their minds when opportunity offers".

But he also claims and implies that the passions and desires which he sees as defining human nature are in fact the products of various aspects of the human condition and that they may thus change and take on different configurations in different people.

Thus, the affair of the Decemviri shows how easily men are corrupted and "in nature become transformed, however good they may be and however well taught". Though "nature" has made the French ardent at the beginning of a fight and weak at the end, "it does not follow from this that the nature which makes them ardent at the start could not be so regulated by rules as to keep them ardent right up to the end".

The envy which is supposedly inherent to man's nature in fact "may be got rid of". And though there may be a nature common to all, yet different men may have different "natures," as the difference between Manlius Torquatus and Valerius Corvinus makes clear.

More importantly, perhaps following an Aristotelian metaphorical locution, Machiavelli on several occasions refers to the populace of a particular political society as "matter" and "material" which, depending upon how it is treated and worked upon, is "good" and "virtuous" or "bad" and "corrupt". This way of speaking about people is confirmed by the way Machiavelli continually distinguishes between the early days of the Roman republic "when men were good," and the later days when "men have become bad".

It is further confirmed by his claim that "anyone seeking to establish a republic at the present time would find it easier to do so among uncultured men of the mountains than among dwellers in cities where civilization is corrupt; just as a sculptor will more easily carve a beautiful statue from rough marble than from marble already spoiled by a bungling workman". Drawing such an analogy, Machiavelli suggests that he does not think there is anything wrong with man; the problem is with what educators and statesmen usually make of him. Indeed, Machiavelli explicitly takes issue with those who, postulating an inherently wicked human nature, proceed to explain events in terms of it and thereby evade taking responsibility for their own part in them.

Thus he chastises those who account for the extraordinarily wicked conduct of the people of the Romagna before Pope Alexander VI got rid of the lords who ruled it by way of wicked human nature: "it was the wickedness of the princes that gave rise to this, not the wicked nature of man".

While Machiavelli does not here say that man is not wicked, he does reject the postulate of natural human depravity as an explanation of what happened here, and insists that "it was the prince who was responsible" for the "evils" in the Romagna.

This kind of argument, which is also in *The Prince* and which likely owes something to the opening of the *The War with Jugurtha* where Sallust condemns those who blame human nature for their own failings, becomes quite pronounced in the final sections of the *Discourses,* where Machiavelli emphasises that the "nature" of individuals, soldiers, families, and peoples is a product of education, rules, customs, institutions, and ways of life.

Because the passions and desires that constitute the "nature" of men are not in fact inherent to them but are products of how they are educated, trained, brought up, and ruled, because human nature is highly *imitative* and *malleable,* Machiavelli strongly asserts, those princes and republics whose soldiers and citizens have a corrupt nature have only themselves to blame.

Finally, though Machiavelli occasionally associates the passions and desires with vice and contrasts them with some kind of mental vision, reason, conceived as an independent element of human nature which vies with passion and appetite for authority over the soul and which, having won the battle, makes it virtuous, makes no appearance in the *The Prince* or the *Discourses*. And the passions and desires, not to mention the beasts with which man shares them, have much more positive associations with drive, energy, greatness, and even virtue in Machiavelli than they do in the ancients—Cicero criticises those who take after the lion and the fox, while Machiavelli praises them, though Machiavelli still draws a distinction between their natures.

This of course means that Machiavelli also abandons the Aristotelian and Ciceronian view that, in large part by virtue of the rational principle which distinguishes man from the beasts and allows him to reason and speak eloquently, mankind reaches its full development and fulfills itself only through active engagement in political life and/or contemplation.

As Rahe, puts it, Machiavelli's "republicanism is, in fact, grounded upon the conviction that all talk of natural human ends is nonsense". Humans may thus not know the fulfilment of natural ends, but only of the desires and passions which happen to form within them, and though Machiavelli regards some of these desires and passions as being base, he is far from thinking man naturally depraved for being a creature that is possessed and driven by them.

Machiavelli thus does not share Augustine's overwhelming sense of the depravity of human nature, but is pessimistic about what men usually become as a result of the conditions under which they live–it is not an untouched block of marble, but one that has been botched that is difficult to turn into a beautiful statue.

One must take for granted that all men are wicked, that is, not because that is what they are from the start, or because that is what they are powerfully disposed to become, but because that is what they almost always have become as a result of their upbringing (though he also concedes that, like *all* things of this world, man is inclined to deterioration over time).

Emphasizing that the same passions and desires have animated mankind over millenia, and that the particular configuration of those passions and desires is usually a mode of vice or corruption, Machiavelli also asserts that the essential, unchanging being of humanity is a rather amoral, malleable, imitative life-form which, by virtue of a way of life, *becomes* a structure of passion and desire which may be a good or a bad "nature."

Unlike all of the authors we have been considering, Milton in *Paradise Lost* (and elsewhere) thinks of mankind as the product of a deliberate act of creation performed by a beneficent and omnipotent deity, an act that is recounted, mainly on the basis of Genesis, in some detail by Raphael in Book VII and Adam in Book VIII. These accounts, and the numerous other references to God's act of creating man and the world over the course of the poem, make clear that God did not simply make man, but that he made him *to* do certain things, and *for* a particular way of life.

This is suggested early in the poem by the Son when, speaking to God, he presumes that God will not abolish the entire "Creation" (which includes mankind) and unmake for Satan "what for thy glory thou hast made". That God makes man in particular *for* and *to* is confirmed by Raphael in Book VII where he prefaces his account of God's creation of man with the observation that mankind was to be the "Master work" which endu'd:

With Sanctity of Reason, might erect
His Stature, and upright with Front serene
Govern the rest, self-knowing, and from thence
Magnanimous to correspond with Heav'n,
But grateful to acknowledge whence his good
Descends, thither with heart and voice and eyes
Directed in Devotion, to adore
And worship God Supreme who made him chief
Of all his works.

Raphael here indicates that God does not just happen to endow man with reason, but that he does so *so that* he can do things God wishes him to do, such as govern the animals, and acknowledge, adore, and worship God. That God does indeed create man *to* do things such as adore and glorify him, but also to produce other humans who do this as well, is confirmed by the angels immediately after the creation when they observe that God created man in his image "to dwell [on earth] / And worship him," and to "multiply a race of worshippers / Holy and just". As Uriel explains to the disguised Satan earlier in the poem, God made man to serve him, indeed, "to serve him better" than the fallen angels did. And as the narrator, describing Adam and Eve in paradise, explains,

For contemplation hee and valor [was] form'd,
For softness shee and sweet attractive Grace,
Hee for God only, shee for God in him.

In Book IX, responding to Eve's suggestion that they work alone, Adam observes that "not to irksome toil, but to delight / He made us, and delight to Reason joined". After the fall, the Son confirms several of these claims: Eve was "Adorn'd... And lovely to attract" Adam's love, but not his subjection; she was made "for" Adam, whose "part / And person" was to bear rule. Finally, in his terrible lament after the fall, Adam must face the fact that he failed to do what he knows God made him to do: "God made thee of choice his own, and of his own / To serve him, thy reward was of his grace".

These assertions that God made man *for* and *to* have two major meanings, the first of which is that God made him with the *will* and *intention* that he do certain things and exist for the sake of certain things. One of the deepest assumptions of the poem and the unfallen characters in it is that because God made man in this way, human nature has an end or purpose: it is to do the things God wills it to do, to live in the way God intended it to live when he created it and as he continues to sustain it over time.

From one perspective, it may appear that this purpose is manifold, since, in making and sustaining human nature, God wills and intends that it do all kinds of things: besides worshipping, acknowledging, extolling, praising, thanking, and adoring him, mankind is to multiply; to govern their appetites; to subdue and possess the earth and all its creatures; to do the work of body and mind God appoints for it; to be happy and blissful; to love each other (conjugal love is "not the lowest end of human life"; to use and admire the world God framed for him; to eat freely of all fruits of paradise; and to abstain from the tree of knowledge (to "persevere" in not eating of its fruit, as Raphael puts it).

In addition, the poem makes clear that God has distinct purposes in mind for Adam and Eve: Adam is to contemplate and govern Eve, who is to obey and solace Adam, take care of domestic good, cultivate her grace and softness, and bear children. From another perspective, however, there is really only one purpose or end of human nature, since all of these activities are the same in the sense that they are all activities willed by God.

As the narrator elliptically puts it summing up the creation, God is the "Author and end of all things". Adam confirms this, and partly explains what it means for this to be the case when, thanking Raphael for revealing to him the war in heaven and forewarning him, he claims to receive God's admonishment "with solemn purpose to observe / Immutably his sovran will, the end / Of what we are". God being the end of man, man's end or purpose is to do his will.

It would have been possible for God to have made human nature in such a way that it was constrained to do or not to do what he made it to do. But God did not do this, and the poem is most emphatic on this point. God made human nature in such a way that it was capable of both performing the "voluntary service he [God] requires" and not performing it. For as God himself observes,

I form'd them free, and free they must remain,
Till they enthrall themselves: I else must change
Thir nature, and revoke the high Decree
Unchangeable, Eternal, which ordain'd
Their freedom.

Raphael later confirms this crucial point: God "ordain'd thy will / By nature free, not over-rul'd by Fate / Inextricable, or strict necessity". Having ordained that human nature be free in the sense of not being subject to the force of fate and necessity, it *is* free in this sense, and it is not constrained in any way that would prevent it from voluntarily and happily performing the service God requires.

But being free to serve God, man is also free not to serve

him. In these passages, Raphael and God make clear that the freedom of unfallen human nature is a freedom from external forces such as fate, necessity, and God himself, but they and several other characters indicate that human nature is free from the force of other elements as well: it is free, or capable of being free, from the force of appetite and passion which do, however, have the potential to "overrule," "govern," and "enthral" him. God makes this clear when he observes that, as a result of the fall, man's "lapsed powers" are "forfeit and enthrall'd / By sin to foul exorbitant desires" with the result that he is in a "sinful state".

Raphael of course attempts to prevent this from happening by telling Adam to "govern well thy appetite", and warning him to "take heed lest Passion sway / Thy Judgment to do aught, which else free Will / Would not admit". Adam explains to Eve that being free from appetite and passion in this way is a matter of making sure that reason, rather than appetite and passion, governs the will: "

God left free the Will, for what obeys / Reason, is free, and Reason he made right". After the fall, we learn that prelapsarian human nature was indeed free in the sense that the will was ruled by reason and understanding, rather than "sensual appetite".

Unfallen human nature, then, is free in the sense that it is free *from* forces that are external to it (such as necessity and fate) and forces that are internal to it (such as passion and appetite) *to* fulfil his purpose, which is to serve God out of the proper care for him. Man is capable of the voluntary service which is his end because God made human nature free.

It would also have been possible for God, being omnipotent, to have made human nature and its world in such a way that, though free to do what God intended him to do, it could only do so with great difficulty or even pain. This might seem an idle speculation, but there is one point at which Adam himself feels that this is in fact so: to continue to obey God in the face of Eve's disobedience, Adam feels he must endure great pain.

Indeed, he feels that "the link of Nature" and "the Bond

of Nature" draw him not to persist in obedience, but to share in Eve's disobedience. But though this episode may show that there may arise situations in which fulfilling his purpose may involve pain and loss, such situations seldom arise.

They seldom arise because God makes man *for* and *to* not just in the sense that he makes him with the intention and will that he do certain things, but in the sense that he makes him in such a way that, at least in most situations, he can efficiently perform with ease and even delight the things God wills him to do.

This is the point Adam makes when, concerning the act of persevering in not eating of the forbidden tree, he observes, "Let us not think hard / One easy prohibition, who enjoy / Free leave so large to all things else. He and Eve proceed to observe how easy and delightful it is for them to do all the other things—such as working, loving, mating, worshipping, praying, conversing–they rightly feel God intends them to do. As even Satan must confess to himself, that for which God made the angels—"his service"—is not "hard". Human nature is thus not only free to fulfill or not to fulfill its purpose, but it is made in such a way that, should it choose to do so, it can do so well, easily and in a way which is delightful and beneficial to it.

Human nature is, moreover, disposed in and of itself and independently of experience to fulfill its end, though Adam and Eve also display what, in relation to their end, are some wayward dispositions. Eve, for example, displays an inclination towards narcissism which Adam opposes by seizing her hand and reasonably pleading with her. Adam, on the other hand, as he confesses to Raphael, is somewhat disposed to overvalue Eve, to give himself over to the passions and desires she produces in him, to submit to her.

Though, as Raphael claims, "Nature..hath done her part", Adam seems to display some natural disposition to uxoriousness and even idolatry. But it is hardly the case that Adam drags Eve kicking and screaming to the nuptial bower, or that they drag themselves out of their rose-petal bed each day to rule the pesky animal kingdom. On the contrary, Adam and Eve commonly display an alacrity in relation to their ends, they harbor many strong dispositions and instincts which, though not causing them to fulfill their end, clearly incline them to move in that direction and render moving in that direction pleasant to them. If virtue is thought of in terms of dispositions or qualities of character which incline one to fulfill one's end, we can say that unfallen human nature is by nature virtuous.

Human nature, then, has an end in the sense of a purpose, and this end derives primarily from the fact that God made and sustains it with a particular will and intention. This end is freely to serve God out of care for him, and human nature is free to achieve or not to achieve this end.

But God made it in such a way that it is virtuous, disposed and inclined in and of itself to achieve its end, and should it choose to do so, it can easily do so well and with delight. In addition, since acting freely is, according to Adam, God, Raphael, and Michael, a matter of exercising the will in accordance with reason (rather than passion and appetite), and since the end of man is an ongoing act of freely chosen service, man's fulfilment of his nature is grounded in the exercise of reason.

That is to say that man cannot achieve his end of properly serving God unless his reason dictates to his will. The moment reason ceases to dictate to the will, the moment the will is directed by nothing (if that is possible), or anything but reason, it loses its freedom, and having lost its freedom, it is incapable of choosing to serve God and freely serving him. All of this follows from the fact that, as God puts it in a rather Aristotelian-sounding formulation, "reason is but choosing," or, as Michael puts it, "true Liberty... always with right Reason dwells / Twinn'd, and from her hath no dividual being". It is thus not the case, as Stanley Fish has argued, that Milton understands man to achieve his end of serving God on the basis of faith, where faith is belief or will that are entirely independent of reason. Were man to serve God out of faith as opposed to reason, his service would not be free, and if it were not free, it would not count as service.

According to Milton, the consequences of achieving this end are first of all, continued happiness for himself and his progeny. That is to say that what the poem refers to as "happiness" is not, as it is for Aristotle, "that which is always desirable in itself and never for the sake of something else", but only a consequence or even reward of man's achieving his end, which is to serve God voluntarily and in the spirit of gratitude and love of him.

Thus, as Adam tells Raphael, God informed him that the "bitter consequence" of not observing his will would be the loss of "this happy State," and Raphael informs him that he owes his continued happiness to himself, to his "obedience". A further consequence of man's achieving his end is immortality and innocence for himself and his progeny. And though man is granted dominion over the animals, the angels indicate that this rule, too, is really the result, the "reward," of man's dwelling on earth and worshipping God.

There are several indications that further things would have followed upon man's continued fulfilment of his end. First, God has promised them that, if they obey him, they shall give birth to an innocent and immortal progeny who, besides worshipping God, will help them do the work in the garden, work which on their own Adam and Eve cannot adequately perform. Second, after informing Adam and Eve that they must leave paradise, Michael speculates that had he stood, Adam might have remained there, his "Capital Seat," and known the pleasure of receiving all generations who would have come "to celebrate / And reverence thee their great Progenitor".

It also seems that, standing, Adam and Eve would have found their nature gradually to have become the purely spiritual and superior nature of angels. Indeed, commenting on Raphael's account of how this may occur, Adam observes that "in contemplation of created things / By steps we may ascend to God". Moreover, "under long obedience tri'd," Adam and Eve and their unfallen progeny might eventually "open to themselves at length the way" to heaven, "And Earth be chang'd to Heav'n, and Heav'n to Earth, / One Kingdom,

Joy and Union without end". The consequences of failing to achieve his end are made clear in the final books of the poem.

For the purposes of assessing Milton's relationship with classical republicanism, it is important to note that in defining the end of human nature and the consequences of its fulfilment in this way, Milton grants virtually no importance to the life of citizenship and statesmanship which is so central to the ends of human nature as Aristotle and Cicero understand them.

There is, first of all, no indication in the poem that God made man for political society in the sense that he made him with the intention and will that, once there were sufficient numbers of humans, they would exercise civic virtue in a Greek polis, a Roman republic, an Italian city-state, or an early-modern European nation-state.

Certainly, God grants man dominion over the earth and wills that he subdue and rule over it, and he grants Adam authority and rule over Eve. Unfallen mankind, moreover, may be said to exist within a hierarchical cosmic order subject to a law, similar to that imagined by Cicero. But none of this means that Adam and Eve are subjects or citizens existing within what either the ancients or Milton would have thought of as a political society.

The society of Adam and Eve is essentially a domestic, familial society, an oikos rather than a polis, and all indications are that, as long as they had stood, it would have remained as such, regardless of how many children they had. Adam's generations would have returned to paradise to revere not their lord, king, consuls, nobles, senators, ephors, guardians, tribunes, ministers, podesta, or rulers, but their father, their "progenitor," and while for seventeenth-century patriarchalists such as Robert Filmer fathers were lords by virtue of being fathers, Milton shows no inclination to think so either in his epic or elsewhere.

The implication is that the life of the citizen and statesman is not the life God intended man to live, not when there were two living in blissful solitude, not when there would have been enough humans to take care of all the work in the garden, not when there would have been a human race "to fill the Earth".

And though it might be argued that Adam and Eve are made in such a way that they are capable of performing the tasks of citizens and statesmen well as the ancients understood them, there is no indication that they have been endowed with an impulse or desire to live and exercise civic virtue within political society.

Neither is there any indication that Adam and Eve and their race need a political society in order to fulfill and perfect themselves, as Aristotle and Cicero say humans do. Indeed, once Adam and Eve are married, they exist in "blissful solitude," as though, excepting the fact that they can not quite keep the garden in order, their domestic society has the self-sufficiency which Aristotle ascribes only to states. Because Adam and Eve neither have any natural impulse to form nor need a political society, neither they, nor God, nor the angels see a future in politics for prelapsarian man.

Adam, however, is formed for "contemplation," and it is difficult here, and in many other passages where Milton uses terms which were standardly used to translate key terms in Aristotle, not to feel an allusion to the Greek philosopher Milton so commonly cites in his political prose. But in Paradise Lost, Milton rarely uses terms standardly used to translate key terms in pagan republican texts to mean what the pagans used those key terms to mean, and his usage of "contemplation" is no exception.

First of all, the contemplation that is proper for man is in no way incompatible, as it would be for Aristotle, with the "work of body" that is also appointed by God for him. In addition, Raphael gently rebukes Adam for wondering about the heavenly bodies and "Ent'ring on studious thoughts abstruse". Informing him that "Heav'n is for thee too high," Raphael instructs him to be "lowly wise" and to "think only what concerns thee and thy being."

In so doing, Raphael seems to direct Adam away from the Aristotelian conception of contemplation as an exercise of speculative rather than practical reason which is grounded in the intellectual virtue of philosophical rather than practical wisdom, and which aims at knowing and understanding, among other things, the heavenly bodies. Learning his lesson, Adam understands that "the prime Wisdom" is "not to know at large of things remote / From use, obscure and subtle, but to know / That which before us lies in daily life".

Having learned this, Adam may well contemplate with ease and delight in the way God intended him to, but as a mode of consideration which will not be directed to "things remote from use," his contemplation will be different in important ways from the activity of Aristotle's philosopher.

Whereas all of the republicans think of human nature as having remained essentially the same over the course of its entire existence, Milton sees it as having existed in two radically different states which are separated from each other by an act performed by the first two human beings. As a chosen, voluntary violation of God's will, as a violation of what God made man for, that act is in God's eye a "revolt", "Treason", a "crime" for which a "penalty" or "ransom" must be paid in order for justice to be served.

Demanding that justice be served, that is, God wills that man pay for his crime. God indicates at the opening of Book III that he will accept two kinds of payment: proclaiming "Die he or Justice must", he indicates that he shall deem justice to have been served by the immediate and total annihilation of mankind. But he adds that he would also deem the death of a just and loving mortal as adequate "satisfaction, death for death".

Observing this second possibility, the Son presents himself as "a sacrifice / Glad to be offer'd," one who, out of filial obedience and love for man, will satisfy God's justice by paying "the deadly forfeiture, and ransom set". This, however, does not let man off the hook–justice will die unless he, too, pays a penalty.

For as the Son observes to God in Book X, in sacrificing himself for love of man, the Son can only "mitigate" and not "reverse" the doom of man, which is "Death". Man, too, must die, not in the sense that he and his progeny be permanently wiped from the face of the earth, but in the sense that every individual human perish after many days. This death, moreover, will terminate an existence which is to be one of misery, pain, and sorrow: expressing God's will by way of his judgment and sentence on fallen mankind, the Son observes that until they "to dust return," Adam and Eve will live, work, and multiply in "sorrow".

As God puts it in his official decree to the angels, now that man has fallen, he wills that he leave the garden, "to Till / The Ground whence he was taken, fitter soil". Willing, as always, that justice live, God thus wills that man's existence be one of "woe" terminated by death. Adam understands: "dust," he says to Eve, is now their "final rest and native home". The end of fallen human nature (what God wills for it) in this world is now the end of human nature (its dissolution and death).

This end differs in two important ways from the end of unfallen man. First, it is not so much a form of choosing and acting as it is a form of suffering and enduring. Certainly, man is to work and to multiply. But willing that man experience sorrow and die, God wills not that man freely, voluntarily do or perform in some way, but essentially that he be subject to various forces and processes. Second, this end is imposed upon him, regardless of what he wishes, thinks, chooses, or wills. Whereas before the fall man is free to fulfill or not to fulfill his end as determined by God's will, after the fall he is not.

For after the fall, human nature is forced, both by what it is in and of itself and by various agents such as the Son and Michael, to experience and do at least part of what God wills for it: Michael and paradise force Adam and Eve from paradise; having been expelled, Adam and Eve, at least as long as they choose to live, have no choice but to till the soil in a harsh clime; they cannot avoid suffering in the new world; they can do nothing to evade their own dissolution.

"Justice shall not return as bounty scorned", God asserts in one of the hardest lines of the poem, because man is not free to scorn God's justice as he was free to scorn his bounty.

Just as unfallen human nature is well suited to do that which God wills for it, so fallen nature is as well. But whereas unfallen human nature is well suited in this respect because

God framed it in a particular way, unfallen nature is well-suited for the existence God wills it to have because of what it becomes as a result of its having committed "the mortal sin original".

That is to say that whereas God intervenes through his angels to reframe the natural world in such a way as to make it a suitable environment for sweat and sorrow, he does not intervene immediately after the fall to recreate man in such a way that he will be suited for the new life of sorrow ending in dust God now has in mind for him.

Rather, human nature becomes this kind of thing on its own as a result of what it does. Thus, in Book IX, having disobeyed, Adam and Eve burn in lust, gratify that lust, sleep, and awaken to find themselves entirely changed. That the narrator does not identify God as being in any way involved in this process is only to be expected since, as God himself earlier insists, "they enthrall themselves".

Immediately after the fall, however, a crucial dimension of human nature is up for grabs, and God must act in order to prevent man from doing something which would result in his having a nature unsuited to his new ends, and which would prevent justice from being done:

Lest therefore his now bolder hand
Reach also of the Tree of Life, and eat,
And live for ever, dream at least to live
For ever, to remove him I decree.

Though God later says that it was he who "provided Death", he here indicates that the act of committing the crime on its own is sufficient to cause human nature to change from being immortal to being mortal. But in order to keep it that way, God decrees that man be banished from paradise and so denied the opportunity to make itself immortal once again by eating of the Tree of Life.

The reason that this fallen human nature is suited for paying the penalty for its crime as God wills is that it is "manifold in sin,", "corrupt," and "depraved." For by virtue of being corrupt, sinful, and depraved, human nature is subject to processes of decay leading to death. "Dissolution" is, as God observes, "wrought by Sin, that first / Distemper'd all things, and of incorrupt / Corrupted".

Sin makes the point when she instructs Death to feast on the plants and animals "Till I in Man residing through the Race, / His thoughts, his looks, words, actions all infect, / And season him thy last and sweetest prey". Manifold in sin, seasoned and infected by it, that is, man is now something which left to itself in its world decays until it dies–his life has become "a slow-pac't evil, / A long day's dying," as Adam observes.

But besides qualifying him for the death God intends for him, what Michael calls man's "natural pravity" also qualifies him well for the misery, pain, sorrow, and sweat which God wills him to experience before that end. First of all, this natural pravity is repellent to the ideal environment of paradise: even had God not evicted him from paradise, the "pure immortal Elements" there would in accordance with "the Law of Nature" have forced him out, since they "eject him tainted now, and purge him off / As a distemper.

The only environment which is now suitable for corrupted mankind is the corrupt, harsh natural environment which is brought about by his own sin and God's decree. In addition, the very processes of dissolution that lead to death will in many cases be a source of terrible pain and suffering, as Michael demonstrates in Book XI.

It is, moreover, clear from Book IX onwards that simply existing in a "sinful state" is painful to humans: though they both feel intoxicated immediately after eating, and take "thir fill of Love and Love's disport," Adam and Eve awaken to find that they are "destitute and bare / Of all thir virtue". Having lost honour, innocence, faith, purity, confidence, and righteousness, they are overwhelmed by the sense of shame and feel "confounded" and "abasht".

They have in addition, as we have already seen, lost their peace of mind, for they are now subject to terrible passions. Despoiled of all their good, the first fallen humans are, in short, "miserable", which is precisely what God, demanding that they be justly punished for their crime against him, wants them to be.

Being manifold in sin further suits and qualifies fallen human nature to fulfill its end because it amounts to a loss of inner freedom. For being in a sinful state, or being "distempered" as the narrator and God also put it, means that passion and appetite have displaced reason as governor of the will, and, as we have seen, the poem asserts that any agent whose will is dictated by passion and desire rather than reason is not free.

Observing at the end of Book IX that as a result of the fall the will is subject to sensual appetite rather than reason, the narrator confirms God's earlier claim that man enthrals himself, and that man's "lapsed powers" are "forfeit and enthrall'd / By sin to foul exorbitant desires". In disobeying God, Michael informs Adam, "themselves they vilifi'd / to serve ungovern'd appetite".

That servitude, he later indicates, is not a punctual action, but a permanent condition:

Since thy original lapse, true Liberty
Is lost, which always with right Reason dwells
Twinn'd, and from her hath no dividual being;
Reason in man obscur'd, or not obey'd,
Immediately inordinate desires
And upstart Passions catch the Government
From Reason, and to servitude reduce
Man till then free.

Having lost inner freedom, man is now incapable of not just freely serving God as he was created to do, but, strictly speaking, of freely doing anything, since you can only voluntarily do something if you act in accordance with reason, and fallen man is incapable of doing that. Were the end of fallen man a form of voluntary service, fallen man would thus by nature in an essential sense be unsuited for his end.

But because the end of fallen man is essentially no longer a matter of choosing and doing (which require reason and freedom) but of suffering and enduring, his being in a state of bondage is entirely compatible with the fulfilment of his end. Indeed, this loss of freedom constitutes a further dimension of the very fulfilment of this end, for simply existing in a state of bondage, simply existing in a state in which one is no longer in control of one's passions and desires but is continually "tossed" by them, as Adam and Eve are in the final books, is in itself sickening.

Those critics such as Lewalski who like to see the poem teaching us "to live as free moral agents and as virtuous citizens who value and deserve personal and political liberty", fail to acknowledge these ways in which the poem insists not only that human nature enters a state of bondage as result of the fall, but also that this bondage is consistent with and indeed part of the fulfilment of its end as determined by God.

The "Eternal purpose" for fallen man, however, is also determined by the will that "Man shall not quite be lost, but sav'd who will". Though out of wrath and justice God wills that man suffer and die, that is, he also out of mercy wills that he (at least some humans) be redeemed and saved. By this he means, as he, the Son, and the angels make clear over the course of the poem, that after having achieved their end of misery and death, some will return with the Son to Heaven where, ultimately, "God shall be All in All".

God thus wills what Michael calls a "happy end" for postlapsarian man. Now, because human nature is depraved, it is totally unsuited and incapable to achieve this dimension of its end. That is to say that in respect of this dimension of its end, there is a profound disjunction between what man by nature is and his end, where his end is defined in terms of what God wills for him.

To put it another way, if by a "natural" end one means that to which a thing is inclined to be or become by virtue of its own internal capacities and instincts, then part of man's end (his happy end) is in relation to him unnatural. In order to achieve the happy end, then, human nature requires the intervention of an agency that is external to itself and that counteracts its own predominant inclinations and dispositions.

That agency is God: man will be saved, God asserts in Book III, "not of will in him, but grace in me / Freely voutsaf't". God will uphold man so "that he may know how frail / His fall'n condition is, and to me owe / All his deliv'rance, and to none but me". This emphasis on supernatural agency in bringing man to his happy end which is, in relation to what he is, unnatural also features throughout the final books.

Thus, the end of fallen human nature (i.e. that which God wills for it) is essentially bipartite and each part is fulfilled in fundamentally different ways: human nature as we know it, simply by virtue of being its own depraved and enslaved self and existing in the corrupt world of nature, suffices to achieve misery and death which are its end in this world; God and the Son bring it, in spite of itself, to the happy end, which is its end in the afterlife.

If, however, human nature could do nothing on its own before it died except suffer, if it was entirely deprived of the ability to choose and act in accordance with that choice, then God could not justly hold him responsible for his existence and make the happy end a reward for it. This, however, God clearly intends to do at the "dread Tribunal" presided over by the Son at the end of time.

That is to say that the hard teaching on fallen nature presented by some passages in the poem conflicts with God's will to punish and reward individual humans on the basis of how they live.

It is partly in order to address this aspect of the theology of the poem that Milton qualifies the vision of fallen human nature as something that can do nothing but till and suffer as it dies. He does so, first, by observing that God acts upon fallen man in such as way as to make it capable once again of choosing and acting freely: even though man's powers are "enthrall'd by sin to foul exorbitant desires," God claims that "once more I will renew" them.

He will, moreover, "clear thir senses dark, / What may suffice, and soft'n stony hearts / To pray, repent, and bring obedience due" as well as "place within them as a guide / My Umpire Conscience".

Here again we have a "to" locution: God acts on fallen human nature so that, or with the intention that, it may freely do certain things such as pray, repent, and obey. This is confirmed at the conclusion of Book X and the opening of Book

XI where we see how God's grace "had remov'd / The stony" from the hearts of Adam and Eve, "and made new flesh / Regenerate grow instead".

In addition, in the final book, Michael informs Adam of how he shall be delivered from the Law, which serves only to "evince thir natural pravity", to a "better Cov'nant," the covenant of grace. After the first coming, the Son will send a Comforter to man "who shall dwell / His Spirit within them" and "the Law of Faith... upon their hearts shall write". Commenting on these passages, Grossman observes that "when the Spirit writes on the heart, man can be released from the self-enthralment incurred by Adam's fall and once again perform his moral part".

This is perhaps too strong since, as the remainder of Book XII makes clear, human nature is far from being restored to its unfallen state by virtue of the covenant of grace, but it does appear to be restored from sin to a state in which it has and may exercise some degree of freedom. Though it is still only as a result of how God and the Son act upon it, fallen human nature, all of these passages suggest, ends up being capable of some degree of voluntary action, of something that would count as "obedience," of something that could justly be punished or rewarded.

There are further indications that there is a realm of freedom within the constraints established by man's fallen nature and a justice which man is not free to scorn. In Book IV, for example, the narrator speaks as though the "wedded Love" enjoyed by Adam and Eve in paradise continued to exist after the fall to drive out the lust in which Adam and Eve burn immediately after the fall and to ground love between fathers, sons, and brothers. Similarly, in Book XI, Michael comments on those who suffer and die of disease as those who "pervert pure Nature's healthful rules / To loathsome sickness", as though the realm of fallen nature is pure, and as though even fallen mankind, as part of the natural realm, may be capable of obeying those rules. This point is perhaps confirmed in Book XII when Michael criticises Nimrod for dispossessing "Concord and Law of Nature from the Earth".

That human nature may retain some of its prelapsarian freedom and even disposition is further indicated by Michael when he corrects Adam who, in the face of the pleasures enjoyed by the sons of Seth and daughters of Cain, observes, "Here Nature seems fulfill'd in all her ends": "Judge not what is best / By pleasure," Michael instructs, "though to Nature seeming meet, / Created, as thou art, to nobler end / Holy and pure, conformity divine".

It seems that even though pleasure may seem meet to fallen human nature, this nature nevertheless has an essentially religious purpose and therefore fulfills itself by living a life that conforms with the holy and the divine. Finally, in his discussion of the loss of inward liberty which supposedly follows from Adam's original lapse, Michael leaves open the possibility of both inner and outer freedom: if reason is not "obscured" but simply "not obey'd," it would seem that man is free to obey reason; if man "permits / Within himself unworthy Powers to reign / Over free Reason," it would seem that he could revoke that permission and thereby regain his inner freedom.

Insofar as the poem asserts that reason is not entirely displaced by passion and appetite as ruler of the will of fallen man, it grants it a degree of freedom, and insofar as it grants it a degree of freedom, it grants it the possibility of virtuous action—virtue is still reason, Michael informs Adam–where virtuous action consists in voluntarily doing those things which God wills him to do. God's will for the fallen human nature that is to a limited extent free as it suffers and dies may be divided into two main parts, the first of which concerns how he is to respond to the grace God may offer him: though he is not free to scorn justice, man is still free to "neglect and scorn" the grace God offers him or to pray for and accept it if granted.

This is in part by virtue of God's giving man the law with purpose to resign him "to free / Acceptance of large Grace". God wills, that is, that man (if only those he has elected above the rest) freely accept his grace; that he repent; that he pray to, appease, and obey him. Even if he is not fully capable of performing these actions well, as long as he endeavours to do them "with sincere intent," he will be doing something that pleases God and mollifies his wrath.

The second main aspect of God's will for fallen man who enjoys limited freedom concerns his response to his punishment, the life of misery and death which he is not free to forego. Though man will suffer and die, he is free to do so in a variety of ways, and much of the instruction provided by Michael in the final books is aimed at describing the proper way.

Exercising his limited freedom in these ways, some fallen men may do as God wills fallen man to do and justly be rewarded with the happy end after their death. Those who do not exercise their freedom in this way will not, however, fail to achieve their end. It is just that, in light of their response to their punishment and his grace, God wills that they be punished again by suffering in hell forever.

As much of the recent commentary on the poem, and the final books in particular, has emphasised, the particular ways in which God wills fallen man to exercise whatever freedom remains to him may include what Aristotle and Cicero would think of as political activity. And over the course of the final books, fallen mankind does display some impulse to form various forms of political society.

But there are no indications that, by founding and governing states, human nature may fulfil itself, or that it may reach its fullest development, or that it will be rewarded in the afterlife. Indeed, the cases of Enoch and Noah suggest that renouncing and abandoning one's political community may in some cases be the only means of avoiding God's wrath and being rewarded. The fact, at least, that one renounces one's own political society and life within it does not mean one cannot achieve one's end, as it does for Aristotle and Cicero.

More importantly, though that dimension of man's end in this world which is answerable to his choice may include political activity, the life of the armed citizen and eloquent statesman can hardly be said to be its core. At the core of the life in this world that is open to our freedom is the Christian life, where the Christian life is grounded not in civic virtue and patriotism but in Christian virtue, and where it is lived not after the example of Cicero, but of the Son. To the extent that the freedom of prelapsarian man survives the fall–and Milton is ambivalent about this—so does his end, which is not to found and hold office in republics, but to serve God out of the care to please him. Humans are to lead "lives Religious," as the Sons of God did before they chose to "yield up all thir virtue".

There is no short, simple answer to the crucial question of how Milton's vision of human nature in Paradise Lost is related to the republicans' vision of human nature. This is because there are major inconsistencies within the works of major republican figures, important differences between these figures, and major complications concerning this issue in Paradise Lost.

But, attempting to take into account some of these difficulties, we can say that Milton follows the classical republicans (but not Machiavelli) in thinking of the human agent (both pre and postlapsarian versions) as a composite that includes a rational element and an appetitive, passionate element. In addition, he is generally inclined to share the classical republicans' basic understanding of both virtue and inner freedom in terms of the rational element's rule over the appetitive, passionate element.

Milton departs from the republicans, however, in many important ways. Though on some occasions (such as his discussion of religious toleration in Book XII) he resorts to a dualistic vocabulary to discuss this composite human nature, on others he explicitly asserts a monistic ontology which is at odds with the dualistic interpretation of man's composite human nature that prevails in Cicero and other republican historians such as Sallust.

In addition, Milton's vision of human nature as part of God's creation stands in stark contrast to the vision or assumption of the naturalistic origins of man in the republicans (though they sometimes see him as a product of a personified Nature). Understanding human nature as God's work, Milton sees it as having an end or purpose in the sense that it was made and is sustained by a deity that wills and intends things for it.

None of the republicans we have considered, with the possible exception of Cicero, sees human nature as having an end in this sense–those republicans who see it as having an end or purpose define this end in terms of the exercise of faculties unique to human nature, and the full development and perfection of capacities and instincts that are internal to it. Milton thus ascribes to human nature a kind of end or purpose which the republicans seldom ascribe to it.

Though he sees it as having an end of this kind, however, Milton also sees it as having an end of the kind attributed to it by the classical republicans: he sees it as having innate instincts and dispositions to do and become certain things. But Milton also differs profoundly from the republicans concerning the content of the end of human nature conceived in this way: whereas the classical republicans understand human nature as we know it in various degrees to have a capacity for and to be disposed to exercising reason as a citizen (and as a philosopher in the case of Aristotle), Milton understands it to be primarily disposed in and of itself to corruption, suffering, and dying, though he also grants it a residual capacity for virtuous action.

This is not to say that the republicans do not see human nature as being prone to decay and death–they do, but they do not see decay, depraved behaviour, and death as something to which human nature is actively, inherently, and ineradicably disposed as Milton does in this poem. In addition, the life of divine service as Milton understands it might include activities such as founding states and administering justice in them, but it need not, and it would seldom include those military activities which are central to citizenship as both the ancients and Machiavelli understand it.

Milton's understanding of a particular kind of religious life as part of the end of fallen man is also at odds with the basic understanding of religion as something that should be serviceable to good citizenship and the state which is expressed by Aristotle, Cicero, and Machiavelli. Milton understands of that to which human nature is disposed in and of itself as not just suffering, but as punishment for a crime, as the satisfaction of justice, is also alien to the sensibility of those republicans we have considered here.

And whereas for Milton the consequences of achieving these natural ends include eternal bliss in heaven, the consequences of achieving the ends of human nature for the republicans (again with the possible exception of Cicero) are confined entirely to this world.

One reason Milton differs from the republicans in these way is that he understands human nature as we know it (i.e. fallen human nature) to be guilty and infected by sin as a result of an act that it committed in the distant past, an act which for the republicans never occurred. Such an inherently depraved nature that disposes us to commit more sin is foreign to Aristotle's prevailing view that we are by nature neither virtuous nor wicked but naturally adapted to receive moral virtue which we may cultivate and perfect by way of habit.

It is also alien to both the "natural goodwill and kindliness" Cicero sometimes sees in man and the raw, malleable human "material" which Machiavelli, following an Aristotelian usage, felt could be made into a good or bad nature by different forms of education and upbringing.

Though we have focussed on descriptions of human nature in Milton and the republicans, it has become clear that because Milton differs from the republicans on this issue, he differs from them on other issues, positions on which are more commonly taken to be at the heart of republican tradition. Thinking of human nature the way he does, for example, Milton obviously thinks about history and virtue in a way which is profoundly at odds with republican thinking on these subjects.

In light of these differences, the reading of Paradise Lost as a poem that affirms or is even consistent with the basic political principles of Aristotle, Cicero, and Machiavelli is untenable. This is not, however, to say, that the case for the poem's participation in and extension of the tradition of republican political thought is without merit. For in many cases, traditions of thought and writing are extended and perpetuated by authors who are hostile towards elements of those traditions.

This is why, for example, those scholars who observe that Machiavelli radically departs from the classical republicans on several major issues nevertheless continue to see him as a central figure of republican tradition.

This is why those critics who observe Milton's hostility towards pagan epic nevertheless see him as participating in the tradition of western epic poetry. As the current scholarship on the issue indicates, there is a case to be made for Milton's response to and participation in republican tradition, but this case needs to take into account the ways in which he not only differs from, but openly repudiates major aspects of it.

Chapter 15

L'Allegro; Il Penseroso; Arcades; Comus

The recognition of this is the most important thing in the study of the first stage of Milton's poetical career. It was a few years before the executive mastery rendered the critical control regulative rather than prohibitive or suspensory; but very few. The famous Shakespeare lines are probably a little, and even not a very little, earlier than the date of the second folio, in which they appeared, and, if not perfect intrinsically, are admirable as from a young disciple to a dead master.

The Hobson pieces, though quite out of Milton's line and much less well done in their own than they would have been by Cleiveland or John Hall, are, at least, curious. *An Epitaph on the Marchioness of Winchester* is a notable study for the verse of *L'Allegro;* and its companion *Arcades,* of which more presently, is a more notable study for *Comus.* A hint from Peele—not the last—and a suggestion from Shakespeare, matter nothing: Milton was to be always a literary poet. These things mark the full initiation, the final winning of the spurs.

From *L'Allegro* itself to *Samson Agonistes,* we have to do with the adept and the knight. The comparative valuation of the various poems of these forty years may be left to others, for it depends partly upon personal preferences, partly upon considerations of scale and subject and other things that can never be brought to a satisfactory common denominator of criticism. But the positive quality of poetry is in and over them all, from first to last, unmistakable by those who have been born or taught to recognise it.

And it is this positive quality, in its various individual manifestations, and in its relations to the general history and development of English poetry at large, that we have now to disengage and study in chronological order, only neglecting this latter in the case of the *Sonnets*, so as to group them together, as is usually done, in what is the actual place of most of them,—the gap between *Lycidas* and *Paradise Lost*.

The twin studies of cheerfulness and melancholy will, of course, come first, for it is impossible to admit the ingenious attempt (above referred to) to postdate them. Their extraordinary felicity has not met any important gainsayings. That some of the details are not quite accurate, as natural history, would matter extremely little in any case, and has even a certain interest in connection with the peculiarity (to be noticed later) of Milton's poetic painting.

Another interesting point is the skill with which the full or shortened octosyllabic couplet, with iambic or trochaic cadence at pleasure, is handled. This famous old measure, handed down from *The Owl and the Nightingale*, if not earlier, had been fingered into new beauty by Shakespeare and others in the last years of the sixteenth century and had been specially cultivated by Fletcher, Browne, Wither and others in the earlier seventeenth.

Its capabilities have never been so perfectly and variously shown as in these two charming poems, which are also, as it were, diploma-pieces, exhibiting Milton's almost unsurpassable combination of bookishness and natural imagination, the art of phrase which still has all the gracefulness of youth, the power over imagery and association, the whole suffused with a temper which is soft even when sad, and which never jars or thorn-crackles even at its most mirthful.

When the beautiful fragment *Arcades* (to return to it for a special purpose) was written is not known; it must have come before *Comus*, but may be of any year between 1630 and 1634. It was addressed to Alice, countess dowager of Derby—the same lady who, as lady Strange (she was by birth lady Alice Spencer) had been the recipient of Spenser's *Teares of the Muses* forty years before, and who, after the death of her first husband (Strange, it must be remembered, was then the second title of the earls of Derby), had married lord keeper Egerton, afterward lord chancellor viscount Brackley.

The masque was performed at Harefield in Middlesex, not far from Horton, and it is supposed, though not known, that the music was by Milton's friend Lawes. Fragment as the libretto is, the songs, especially the second, "On the smooth enamelled green" are perfection; and the decasyllabic couplets of the Genius's speech have deep interest as being Milton's most considerable serious attempt in this form.

He takes, as was natural, the enjambed variety, but carefully avoids the breathless overlapping of his seniors Browne and Marmion and Chalkhill and his younger contemporary Chamberlayne.

The connection of *Comus* with *Arcades* is so close in all ways that it is scarcely improper to regard it as deliberate. The earl of Bridgewater, for whom it was written, was lady Derby's stepson through her second husband, and his wife was her daughter by her first. He was president of Wales, and, in virtue of his office, lived at Ludlow castle, where *Comus* was acted.

His daughter Alice, who acted the Lady, must have been named after her double grandmother. Lawes here certainly wrote the music, and he acted the Attendant Spirit. As for the story, it was partly supplied (beyond all question) by Peele's *Old Wives Tale,* largely supplemented from Milton's classical and modern reading (especially the *Comus* of the Dutchman Puteanus (1608)) and his own imagination; partly derived, at least according to tradition, from an actual adventure of lady Alice and her two brothers.

But it has not always been sufficiently noticed that the whole, as it were, is a filling up of *Arcades*—the Genius of the Wood dividing himself into good and evil parts as Thyrsis and Comus, the merely accidental songs being adapted and multiplied to suit the action, and that action itself being devised, in full colour and body, to take the place of a mere occasional situation, like that of the earlier piece.

The amplification was more than justified, and in a

surprisingly large number of ways. The actual dramatic effect of the piece is not great; and, on the other side, it has been pronounced too much of a fully equipped drama to be a masque.

But, putting questions of words and names apart, it is a most admirable poem; and there have even not been wanting those who put it, for length and poetic quality combined, first of all its author's works, while admitting the superiority of *Lycidas* in the latter respect and the three great later pieces in the first.

One special point of interest is that Milton here discards for his "tragedy," as Sir Henry Wotton called it (*i. e.* the body of his dialogue), the couplet which he had used in *Arcades*, and adopts blank verse; while the rest of the piece is in octosyllabic couplet or lyrical measures which are almost an improvement on *L'Allegro, Il Penseroso* and *Arcades* itself.

Something more will be said of the form later: the substance is amply worthy of it and, like it, duplex in character—an ethical height and weight which the poet had never reached before being matched with unimpaired grace in the lighter parts. It would be difficult to find a poem where profit and delight are more perfectly blended.

Chapter 16

Lycidas

In *Lycidas,* the delight reaches an even higher pitch. For once, there is no need to quarrel even with such an apparent hyperbole as Pattison's "high-water mark of English poetry"—especially as high-water mark is not a thing that can only once be reached.

The circumstances, form and character of this exquisite poem have been the subject of a great deal of writing. It formed part of a collection of epicedes on Edward King, a slightly younger contemporary of Milton at Christ's who had become fellow and tutor, and had intended to take orders, but was drowned on a voyage to Ireland in the summer of 1637. Milton's contribution is signed "J. M." only.

The general scheme is that of a classical pastoral elegy; the verse form is a very peculiar, in fact, up to its date, unique, arrangement of stanzas and lines of unequal length, for the most part irregularly, and not entirely, rimed, but terminating in a regular octave. To what extent the poem expresses personal sorrow has been largely, but very unnecessarily, questioned; as an elegy, it has, poetically speaking, no superior even in a language which contains the various laments on Sidney before, and *Adonais* and *Thyrsis* after.

The whole poem is a tissue of splendid passages, not unconnected, but sewn cunningly together rather than woven in one piece as regards subject. One, however, of these passages contains, for the first time, a note "prophesying war." Up to this date, Milton's verse, though abstaining alike from the passionately amorist tone of contemporary profane lyric, and from the almost erotically mystical tone of contemporary sacred poetry, had contained nothing polemical; and, even in the frequent eulogies of chastity in *Comus*, nothing positively austere.

Here, St. Peter, coming among other symbolical figures to bewail the dead, is made to deliver a tremendous denunciation of what Milton later directly entitled "the corrupt clergy" of the time, and a prophecy of their ruin. The strict propriety of this has been questioned, even by some who agree with Milton's views on the subject: the force and fire of the expression (not injured by a little obscurity, which, perhaps, was a necessary precaution) may be admitted by the most thorough admirer of Laud.

And all the rest (except from the point of view of an objection to pedantry which is itself ultra-pedantic) is absolutely proof against criticism. There cannot be better verse than *Lycidas*.

Chapter 17

Milton's Sonnets

The few, but extremely interesting, *Sonnets* derive their interest from various sources. Except the earliest two, and the batch of Italian pieces which follows, they bridge the interval between Milton's first poetical period and his last—dotting the twenty dark years with spots of light.

It is true that the evil spirit of the prose pamphlets retains some influence here, that his footing is seen in the *Tetrachordon* sonnets, in the tail-sonnet (twenty lines, the fifteenth and eighteenth of six syllables only) *On the new forcers of Conscience* and, to some, though less, extent, in the political sonnets to Fairfax, Cromwell and Vane.

It is true, also, that one (xiv) *On the Religious Memory of Mrs. Catherine Thomson* is the most commonplace thing that-Milton ever wrote. But, even were the best and the most of them less good, they would be interesting as resuming (with little following for more than another century) the Elizabethan practice of this great form, and as bringing it nearer to the commoner Italian model. Individually and intrinsically, they do not need any allowance.

Wordsworth's hackneyed praise is not very specially applicable to most of them; and Johnson's contempt of the form itself, no doubt slightly accentuated by dislike of the author. Taken dispassionately, Milton's sonnets are examples, curiously various considering their small number, at once of the adaptability of the kind to "occasional" purposes, and of the absence of any necessity that this adaptability should be abused, as Wordsworth himself certainly abused it, and as lesser men have abused it still more.

Nowhere, moreover, and this is natural, is the poet's tendency to be autobiographical shown in a more interesting way. The pretty overture to the nightingale not only shows the true Miltonic style very early, but gives us a Miltonic person who might have developed very differently. The other side—the side which did develop—appears in the "three and twentieth year" (vii), and at once foretells the compensations for the loss of the less austere personage.

And all the better later examples give that compensation, with lighter touches here and there in the sonnets to Lawes, Lawrence and Cyriack Skinner. The grace of these; the splendour of *On the late Massacher in Piemont* and the sonnet on his blindness; the dignity, even in partisanship, of the three political addresses; the idealised tenderness of the finale on his dead wife—give us not merely great poetry, but invaluable comment on the other great poetry which was to follow them.

The year 1645, however, saw a more important event in Milton's literary biography and in the history of English literature than the move to Barbican, or the reconciliation with his wife, or even the downfall of the royal cause. Hitherto—in this respect following a considerable and respectable, though inconvenient and dangerous, Elizabethan tradition—he had been very shy of printing his poems. The Shakespeare lines were merely a trimming to the edition of Shakespeare in which they appeared, and we do not know exactly how they came there. *Lycidas* had formed part of a collection containing other men's work; Lawes's edition of *Comus* was anonymous.

But now, at a time when his mind was occupied with things very different from the composition of poetry, Milton consented to the publication of his earlier poetical work (by, and at the instance of, the bookseller Humphrey Moseley) as *Poems of Mr. John Milton, both English and Latin, Compos'd at several times* ... 1645.

It has been supposed that this publication, with its accompanying commendatory poems, was intended as a sort of self-vindication, or countersally, in respect of his polemical, and, in parts, highly unpopular, prose pamphlets. This seems very doubtful; for anything like excuse, or plea in mitigation, was absolutely alien from Milton's undoubting self-confidence and his positive contumacy of spirit. Nor does the motto

Baccare frontem
Cingite, ne vati noceat mala lingua futuro

necessarily involve any such intention. "Good luck and escape from the evil eye and the evil tongue to the poems" is all it invokes.

Probably, there was nothing more behind the matter than the fact that, since Milton returned from Italy, he had had other things to think about; and that Moseley's direct solicitation (a fact recorded in the preface) was the main, if not the sole, occasional cause of the appearance.

The book had a bad portrait, with a Greek inscription, by Milton himself, stigmatising the badness. For twenty years and more after this he did not publish any poetry.

Chapter 18

Milton's "Plagiarism"

Again, fact assures us that the matter of the poem was largely the result of general reading. Fancy, which has sometimes deserved a harsher name, goes further and tries to assign particular sources. The lies of Lauder—who actually took portions of Hog's Latin translations of Milton, garbled them into divers more or less obscure writers and put them forth as Milton's originals, plagiarised by him—stand by themselves here; though, from another point of view, they have an ungoodly fellowship of literary mystifications and forgeries to keep them company.

But the parallel-hunters and the plagiarism-hunters and the source-hunters have spent immense pains—by no means always or often with malicious intent—to show that Milton imitated, borrowed from, or, in this way and that, followed, the *Adamo* of the Italian dramatist Giambattista Andreini (1613), the *Lucifer,* also a drama, of the Dutch poet Vondel (1654), the *Adamus Exul* of Grotius (1601), Sylvester's *Du Bartas* (1605) and even Caedmon, whose *Genesis* was published by Milton's friend Junius, in 1655.

Even more than most such things, these suggestions, if they insinuate what is properly called plagiarism, deserve simple contempt; and, if they only infer acquaintance, are matter of simple curiosity at most.

Supposing Milton to have read all these books, *Paradise Lost* remains Milton's; and it is perfectly certain, not merely that nobody else could have constructed it out of them, but that a syndicate composed of their authors, each in his happiest vein and working together as never collaborators worked, could not have come within measurable distance of it, or of him. For, after all the detraction and all the adulation (the latter, in some cases, as damaging as the former or more so) which *Paradise, Lost* has received, it remains unique. It is not, as it has been foolishly called, "the only great poem" in existence; but it is the only poem as great in a particular way, or, rather, it is quite alone in its kind of greatness.

It will be found that all objections to it, when examined, involve a sort, or different sorts, of *petitio principii.* "It has no hero (for Adam is hardly such and Christ's victory does not come till later) or a bad and unsuccessful hero in Satan." Why should it have one?

"The story is known beforehand." This applies practically to all classical epic and drama. "It, or part of it, is dull." That is a matter of taste. "Its religious ideas are exploded." That is a matter of opinion. The list of thrust and parry might be largely extended; but this may suffice.

On the other hand, it can show a sustained magnificence of poetic conception, and of poetic treatment in the solemn and serious way, which has practically never been denied by any competent critic. It would be difficult to find any two persons who differed from each other more than Voltaire and Johnson, or any two who, for different reasons, disliked Milton more.

Yet Johnson practically admits, though without enthusiasm, the magnificence above claimed, and Voltaire is only enabled to shrug it off—he hardly denies it—by the aid of a certain incompetence to appreciate it if he would. It has been pronounced not delightful by persons not incompetent: it can never, by any such, be pronounced not great.

That the whole is not quite at the height of the first two books may be granted; but, even the lower level would be a mountain top in other poetry. It matters little whether it be approached from the side of form, or from that of spirit. As regards form, it practically endowed English with a new medium for great non-dramatic poetry: what, at the very time of its completion, was being pronounced "too mean for a copy of verses," was made great enough for the greatest poem.

As regards spirit, we find the loftiest height of argument, the most gorgeous description, action not extremely varied but nobly managed, character not much individualised but sufficiently adapted to the action, above all, a suffused imaginative dignity, not merely unsurpassed, but unparalleled elsewhere.

PARADISE REGAINED

The exact relations of *Paradise Lost* and its sequel or pendant are rather uncertain. It is so perfectly natural that Milton should have written this sequel that, perhaps, some people may hardly look further; and it is equally natural that some time should be allowed to pass between the successive publications. It has, however, been customary to accept the statement of the aforementioned quaker Ellwood to the effect that he, visiting Milton at Chalfont during his retreat before the plague, "pleasantly" said to the poet, "Thou hast said much here of 'Paradise Lost,' but what hast thou to say of 'Paradise Found'?"

Whereupon Milton answered nothing and "sat some time in a muse"; but, next year, in London, showed Ellwood the poem. Of course, if this be true, it was finished-considerably before the publication of *Paradise Lost*. There is, however, a good deal that is suspicious about this statement; it is not confirmed or supported by Phillips or any other contemporary authority; and there is against it strong evidence of a kind which receives too little general attention—the evidence of prosody.

Critics who take very different views of Milton's versification admit equally that there is a difference between that of the two poems—a difference specially suggesting some interval between their composition; but less between that of *Paradise Regained* and its companion in publication *Samson Agonistes*.

At any rate, these two were published together in 1671 by one John Starkey, who lived at the prelatical sign of The Mitre in Fleet street. They had been licensed (again by Tomkyns) on 2 July, 1670. Of the details—copies printed, terms of publication and so forth—we do not, in this instance, know anything; but, as the book is said to be "Printed by J. M.," it has been supposed that it was an independent venture of the poet's own.

The sale was less rapid than that of *Paradise Lost*, or (which is improbable) the edition was much larger—at any rate, it was not exhausted for nine years, and the tradition of the comparative unpopularity of the poem is early. Phillips says that it was "generally censured to be [*i. e.* criticised as being] much inferior to the other, though *he* [his uncle] could not hear with patience any such thing." He would have had more than his usual uniqueness if he could have heard it with patience; but an author's partiality need not bear all the blame of his impatience.

The inferiority which the "general censure" of *Paradise Regained* has continued to ascribe, though it may be admitted to some extent, is an accidental, and, so to speak, artificial, inferiority. The subject is certainly less interesting: partly because it allows of less addition, traditional or original, to the scriptural narrative, and, partly, because the conclusion is even more foregone.

It is probable that, to Milton, with his semi-Arian views, the succumbing of Christ to temptation was a sufficiently epical contingency: to the orthodox and the infidel alike, it lacks that element. The poem is rather long for the actual action and yet rather short in itself—a mere episode in the real "Regaining of Paradise." And there are other objections which may be made, some from what may be called the point of view of the professional critic, some from more popular approaches.

But, in purely poetic value, *Paradise Regained* is little inferior to its predecessor. There may be nothing in the poem that can quite touch the first two books of *Paradise Lost* for magnificence; but there are several things that may fairly be set beside almost anything in the last ten.

The splendid "stand at bay" of the discovered tempter—"'T is true I am that spirit unfortunate"—in the first book; his rebuke of Belial in the second, and the picture of the magic banquet (it must be remembered that, though it is customary to extol Milton's asceticism, the story of his remark to his third wife, and the Lawrence and Skinner sonnets, go the other way); above all, the panoramas from the mountain-top in the third and fourth; the terrors of the night of storm; the crisis on the pinnacle of the temple—are quite of the best Milton, which is equivalent to saying that they are of the best of one kind of poetry.

SAMSON AGONISTES

Our diminishing acquaintance with the circumstances of *Paradise Regained* as compared with those of *Paradise Lost* dwindles to almost nothing when we come to *Paradise Regained*'s companion in print. No Ellwood boasts its suggestion; although there are two Samson subjects for dramas in the Cambridge list neither of these has any detail appended to it, and one refers to an early episode (the fox tails and fire brands) of the hero's life.

And, though the other, *Dagonalia,* is concerned with the catastrophe, it does not follow that the subject would have been treated in the actual way of *Agonistes.* Nor is much to be learnt from the short preface "Of that sort of Dramatic Poem called Tragedy."

Although longer and less defiant than the afterthought on "The Verse" of *Paradise Lost,* it is mainly explanatory of differences from the accepted English form, the poet specially objecting to tragicomic admixture, disclaiming stage intention and maintaining the unities of action and time, without mentioning that of place, which, however is, in fact, observed. His comment on his choric metres is less enigmatical than that on the Rous ode in Latin which, however, should be taken with it. It merely disclaims regular strophic arrangement.

The poem itself is of the very highest interest, and does not need any doubtful—hardly any certain—external support. There is scarcely anything, in poetry—Dante again excepted—which combines poetical and personal appeal in so striking a fashion. The parallel of Samson and Milton himself is extraordinary, even at first blush, and the poet, with his strong autobiographical tendency, has brought it out still further. The blindness, the triumph of political enemies, the failing strength and closing life (see, especially the poignant lines "So much I feel my genial spirits droop ... And I shall shortly be with them that rest"), the unbroken and undaunted resolution—all are in both.

And there are less certain, but most suggestive, added touches. There is no need to make the story of the first marriage worse by confounding Mary Powell with Dalila, nor can the cases be made to cover each other by the utmost violence or the most perverted ingenuity.

But, in the Dalila passages of *Samson,* there certainly is that combination of susceptibility to feminine charms and distrustful revolt against them which is thoroughly Miltonic. One cannot but see in the altercation with Harapha what Milton would have liked to say—if he never said it—to an "over-crowing" malignant; and the whole tissue of situations is worked into similarity, now actual, now allegoric.

But, quite independently of this, *Samson Agonistes,* from the purely literary point of view, is a poem of the highest interest and of the greatest beauty. An acting play, we are told, it was never meant to be; but, even of the acting quality, it has probably as much as any English play on the strict classical model can have. It has certainly more than either *Cornelia* or *Philotas,* than either *Merope* or *Erechtheus.* As a poem, dramatised in a given form, it needs no allowance and no apology.

Both the style and the versification, to some extent, show that "drooping of the genial spirits" which has been quoted: they are harder and stiffer. But there is even more art, if less "bloomy flush of life"; and the art is almost more imposing than ever, if less graceful. When Mark Pattison thought that, to critics who maintain that beauty is the only characteristic of poetry, *Samson* "will seem tame, flat, meaningless and artificial," he showed clearly that he did not understand the point of view to which he was referring.

Above all, the choruses give us not only much splendid verse, but an extraordinary abundance of special points of interest. To begin with, there is—and this point is not

Samsonic—the submission to the once loved, then slighted, enchantress rime. The first two or three choruses or choric scenes are blank; rime, not regular, but on a sort of further unregularísed *Lycidas* scheme, reappears with the striking *epiphonema* "God of our Fathers, what is man"and is never wholly abandoned afterwards.

Nevertheless, the poet continues his ceaseless experimentation in the mere forms of verse, putting rime out of the question—varying the assortment of his lengths, associating different feet on an extension of the same bold principle which had underlain the versification of *Paradise Lost* and, in places, venturing on entirely new rhythms, his intention in which is not yet quite certain, as in the famous "O how comely it is and how reviving" and "When their hearts were jocund and sublime."

And all this art is used for the presentation of a picture of really great action and high passion, a picture which, if we were ignorant of, and insusceptible to, all Biblical associations, if we knew nothing about Milton's personal history, would appeal to the eternal human interests. It may be that, in his central and, as the phrase goes, greatest, works, Milton had sometimes forgotten this appeal. He had not done so in his earlier and happier period; and though the time was late and hardly happy, he had returned to it now.

Chapter 19

Milton's Prose Works

The subject of Milton's prose work is not a very easy one, and it has often been neglected—comparatively, at least—in general surveys of his work. So long, indeed, as criticism was mainly coloured by the critic's agreement or disagreement with the author's views, it was almost impossible that anything valuable should be said on the subject. There could not be any critical edification in discourse which tended, on the one side, towards a sermon on the 30th of January and, on the other, towards a Calf's Head club harangue.

But, even if the king be kept as entirely as possible out of the matter, many difficulties, not merely troublesome but, as Milton's own time would have said, "disgustful," remain. That poets have usually been good prose-writers is a commonplace; and that some of Milton's prose passages are among the finest in English is hardly denied by anybody. Yet, even here, there have been gainsayers who were not political partisans, and whose competence was not to be questioned; while, if we stop short of absolute gainsaying, there has been hardly anybody, whose competence and impartiality are not questionable, to praise without abundant and uncomfortable allowance and exception.

The difficulty arises mainly from the fact that, except in the *Education* tractate, and in the curious *Histories*, Milton was always "fighting a prize" in his prose compositions; and that, hardly ever, except in *Areopagitica*, had he a prize before him which was worth the fight in a literary sense. This, to some extent, might have been compensated if he had been a born "Swiss of Heaven" in his controversies—if he had known how to make the most of his case without positive passion. But he did not. One would suppose that no one, unless entirely carried away by sympathy with Milton's causes, could approve Milton's controversial methods. His capital fault is that he never succeeds in bringing, or, apparently, attempts to bring, the matter under any consideration, or upon any ground, which his opponents can be imagined as sharing, or reasonably invited to share. To convict your adversary on your own statement of case is quite idle: and this is what Milton is constantly doing.

Even if his manner were less offensive than it is admitted to be, this peculiarity would be nearly fatal. His arguments against Ussher and Hall are not merely indecent in form towards one of the most learned men in Europe and one of the leaders of English literature, both of them aged divines of unblemished reputation: they have the further drawback of constantly taking for granted premisses which Hall and Ussher would utterly, and on strong reason, deny.

In his divorce tracts, when he is not (with a curious mixture of the pathetic and the ludicrous) urging (under whatever general shield) his own painful situation, he has recourse to such arguments as the opinion of Lutheran divines on Henry VIII's conduct—which is about as valuable as the opinion of Amphitryon's guests as to the identity of Amphitryon. In the Salmasius and Morus controversies and in the minor political or ecclesiastical pamphlets, it is even worse. Cut the abuse out, and there is not much left of them: cut out subsequently what cannot be admitted by the *communis sensus* as real argument, and there is almost nothing left.

Even so, however, it would have been possible for Milton—if he had been a cool-headed person with a dominant rhetorical faculty, or even a strong sense of prose art, mastering his personal convictions, as his poetic faculty and his sense of poetical art mastered them in the other division—to make his prose work, unpromising as is most of it in subject, a success in treatment.

But Milton was never cool-headed; and when he was out of his singing robes, the poetic warmth was exchanged for a less genial variety. Hypocrisy—even of that modified sort which makes every rhetorician (if not, indeed, every artist) a v[char] of a kind—was impossible to him. And it so happened that some of his special characteristics of style, which were harmless and even beneficial in verse, were dangerous, more especially at the time, in prose.

He was very fond of long sentences—the very first of *Paradise Lost* contains sixteen lines, and, perhaps, six score words, while there are others longer. In verse, this did no harm, and much good—indeed, without it, he could hardly have achieved, as will be duly pointed out elsewhere, his famous "verse-paragraph."

His unerring sense of verse-form prevented these sentences from being in any way formless. But, in prose, it was different. Destitute of the girth and band of the line, enabled to expand and expatiate, to indulge in parenthesis, and epexegesis, and additional relative clause, by the treacherous confusion of English and Latin grammar which prevailed, his sentences too frequently become a mere welter; and, in citing some of the finest, it is customary to commit the minor fraud of stopping short where he ought to have stopped, but did not.

If there had been—as it was practically impossible that there should be then—an accomplished critic who, at the same time, was not a political or ecclesiastical partisan, he must have been genuinely distressed by *Of Reformation touching Church-Discipline in England*, when it appeared in 1641. It is impossible to read a page or two without seeing that here was a writer who united the gifts of striking phrase and of rhythmical adjustment as, even in that age of marvellous achievement in these respects, few had done; but who exaggerated the defects of composition, usual after Hooker's time, in an almost unbelievable way.

The second sentence, not without premonition of the great flights later, is almost a pattern of Milton's style when not at its best—that style, even at its best, retaining a general likeness in composition, and (as Dryden says) *ordonnance*, to it:

Sad it is to think how that doctrine of the gospel, planted

by teachers divinely inspired, and by them winnowed and sifted from the chaff of overdated ceremonies, and refined to such a spiritual height and temper of purity, and knowledge of the Creator, that the body,

With all the circumstances of time and place, were purified by the affections of the regenerate soul, and nothing left impure but sin; faith needing not the weak and fallible office of the senses, to be either the ushers or interpreters of heavenly mysteries, save where our Lord himself in his sacraments ordained; that such a doctrine should, through the grossness and blindness of her professors,

And the fraud of deceivable traditions, drag so downwards, as to backslide one way into the Jewish beggary of old cast rudiments, and stumble forward another way into the new-vomited paganism of sensual idolatry, attributing purity or impurity to things indifferent, that they might bring the inward acts of the spirit to the outward and customary eye-service of the body,

As if they would make God earthly and fleshly, because they could not make themselves heavenly and spiritual; they began to draw down all the divine intercourse between God and the soul, yea the very shape of God himself, into an external bodily form urgently pretending a necessity and obligement of joining the body in a formal reverence and worship circumscribed; they hallowed it, they fumed up, they sprinkled it, they bedecked it, not in robes of pure innocency,

But of pure linen, with other deformed and fantastic dresses, in palls and mitres, gold, and gewgaws fetched from Aaron's old wardrobe, or the flamins vestry: then was the priest set to con his motions and his postures, his liturgies and his lurries, till the soul by this means of overbodying herself, given up justly to fleshly delights, bated her wing apace downward: and finding the ease she had from her visible and sensuous colleague,

The body, in performance of religious duties, her pinions now broken, and flagging, shifted off from herself the labour of high soaring any more, forgot her heavenly flight, and left the dull and droiling carcase to plod on in the old road, and drudging trade of outward conformity. Now the reader of this, struggling like Robinson Crusoe with the waves that, though they washed him ashore, all but strangled and crushed him in the process, may naturally protest with all the breath he has left on his deliverance.

And he certainly would not lack sound critical objections. There is no necessary harm in the long cumulative sentence: it may be found (for instance in Ruskin) of something like double the above length, but building up a picture whose every stroke is a clear and congruous addition. Milton's, at first sight and not at first sight only, is a daub of plastered touches.

One or two of the sections (if they can be called sections) could, indeed, be kept clear by punctuation. But, for the most part, they are not hinged and jointed together; they are thrust bodily into each other's substance so far as composition goes, while the actual words could be thinned out, with, in many cases, almost infinite advantage.

But, a little further thought will discover no small "condolences and vails" of the kind indicated above. In the first place, the reader's sufferings would be considerably mitigated in the case of the hearer, if the thing were cunningly declaimed. Now the ancients never could rid themselves of the idea that poetry and oratory were very close together: and Milton was largely an ancient. Secondly, let it be considered how little it would take to turn the passage into a blank verse tirade, not quite of *Paradise Lost* quality, but of good *Comus* type.

And, thirdly, let the positive excellencies be noted. If the word-selection be sometimes bad, it is not always so. How much better is "overdated" than our "out of date"; how fine the kindred "overbodying herself"; how happy the reversal of epithet order (always a favourite device of Milton) in "a formal reverence and worship circumscribed"! While, all through, even if half whelmed by the over-sentencing, there rings the wonderful prose cadence which we never find in English—not even in Malory—till the early translators of the Bible got it somehow from their orginals and infused it into our literature for ever.

This passionate, voluminous, eloquent, unequal medium served Milton, when he did not use Latin (in which his manner was not very different), throughout his life, and on almost all occasions. An intenser passion, with a nobler subject, elevated it into the noble, but even then not always faultless, style of the great *Areopagitica* passages; of the fine prayers at the close of *Reformation touching Church-Discipline in England;* of the enthusiastic autobiography of *An Apology [for] Smectymnuus;* of some parts even of the unfortunate divorce tracts.

Less fortunate occasions and a lower mood degrade it into the "rude railing and insolent swagger" of *Eikonoklastes,* which Mark Pattison, for all his liberalism and his Milton-worship, describes as "grossly indecent"; or into the inconceivably dreary horseplay—or worse—of the *Animadversions upon the Remonstrant's defence.* With passion and "interest" (in the doubtful sense) almost entirely absent, it composes itself into the sobre, businesslike, yet very far from inelegant, vehicle of the *Education* tractate.

It is really curious to see how, for the most part, the sentences shorten themselves, how the composition is clarified, the epithets are thinned and carefully sifted, in this tract. And it is still more curious to note the exceptions to this—as in the sentence of the third paragraph beginning, "And for the usual method of teaching arts," where the unblessed memory of his tutor occurs to him, where he loses his temper, his head, his command of the rudder of style, and once more welters and wallows through clause after clause of ill-jointed afterthought and ill-selected abuse.

Lastly, it finds its way into channels again different—those of the two *Histories;* and has something of surprise for us still. Most people who have read it have been more or less fascinated by the little *History of Moscovia.* The oddity of it is, of course, less than it may seem to the modern reader. The seventeenth century was, perhaps, the most learned of all centuries; but—some might say because—it was not largely provided with ready-digested learning. Men, therefore, had to make their digests, their conspectus, their abstracts for themselves: and this is a specimen.

It is singularly well done—quite a model of *précis,* with a little expatiation and ornament betraying the poet's hand.

The sentences are mostly quite short, but not in the least snip-snappy. The touches that had struck the writer's own attention are selected and composed admirably to catch the reader's. Manners, incidents, local colour—all are used to relieve the mere gazetteer- or chronicle-effect; and, where the piece becomes more dramatic and less summary (as in the rather well known interview between Ivan the Terrible and Sir Jerome Bowes), the style is perfectly equal to the occasion. The reason, of course, is that there is nothing in the subject which is *cinis dolosus;* and so the foot never breaks through the crust, and no "curling tempests" of wrath and incoherence burst out.

This is not quite the case with the much longer and very much odder *History of England,* where Milton gives himself the trouble to tell over again what he well knew (and admits that he knew) to be merely "modern fable." His reason is frankly given and it makes us like him all the better—"be it for nothing else but in favour of our English poets and rhetoricians, who by their art will know how to use them judiciously" as (let us say, though he does not) Shakespeare had done in *King Lear* and Milton himself in *Comus.*

Here, there was certainly "miching mallecho" if wanted—monks and popes and painted images and other dangerous things. But either the "kind calm years" (he revised it in 1670), or the distance of time, or the blessed influence of romance, though under the mask of history, kept the coals from blazing; and the curious power of dramatic recitative, little associated, as a rule, with Milton, reappears. In the story of Edwin and Paulinus, he passes slightly over the famous incidents of the bird flying through the hall, and the violent apostasy of the high priest, to dwell on the sign of the imposition of the right hand.

It is to be feared that we can account for his slighting the heroism of Boadicea "as if in Britain women were men and men women." But the Caesarean invasions are told with remarkable spirit; and the use of the historic present in the account of the war between Brutus and the Greeks is excellently vivid. Even the curious parallel introduced (in later editions) at the beginning of the third book as to "the late troubles," though, of course, one-sided, never lapses into the feverish incoherence of the earlier treatises; and it remains a strange Epimethean criticism of the actual facts.

In these later years, too, he composed the longest of his prose works, the Latin *De Doctrina Christiana,* which, after lying unnotice[char] the State Paper office for a century and a half, was printed in 1825 by Sumner, and served as peg, though hardly as subject, to Macaulay's essay. It is a curious document of its author's tendency to "ray out" nonconformity in almost all directions and on almost all subjects: being pantheistic in philosophy,

Arian in theology, millenarian in eschatology, semi-Antinomian in ethics (with advocacy of polygamy) and individualist as regards church government, the whole, of course, being professedly Biblical in origin. The recent attempt to attribute to Milton a Latin religious romance entitled *Nova Solyma* will hardly commend itself either to any impartial judge of evidence or to any competent literary critic.

A complete list of Milton's prose will be subjoined; and it seems better to deal with it here in the manner adopted in the foregoing pages than to tag more or less slight critical *aperçus* to the several titles. More emphatically, perhaps, than is the case with any portion of the work of an author of equal eminence, it is a by-work.

Except *Areopagitica,* there is hardly a piece of it that can be said to be, in the common phrase, worthy of its author, as a piece of literature; and there is much in it that is painful, much that is even offensive, to read. Yet it may be questioned whether, from any literary point of view, one can wish that it had not been written.

In the first place, it tells us a great deal about the author's literary, as well as even more about his personal, character; and it explains to us at once how the strong pleasure which he found in form and the strong constraint which it imposes were needed to produce the perfection of his poetic style, and how the volcanic quality of his genius forced even that constraint to permit the variety, the pulse, the fluctuation, which made English blank verse of the non-dramatic type. In the second, it has given us passages—the longer of them well known by quotation and selection, the shorter constantly, as has been said, to be found in all the welter and confusion of the mass—of extraordinary beauty, passages without which the crown of English prose writing would show miserable gaps and empty socket-holes.

In the third, it is the strongest possible historical document as to the necessity of an alteration—for a time, at any rate—in the dominant character of English prose style. In the other greatest pre-restoration prose writers—in Donne, in Taylor, in Browne—the solace is altogether above the sin. In Milton, it is not.

Take them, and you may say "Well, under this dispensation, a great writer may slip, but look what he can do constantly without slipping!" Take Milton, and the most that can be said is "Such a writer could never have written so ill so often under the other dispensation; but, at any rate, there are some passages, and those very precious ones, which he would only have been likely to produce under this."

HIS LATIN WRITINGS

Glances have already been made, for special reasons, at some of Milton's Latin works, but, when they are taken as a whole, their interest is very considerable; and it is unfortunate—with a misfortune not likely now to be decreased—that few people know them at first hand. Here, also, there is no comparison between the verse and the prose—in fact, the latter is worse off even than its English companion.

A Latin *Areopagitica* would have given opportunity for that stateliness, which is almost as characteristic of Milton's prose as of his verse, to show itself almost unhindered. There are flashes and glimmerings of it in the Latin pamphlets as it is. Even the dull and discreditable Billingsgate against Morus is relieved, so far as literary relief goes, by the passage on the consolations of Milton's blindness and by the encomia on

Christina and on Cromwell. But these things are almost perforce drowned in matter of a very different quality.

The most enthusiastic devotee of the classics, if he retains any critical faculty, must pronounce the usual controversial style, even of Greek, but, much more, of Latin, to be deplorable; and the comparatively few people who have studied technical classical rhetoric know why it was so. The whole thing was conducted on more or less cut-and-dried rules, which were only neglected—and that not always—by irrepressible genius like that of Demosthenes, or by eccentric individualities of late date like that of Lucian.

With Lucian, Milton had nothing in common: with Demosthenes, he had something, but not enough for the purpose. His models were Latin; and not so much the terser and more austere phrases of Tacitus of the vivid cleverness of Sallust, as the academic and parliamentary volubility of Cicero, largely adulterated with the ditch water of many of the renascence Ciceronians.

The consequence is that the compositions are merely large themes, patched together with commonplaces of the stalest kind. With a perfect command of such Latin as he chose to use, Milton rarely, if ever, lets himself go into a sublime or eloquent passage such as those which lighten the darkness of the English polemic.

The inability to carry the actual argument into any equal court is the same, or greater; but the purple patches of declamation are rarely present. There is a good deal of bandying of authority and of wearisome rebutting on particular points.

But, on the whole, the two sentences "Salmasius is an old fool" and "Morus is a rascally and vulgar libertine," represent the whole gist of the two *Defensiones* and their supplements, watered out into hundreds of pages, with floods of bad jokes, trivial minutiae and verbose vituperation.

The verse, for the most part, is free from this great drawback: and, though it has something of the same quality of *pastiche,* stock diction is more tolerable in poetry than in prose. Moreover, these pieces have the distinction of belonging to a body of composition which was the favourite literary exercise of good wits, and was cultivated all over Europe for at least three centuries, if not more, besides that of being written by the greatest poet who ever indulged in this exercise.

Many of them are only schoolboy or undergraduate taskwork; but some, even of these, especially that entitled *In quintum Novembris, Anno ætatis* 17, have interest; and three of the later, *Ad Patrem, Mansus,* a graceful tribute to his old Neapolitan friend, and *Epitaphium Damonis,* an elegy on the companion of his youth Charles Diodati, have much more.

Perhaps the unusual opportunity of comparison with *Lycidas* has somewhat enhanced the appreciation with which *Epitaphium* has been sometimes received; and one may not be quite sure that, if we did not know that diodati was really a friend, and King but an acquaintance, we could discover it from impartial reading of the poems.

Perhaps, the extreme rarity of acquaintance with the voluminous *deliciae* of the sixteenth and seventeenth centuries has also enhanced opinion of this piece among those who are competent to read it, but do not know much of the *corpus* to which it belongs. But it certainly has both elegance and pathos.

What seems to have been Milton's last Latin verse of importance, though it is not exactly a success in itself, has extraordinary, and generally overlooked, interest of form. *Ad Joannem Rousium* is an attempt (explained carefully in scheme by Milton himself) at a Latin strophic ode, in which the most singular liberties are taken with the construction and correspondence of the lines and, indeed, with the whole arrangement.

His explanation leaves us a good deal in the dark, and, whereas he says that he has "looked rather at a method of convenient *reading* than at one of *singing* on old modes" it seems more like a sort of musical chase of a chain of motives through variations of metre. But it is very valuable for purposes of comparison with the choruses of *Samson;* and it could hardly be more so as an indication of Milton's own interest in metrical experiment.

Chapter 20

Milton's Literary Form

At this point, we may naturally pass to a general consideration of Milton's literary form, which, in his case, is almost more important than in that of any other very great English writer. In general style, Milton's peculiarity appears, as has been pointed out, so early as the poem *On the Morning of Christ's Nativity:* and it perseveres until *Samson*. Even the furious welter of the prose cannot prevent the calm and stately phraseology from emerging—at least occasionally—the mighty rhythm from subjugating the chaotic throng of words, now and then.

In the verse, the phenomena go all the other way. It is only on the rarest occasions—when he attempts humour, or when he becomes simply didactic—that the style is other than consummate in its own way. To that way, hardly more than one epithet of praise, in the wider and higher range, can be denied. Milton's style is never exactly natural; it never has even the quaint eccentric nature which the conceit of the time sometimes takes on, as, for instance, eminently in Browne.

It is always confessed and almost ostentatious art: art attained, to some extent, by definite and obvious rhetorical devices, such as apposition; the old Chaucerian posing of the substantive between two epithets for the special purpose of drawing attention to some connection or opposition between the two; the reversal of the order of noun and adjective in the same line, or clause.

In his poetry, he particularly affects proper names of resonance and colour—scattering them over his verse paragraphs with an effect that is almost pyrotechnical.

But these verse paragraphs themselves are almost the central secret and peculiarity of the Miltonic manner—serving as a bridge between his style proper and his versification. It is perfectly clear that he was dimly aiming at something of the same kind in prose; and he sometimes came near it. In verse, he attained it very early, and perfected it more and more. The thing is not, of course, of his own invention: it is an inspiration from drama and, especially, from the soliloquies of Shakespeare.

But non-dramatic blank verse had been little practised by anyone, and the first and chief example of it, Surrey's translation of the *Aeneid,* though Vergil gives excellent opportunity, was not likely to arrive at any such mastery. The early blank verse writer was too glad to get safely to the end of his line to think about playing tricks with that line, so as to put it in concatenation with others.

But the dramatist had to do this; and, in doing it, he discovered—in Shakespeare's case perfectly, in others less so—the various secrets of the mystery. And the average dramatist had not only discovered them, but, about the time when Milton entered upon serious verse writing, had begun to abuse and degrade the art—making his lines battered deformities and his verse sentences ruinous heaps.

To Milton's sense of stately order, such things must have been abhorrent; and his musical training, no doubt, strengthened his aversion. His first finished poems are in tight, not loose, verse—the sonnet, the solemn stanzas of *On the Morning of Christ's Nativity,* the easy, but fairly regular and uniform, as well as uncomplicated, sevens and eights of *L'Allegro* and its companion.

When he makes a serious attempt with blank verse in *Comus,* there is even noticeable a tendency to fall back on the single-moulded line of Marlowe, accurately constructed in itself and correctly accumulated, but not jointed, and continued, and twined into a contrasted pattern of various but homogeneous design.

Yet, even here, the power of his own genius for verse, and his matchless daring in experiment, introduced variety. And when, some twenty years after, he perhaps began, and some thirty years after definitely set to work on and completed, *Paradise Lost,* he had become an absolute master of the blank verse line, single and combined.

HIS VERSIFICATION AND STYLE

The exact principles of Miltonic versification, in the epics and *Samson,* have been matters of sharp controversy; and, in such a *History* as this, it is the duty of a writer to be an expositor and not an advocate. The various opinions on the subject may be reduced, with less violence than in some other cases, to the usual three.

The older opinion—long considered the orthodox one and still held by some, though chiefly by foreign, critics—is that Milton's blank verse lines are strictly decasyllabic, apparent exceptions being due to actual elison or running together of syllables; and that, though it cannot be said that they are all strictly iambic or arranged in rising stress, variations from this are due only to wrenched accent, "impure" construction for the sake of preventing monotony and so forth.

The opposite view is that Milton, not more from his study of the classics than from that of English poets and, especially, Shakespeare, was fully conversant with the practice, if not the theory, of substitution of equivalent feet—disyllabic or trisyllabic, trochee, spondee, dactyl, anapaest—for the iambic; and that he used this deliberately for the purpose of obtaining varied and concerted music.

This opinion, which is that of the present writer, grew up slowly during the eighteenth century, but has been increasingly common in the nineteenth, though not often thoroughly worked out.

Between the two, and held by some critics of great distinction, is a theory (or, perhaps, more than one) according to which Milton always intended the strict five-foot ten-syllabled line, but gave himself certain intricate dispensations, capable of being more or less rigidly systematised, by which a larger number of syllables than ten could be written in the line; could (in some cases, though not in all) be actually pronounced in it; but could be metrically elided. To put the thing, perhaps, more intelligibly by examples: according to theory (i) "ominous," when the *i* makes an eleventh syllable, and "the Eternal," when *the* is in the same case, should be pronounced "om'nous" and "th' Eternal" and, in at least the latter case, printed so.

According to (ii) "ominous" and "the Eternal" should be written in full, pronounced in full, and reckoned metrically as trisyllabic feet, or (in another notation) as combinations of two unaccented syllables and one accented. According to (iii) they should be written and pronounced in full, but the *i* and the first *e* should be regarded as metrically "vanished."

Putting aside this capital point, on which the student must make up his mind after full consideration of the subject, there are not a few lines of Milton where unusual combinations of foot or arrangements of stress give rise to difficulty.

On another great general feature, there is not, nor can there be, any difference of opinion as to fact; and this is that Milton pays no attention to the supposed necessity, or, at least, propriety, of putting a pause near the middle of the line, and that his freedom of handling here is vital to his versification.

On the propriety, as distinguished from the fact, of the variation, such unanimity has not prevailed. The more rigid eighteenth century critics regarded the central or centripetal pause as an absolute law, the breach of which was to be justified by no success of result.

Johnson was not quite so strait-laced as this; but as, with him, regularity of correspondence was the main article of poetry, he objected to such confusions of "the methods of the poet and the declaimer"; and, consistently enough, disliked blank verse altogether. It is, at any rate, certain, that it is by variety of line material (attained by whatever means), and by further variation of pause, that Milton achieves the extraordinary freedom from monotony, and the force of character, which distinguish his verse.

And it has been recognised, with increasing decision, that he does not employ these means in a fashion merely continuous or strung together, that his verse construction is really periodic or paragraphic—the sections corresponding in division of sense and substance, as it were, to long but unequal stanzas or strophes of verses identical at first sight, but individually variable.

If the reader will compare the sketches of the progress of English prosody given at intervals in this *History;* if he will remember that Milton was a careful scholar and a fluent writer of Latin verse; and if he will pay particular attention to the Rous ode in Latin, and to *Samson* in English—he will not have much difficulty in appreciating the position of the poet in regard to quality of versification. So far as Milton's historical position is concerned, he is almost the central figure in the whole history of our verse. Brought into definite form as that verse had been, after two centuries of experiment, by Chaucer; restored and reformed, after nearly two more of disarray, by Spenser; enormously varied and advanced by Shakespeare and the later Elizabethans—Milton found it liable to fresh disorders.

He did not so much directly attack these as elaborate, for non-dramatic poetry, a medium practically involving all the order and all the freedom possible in English verse—yet without rime. And, in *Samson,* he returned to rime itself in choruses, though not universally or regularly, but, rather, with an extension of the occasional use which he had tried in *Lycidas*.

In the larger sense of style, Milton holds so great a place that we may almost let the arrangement of this chapter pass here into a conclusion-summary. He is, admittedly, in the least disputed sense of that much debated term, "the grand style," the grandest-styled of English poets.

He never, indeed, attains to the absolute zenith of expression—as does Shakespeare often and, perhaps, Dante sometimes. He is, unlike them, strangely unmodern; he has, indeed, it has been quite correctly said, little even of the renascence about him, except those tricks and fashions of form which have been noticed. Biblical, classical and medieval influences almost alone work on him—especially the former two. Under their joint pressure, he has elaborated a manner so all-pervading, that, if it were not also great, it might, or must, be called a mannerism. But it is always a mannerism of grandeur and never—this is another of the points in which Milton is unique—one of grandiosity.

It does break down sometimes, though rarely, when he attempts humour; when he lets himself prose, and so forth; but, even then, it does not become grandiose, still less bombastic: it is merely flat and dull or, sometimes, grotesque. Almost everywhere, the magnificent state and ceremony covers and carries off the occasion, the subject, resistlessly.

This manner has some modes and phases which are worth particularising, especially in the attempt to complete the presentation in little of the work and figure of so great a poet. One of the most remarkable of these is the famous "Miltonic vague"—the preference of vast but rather indeterminate pictures, tinted with a sort of dim gorgeousness or luridity, as the case may be—to sharper outlines and more definite colours. Another—as it may seem in a different sphere of thought—is the peculiar moral atmosphere of a kind of magnanimous *intransigeance* which pervades the whole.

The common saying that "Satan is the hero of *Paradise Lost*" is merely a way of expressing this wider truth to the vulgar mind. It is not at all probable that Milton meant anything of the kind; according to "the rules," a hero ought to be victorious, and Satan's victory is exceedingly Pyrrhic; according to "the rules," he ought to be good, if not faultless, and certainly Milton did not think Satan good.

But he has made Satan the most interesting person, and his unflinching nonconformity the most interesting thing, in the poem. In *Paradise Regained,* he enjoys a double presentation of this kind—the persistence of Satan, unconquered by past or future certainty of defeat, and the resistance of Christ, to which Milton's semi-Arian views must, as has been said, have given a peculiar interest.

As regards *Agonistes*, the other common saying, that "Samson is Milton," contains the general truth again. Samson is incarnate resistance; he has resisted grace and the Philistines alike, in the past; his repentance and atonement consist in resisting his father, the chorus, Harapha, the officer, the lords,

Dalila, everybody; and his final simulated compliance is only to obtain the means of making this resistance triumph.

Even some forty years earlier, the centre of *Comus* is the invincible resolution of the Lady; and the real inspiration of *Lycidas,* apart from the poetry, is the defiant denunciation—utterly different from the parallel and, no doubt, suggesting passage in Dante—of St. Peter. Now this pervading irreconcilableness, wherein Milton and Dante, to some extent, come together again, can only be made poetical by a style of severe splendour; and it meets this eminently in both, but more exclusively and restrictively in Milton.

It is almost a necessary consequence of this peculiar kind of magnificence that Milton has always been more admired and written about than loved and read, except in his earlier and smaller poems. Some have been bold enough to say that even *Il Penseroso* is generally known only in a few passages of its brightest purple; and the extraordinary beauty of the latter part of *Comus* has not prevented persons who united cultivation with frankness from pronouncing it heavy. That this is unfortunate need hardly be said. To begin with, it is a loss, to him who does not read it, of some of the greatest poetry in the world—of poetry which scarcely ever declines below a level that most poets scarcely ever reach.

But the loss is greater than this. Careless folk are sometimes found who decry the historic estimate altogether, and who maintain that a minor poet of the twentieth century is better worth reading than a minor poet of the thirteenth, though the later, for the most part, is simply a hand at the machine which the earlier had helped to construct. But Milton is not a minor poet, and his influence is omnipresent in almost all later English poetry, and in not a little of later prose English literature. At first, at second, at third, hand, he has permeated almost all his successors.

Without Milton, you cannot understand, in the real sense of understanding, writers so different as Landor and Tennyson, as Thomson and Wordsworth. He might walk through English letters and, like the unwelcome apparition in one of Dickens's shorter stories, ejaculate "Mine!" as he laid his hand on rhythm after rhythm, phrase after phrase, design after design, in poetical arrangement.

Although there was some plagiarism, even from his early poems, by men like Baron and Benlowes, he was not much followed immediately; but, as usual, the long germinating seed took the deeper and wider hold, and bore the most abundant and perennial crops.

In particular, he, with Shakespeare, maintained the citadel of true English prosody through all the deviations and shortcomings of the eighteenth century. With whatever allowance, in however grudging a manner, the greatness of these two was always allowed, and could be taken as pattern when the time came.

But this reflected and incidental glory, of course, is not the whole, or, with most people, the main, glory of Milton. His praises have been the theme of many excellent discourses; and it is quite superfluous, especially in such a place as this, to be rhetorical in regard to him. But the indication—if only the reindication—of the special quality and quiddity of writers great and small cannot be superfluous in a history of literature.

Although Dryden was merely repeating the common criticism on Homer and Vergil in ascribing "loftiness of mind" to the first and "majesty" to the second, and although his claim for a combination of the two in Milton is a sufficiently obvious figure of rhetoric, yet there was more of his own great critical genius in the hyperbole. One would, perhaps, rather choose "variety" and "nature" for Homer, "grace" and "perfection of art" for Vergil. But "loftiness of mind" and "majesty" (of expression, which, no doubt, was understood) remain true and keep their combination in regard to Milton.

Great variety he has not; in his longer and later poems certainly not; while the contrast of later and earlier only supplies it to a limited extent.

Although he is never unnatural, nature is never the first thing that suggests itself in him; and, though he is never (except in the rare instances often referred to) ungraceful, yet grace is too delicate a thing to be attributed to his work, at least after *Comus*. But in loftiness—sublimity—of thought and majesty of expression, both sustained at almost superhuman pitch, he has no superior, and no rival except Dante.

That, despite this, he has had few admirers out of England and those few (like Scherer for instance) for more or less special reasons, is not surprising. For, in order to appreciate Milton, it is necessary to know the English language not merely, as has sometimes been said, with more than usual acquired scholarship, but thoroughly, and with a native intimacy. His subjects may attract or repel; his temper may be repellent and can hardly be very attractive, though it may have its admirers. But the magnificence of his poetical command of the language in which he writes has only to be perceived in order to carry all before it.

Bibliography

Brown, Cedric. John Milton: A Literary Life. New York: Palgrave Macmillan, 1995.

Campbell, Gordon, ed. A Milton Chronology. New York: Macmillan, 1997.

Darbishire, Helen, ed. The Early Lives of Milton.

London: Constable & Co., 1932. (Repr. 1965)

Reprinted, Scholarly Press, 1971.

Diekhoff, John. Milton on Himself: Milton's Utterances Upon Himself and His Works.

Oxford: OUP, 1939. Reprinted, London: Cohen & West, 1965.

Fletcher, Harris F. The Intellectual Development of John Milton. 2 vols.

Urbana: University of Illinois Press, 1956-1961.

French, Joseph M., ed. The Life Records of John Milton. 5 vols.

New Brunswick, NJ: Rutgers University Press, 1949-58.

Reprinted, New York: Gordian Press, 1966.

Hanford, James H. John Milton, Englishman. New York: Crown Publishers, 1949.

Lewalski, Barbara K. The Life of John Milton: A Critical Biography.

Williston, VT: Blackwell Publishers, 2001.

Masson, David. The Life of John Milton. 7 vols. London: Macmillan, 1859-94.

Parker, William R. Milton: A Biography. 2 vols. 2nd ed. rev.

Gordon Campbell, Ed. Oxford: Clarendon Press, 1996.

Shawcross, John T. John Milton: The Self and the World. Lexington: University Press of Kentucky, 1993. (Repr. 2001)

Wilson, A.N. The Life of John Milton. Oxford: Oxford University Press, 1983. (Repr. 1996)

Ayers, Robert W., ed. The Complete Prose Works of John Milton. Revised Ed.

New Haven: Yale University Press, 1980.

Bush, Douglas. The Portable Milton. New York: Viking Penguin, 1976.

Flannagan, Roy C., ed. The Riverside Milton. Boston: Houghton Mifflin, 1998.

Hughes, Merritt Y., ed. John Milton: Complete Poems and Major Prose.

New York: Odyssey Press, 1957.

Patterson, Frank A., ed. The Works of John Milton. 20 vol.

New York: Columbia University Press, 1931–40.

Shawcross, John T., ed. The Complete Poetry of John Milton. Revised Ed.

New York: Anchor Books, 1971.

Armitage, David, Armand Himy, and Quentin Skinner, eds. Milton and Republicanism. Cambridge: CUP, 1995.

Cummins, Juliet, ed. Milton and the Ends of Time. Cambridge: CUP, 2003.

Daiches, David. Milton. Reprint. New York: W. W. Norton & Co., 1966.

Danielson, Dennis. The Cambridge Companion to Milton. 2nd ed. Cambridge: CUP, 1999.

Dobranski, Stephen B., and John P. Rumrich, eds. Milton and Heresy. Cambridge: CUP, 1998.

Evans, Martin J., ed. John Milton: Twentieth Century Perspectives. 5 vols.

New York: Taylor & Francis (Routledge), 2002.

Fallon, Stephen M. Milton among the Philosophers: Poetry and Materialism in Seventeenth-Century England.

Ithaca, NY: Cornell University Press, 1991.

Ferry, Anne D. Milton's Epic Voice: The Narrator in Paradise Lost. Reprint.

Chicago: University of Chicago Press, 1983.

Flannagan, Roy C. John Milton: A Short Introduction. Oxford: Blackwell Publishers, 2002.

Freeman, James A. Milton and the Martial Muse: Paradise Lost and European Traditions of War.

Princeton: Princeton University Press, 1980.

Geisst, Charles R. The Political Thought of John Milton. London: Macmillan, 1984.

Hunter, William Bridges, C. A. Patrides and J. H. Adamson, eds.Bright Essence: Studies in Milton's Theology.

Salt Lake City: University of Utah Press, 1971.

Kermode, Frank, ed. The Living Milton: Essays by Various Hands. Reprint.

London: Routledge & Kegan Paul, 1960.

Lieb, Michael and John T. Shawcross, eds. Achievements of the Left Hand: Essays on the Prose of John Milton.

Amherst: University of Massachussetts Press, 1974.

Luxon, Thomas H. Single Imperfection: Milton, Marriage and Friendship.

Pittsburgh: Duquesne University Press, 2005.

Marjara, Harinder Singh. Contemplation of Created Things: Science in Paradise Lost.

Toronto: University of Toronto Press, 1992.

Nicholson, Marjorie. John Milton: A Reader's Guide to his Poetry

New York: Farrar, Straus & Giroux, 1963.

Patrides, C.A. Milton and the Christian Tradition. Oxford: OUP, 1966.

Patrides, C.A., ed. Milton's Epic Poetry: Essays on 'Paradise Lost' and 'Paradise Regained'.

London: Penguin Books, 1967.

Revard, Stella P. The War in Heaven: "Paradise Lost" and the Tradition of Satan's Rebellion.

Ithaca: Cornell University Press, 1980.

Shawcross, J. T., ed. Milton: The Critical Heritage. London: Routledge & Kegan Paul, 1970.

Steadman, John M. Milton and the Paradoxes of Renaissance Heroism.